Bourbon's Backroads

Bourbon's Backroads

A Journey through
Kentucky's Distilling Landscape

Karl Raitz

Cartographic Design and Production by Dick Gilbreath,
Gyula Pauer Center for Cartography and GIS

south limestone

Published by South Limestone Books
An imprint of the University Press of Kentucky

Editorial and Sales Offices: The University Press of Kentucky
663 South Limestone Street, Lexington, Kentucky 40508-4008
www.kentuckypress.com

Unless otherwise noted, photographs are from the author's collection.

Library of Congress Cataloging-in-Publication Data

Names: Raitz, Karl B., author.
Title: Bourbon's backroads : a journey through Kentucky's distilling
    landscape / Karl Raitz.
Description: Lexington, Kentucky : South Limestone Books, [2019] | Includes
    bibliographical references and index.
Identifiers: LCCN 2019024294 | ISBN 9780813178424 (hardcover) | ISBN
    9780813178448 (pdf) | ISBN 9780813178455 (epub)
Subjects: LCSH: Bourbon whiskey—Kentucky—History. |
    Distilleries—Kentucky—History. | Distilling
    industries—Kentucky—History.
Classification: LCC TP605 .R35 2019 | DDC 338.4/7663509769—dc23

for Carol

Contents

Introduction

Bourbon, Kentucky's signature spirit, can be defined with some precision. It is a type of whiskey made primarily from corn, with rye or wheat as a secondary grain; adding small amounts of malted barley increases the efficiency of the fermentation process. A federal law decreed in 1964 that the term "bourbon" refers to a spirit distilled at no more than 160 proof from a fermented mash of not less than 51 percent corn and stored at no more than 125 proof in new, charred oak barrels. Spirits so produced can legally be identified as "bourbon whiskey."[1]

The term "backroads" is less precise. Its meaning is prescribed not by law but by convention. A backroad is any lesser-used overland route that traverses countryside and connects places that constitute the fundament of the local and regional culture and economy. Residents of backroads country are dependent on it; appreciative outsiders find backroads of interest in part because they reveal how places work. Backroads pass through landscapes where people conduct their lives; these landscapes contain the natural environments, structures, farms, fields, towns, and industries from which these people earn their living. Backroads can also be interpreted metaphorically—as historical places that possess venerated traditions, or as the backstory behind how something is made, how it works, the form it takes, and how it came to occupy the place (actual or perceptual) where it now resides. In short, the backstory explains how landscapes are made. This book is about one of Kentucky's signature industries: whiskey distilling. It is also about the landscape the industry created and the heritage it represents.

Bourbon's Backroads can be read in the traditional way: simply retire to an armchair and read about how distillers make that bright amber liquid in the cut-glass tumbler standing on your side table. Alternatively, you can use the book as a guide to visit and experience the places where bourbon's heritage was made: distilleries long standing, relict, razed, or brand new; distiller's homes on Main Street; villages and neighborhoods where laborers lived; storage warehouses on Whiskey Row; river landings and railroad yards; and factories where copper distilling vessels and charred white oak barrels are made. Reading the story of fine bourbon distilling can be engrossing; standing in the landscape where it began and continues to thrive is akin to participating in an interactive theater performance!

Part I, "Making Bourbon, Making Landscapes," consists of five topical chapters that introduce the practical aspects of establishing and operating a distillery, such as the role of "pure" spring water, the tradition of family recipes for yeast making and mash bills, and strategies for storing and aging whiskey spirits. Part II, "The Lands of Fine Whiskey Distilling," contains three regional chapters that offer insight into the variety of opportunities and possibilities available in different environmental contexts. Why did whiskey distilling grow into one of the state's signature industries? Why were some regions attractive to large-scale commercial distilling, while others were not? How has all this been recorded on the landscape, whether in modern-day distilleries, vacant and aging warehouses that have been converted to business offices, or grain elevators that have found new life as restaurants? The answers await on the backroads.

I

Making Bourbon, Making Landscapes

Kentucky's Distilling Heritage

American spirits distilling grew from European and colonial traditions. New England distillers, among them John Hancock and Samuel Adams, made rum out of fermented Caribbean molasses to supply local tipplers with spirituous drink, to stock merchant and whaling ships with the makings for grog, and to serve as currency in the Triangular Trade.[1] In the Middle Colonies, German settlers on southeastern Pennsylvania's Piedmont and in the adjacent Maryland counties distilled spirits from rye, as did George Washington in eastern Virginia. Protestant Scots-Irish from Ireland's Ulster country and Catholic Irish immigrants brought a thousand-year-old whiskey-making tradition to western Pennsylvania and the Ohio River Valley in the trans-Appalachian West.[2] In 1794, upon finding themselves subject to federal enforcement of Alexander Hamilton's excise tax on the whiskey they made, some 2,000 farmer-distillers in western Pennsylvania migrated west, many of them to Kentucky.[3] These Whiskey Rebellion refugees reinforced frontier Kentucky's rapidly developing distilling economy.

Pioneers and innovators are often cited in the legends and lore that constitute a founding myth as being the "first" to accomplish something. Evan Williams, Elijah Craig, and other eighteenth-century Kentucky distillers are often so acknowledged, but absent definitive documentation, only general recognition can be given. It is sufficient to know that distilling was commonplace in 1780s Kentucky.[4] Second-generation distillers were providentially positioned to see their accomplishments recorded as literacy rates increased, personal travel reduced isolation, and communication improved with the establishment of local newspapers. Accordingly, the contributions of James C. Crow are more fully understood and illustrate how a talented individual influenced the development of quality whiskey. "To him, more than any other man, is due the international reputation that Kentucky enjoys, and the vast distilling interests of the country are largely the result of his discoveries," pronounced a New York publication in 1897.[5] Crow was born in Dirleton, Scotland, in 1779. A "Presbyterian of the John Knox type," he graduated from the College of Medicine and Surgery in Edinburgh in 1822, trained as a physician and a chemist. The following year he moved from Philadelphia to Kentucky, where he entered the distilling business on Glenns (also spelled Glens or Glenn's) Creek, near Millville in Woodford County. Distilling at the time was rarely directed by rules; nor was it exacting in terms of quantity and proportion of ingredients, critical temperatures, or precise timing. Though his still house had a very limited capacity—only two to two and a half gallons per day—by embracing chemistry as a hobby and experimentation as a practice, Crow applied scientific method and advanced instrumentation to his distilling practice. Eventually, he was able to consistently produce a superior corn spirit and, in the process, changed whiskey distilling from an idiosyncratic folk craft to something resembling a science. Brisk sales soon followed, and Henry Clay, Andrew Jackson, William Henry Harrison, and Daniel Webster were among his better-known customers.[6]

Kentucky's frontier folk, whatever their heritage, often engaged in small-scale farm distilling, producing corn spirits for themselves and perhaps enough to sell to neighbors or ship to southern markets if they had ready access to one of the Ohio River's navigable tributaries. Kentucky's first *commercial* distillery may have been operating in Louisville, at the Falls of the Ohio, in 1783. Many of the skilled coopers who built the wooden tubs and barrels used to distill and store whiskey had served apprenticeships and worked in Virginia, Maryland, and Ohio, as well as in Belgium, France, and Germany. Distillers who wished to increase the scale of operations beyond their family members' capacity hired itinerant and immigrant laborers or depended on enslaved African Americans to provide the workforce.

A Distilling Primer

Grain starch is the only ingredient used in the manufacture of whiskey. Millers perform the first step in the distilling process by milling corn and rye or wheat to the consistency of fine meal. Maltsters subject barley to a wetting process that causes the grain to sprout; thereafter, the malted barley is dried and milled. Distillers add boiling water to their milled grains to create a mash. Traditional distillers cooked their mash in large wooden tubs. Once the mash temperature cools to about 152°F, the distiller adds the barley malt, and the conversion of grain starches into glucose or grape sugar becomes robust. Starch conversion is enhanced by the malt, which contains enzymes that convert up to 2,000 times their weight into glucose, which then undergoes vinous fermentation. When the starch conversion process is complete, the mixture is cooled, and yeasts begin to ferment the sugars into alcohol.[7] Yeast fermentation, a form of combustion, lasts seventy-two to ninety-six hours. The fermented mash, or distiller's beer, contains alcohol and congeners such as methanol, fusel alcohols, aldehydes, and tannins, which give the distilled whiskey some of its taste and aroma. This process produces a sweet mash; to make sour-mash whiskey, distillers add stillage residue or "back set" from a previous batch to the fermenting vat.

In Kentucky, fine whiskeys were traditionally made in alembics, or onion-shaped copper pot stills; these were subsequently augmented by the vertical column still. In the 1880s commercial-scale column stills were three to four feet in diameter and thirty to seventy-five feet tall. Both still types are comparatively simple mechanical devices whose operation is based on the different boiling points of water and alcohol. Pot and column stills remove alcohol from fermented beer by heating the beer to about 173.1°F, or 38.9°F lower than the boiling point of water. At this critical temperature, the alcohol "goes over," or vaporizes. Since alcohol vapor is lighter than water vapor, it separates, leaving the water vapor behind. The alcohol vapor is then captured and passes through a coiled copper pipe, or worm, where it condenses into liquid ethyl alcohol, also known as drinking alcohol or spirits.[8] This condensed product is termed low wine or singlings, and it is 45 to 65 proof, or 90 to 130 percent alcohol.[9] The low wine then passes into a second still or doubler, commonly made of copper and traditionally heated by a wood or coal fire, to undergo a second distillation. The alcohol vapor produced then passes through a second worm and emerges as high wine or whiskey of roughly 150 proof, or 75 percent alcohol. The distiller adds distilled or local water to reduce the proof to 100 to 110. The water and spent grain, variously known as grain stillage, wash, or slop, is left behind and must be disposed of. The contemporary distilling process has undergone little change, in principle, from that employed in the nineteenth century. The final step in whiskey production is barreling and aging. Nineteenth-century American whiskey barrels held 48 gallons; barrel volume was increased to 53 gallons, or 200 liters, sometime during the twentieth century.[10] The filled barrels are moved to warehouses for aging for a period of two years or more. Fine whiskeys may be aged for a decade or longer.

If the spirit produced in this manner was distilled from a fermented mash of not less than 51 percent corn and stored at no more than 125 proof in new, charred oak barrels, it can legally be identified as "bourbon whiskey." Whiskeys stored in appropriate containers and aged for two years or more are identified as "straight bourbon whiskey."[11] As this standard implies, all bourbon is whiskey, but not all whiskey is bourbon.[12]

Nineteenth-century Kentucky distillers sold bourbon whiskey to wholesalers and retailers in full-size barrels or in smaller containers such as half barrels or kegs. Saloon keepers served customers whiskey from full-size barrels tapped with a spigot. Some distillers sold their whiskey at distillery "quart houses" to customers who brought their own stoneware jugs.

Kentucky: The Center of American Bourbon Whiskey Distilling

How does one explain Kentucky's traditional association with whiskey distilling? Many of the state's eighteenth-century Anglo settlers had a modicum of distilling experience, so the industry enjoyed the advantage of an early start. But folk distilling was also widely practiced elsewhere, from the Carolinas and Tennessee north and west to Indiana and Illinois, well into the nineteenth century. One might presume that the extraordinary concentration of whiskey distilling in Kentucky is a matter of rational economic geography that can be readily explained by an analysis of production costs. Businesses incur costs to purchase, move, and process raw materials; to train and pay a labor force; and to distribute the finished product. For example, bourbon distilling is dependent on the availability of large quantities of grains; therefore, according to best economic practices, distilleries should be located in the most productive parts of the Corn Belt—Indiana, Illinois, and Iowa—to ensure grain availability and low transportation costs. By this analysis, the industry should not be located in Kentucky. Yet in 2014, Kentucky distillers used more than 12 million bushels of corn and 4 million bushels of other grains, and farms outside Kentucky supplied about 50 percent of the corn and 80 percent of the wheat and rye processed by the state's distilleries.[13] Likewise, very little rye or barley was grown in Kentucky during the nineteenth century. In the 1860s and 1870s many distillers bought malted barley from Canadian suppliers, and the majority of contemporary malted barley production is in North Dakota and Saskatchewan.

Moreover, distilling is not concentrated in Kentucky because of superior transport access or freight rate advantages. Distilling has a very low weight-loss ratio; that is, the weight of the raw materials used in distilling is very similar to the weight of the finished product. Transportation costs for finished products are usually higher than those for raw materials, in part because the raw materials can often be handled in bulk by specialized equipment. Finished products may require special handling because they are more perishable than the raw material. Whether bourbon was shipped in barrels, kegs, or jugs during the nineteenth century or glass bottles thereafter, transportation involves concerns about breakage and pilferage. Such industries are most conveniently located near their customers, yet the consumption of spirituous beverages in Kentucky is comparatively low, and 48 of the state's 120 counties are nominally dry.

Distilled bourbon must be aged in American white oak (*Quercus alba*) barrels, often for four years or more, to ensure a quality product. Indeed, cooperage and warehousing costs, insurance, and product loss through evaporation can exceed the costs of raw materials, labor, and overhead combined. Warehousing costs would be similar in other states, so Kentucky does not enjoy an advantage in transforming raw whiskey into aged bourbon.[14]

Given such anomalies in raw material quality and availability and the costs of manufacturing and transport, why is bourbon whiskey production centered in Kentucky? Kentucky distiller John Atherton acknowledged these inconsistencies when he testified before Congress in 1888 concerning internal revenue regulations. "The distillers located in the best grain country (the Middle West and central and northern Great Plains) and with the best railroad facilities would drive other distillers (in Kentucky) out of existence," he said, without the protection of the internal revenue law for fine whiskey production.[15]

Perhaps Kentucky possesses optimal environmental conditions that abet distilling. Corn and wheat thrive in Kentucky's climate and soil, yet rye and barley do not. Accepted lore suggests that early distillers touted the state's "pure limestone water" as a favorable factor if not the primary criterion for the founding and building of Kentucky's distilling industry. Kentucky's groundwater was said to be "pure" and iron free and lent the finished product a particular taste. But distillers in other states likely would have vigorously debated this presumption. The Great Valley is floored with limestone for much of its length from Maryland and Virginia to east Tennessee, as are many of the fertile farming valleys of eastern Pennsylvania. And what about Tennessee? The famed Nashville Basin is also a limestone plain and a near mirror image of the Bluegrass to which it is geologically related. If limestone water was the secret to whiskey production, wouldn't these other places also be favored by distillers? Instead, even though central Illinois was covered in tens of feet of glacial till, Peoria became one of the nation's major nineteenth-century whiskey distilling centers. By the 1840s, distilleries operated in most Kentucky counties regardless of their geological provenance. Limestone is scarce in Kentucky's Appalachian counties and incidental on the Ohio River floodplain downstream from Louisville. Two Kentucky regions, the greater Bluegrass and the Pennyroyal, are deeply underlain by limestones that husband groundwater and are the source of productive springs and wells. Although extensive development of distilling has taken place in the Bluegrass, it has not done so in the Pennyroyal.

Can one argue that distilling succeeded in Kentucky because of favorable social and political attitudes by the public and government officials? Kentucky had an active temperance movement during the nineteenth century. In 1834 the Kentucky Legislative Temperance Society was formed, with Governor John Breathitt (Democrat) as president and Lieutenant Governor James Morehead (Republican) as one of the five vice presidents.[16] Well-attended Temperance Society meetings were often held in towns with large operating distilleries.[17] Temperance activist Carrie Nation was born in Garrard County in 1846, although most of her "saloon-smashing" efforts took place in Missouri, Kansas, and Texas.

Perhaps the most compelling explanation for Kentucky's emergence as the nation's principal bourbon whiskey producer is that, from the earliest decades, Kentucky distillers sought to make high-quality whiskey, an inclination that became an operative requirement by the last third of the nineteenth century. Neighboring states were major whiskey production centers—in fact, Illinois produced a larger volume of whiskey than any other state. But Kentucky distillers argued that those Corn Belt whiskeys were poorly made, insufficiently aged, and tolerable only because of the addition of flavorings. The end product was deemed suitable only for a nondiscriminating market. Kentucky distillers, in contrast, cultivated their reputation for producing a first-class product and expanded their sales through clever marketing and advertising.[18]

We must also acknowledge that Kentucky's successful distilling tradition was built on the knowledge and experience of migrants from Maryland, Pennsylvania, Scotland, and Ireland; their log cabin distilleries were producing unaged white whiskey on Bluegrass farms and in the towns of central Kentucky by 1775.[19] Early whiskey distilling was a craft, a vernacular folkway that was perhaps the first widespread industry in Kentucky, processing local resources—water and grain—into a product that could be readily sold. Distillers sold their product to local customers, but they also exported it by overland trails to river towns such as Louisville and Cincinnati, where it was sold or loaded onto riverboats for delivery to downriver markets. As corn and wheat production moved into the trans-Appalachian West, whiskey distilling followed, and by 1850, Cincinnati had become the largest whiskey market in the world.[20]

Frontier whiskey fit easily into community economies. In central Kentucky, whiskey was used in barter-exchange transactions, primarily in rural areas beyond the reach of merchants and bankers in commercial towns.[21] Distillers used whiskey to barter with farmers; a gallon of whiskey for a bushel of corn was a common equivalence. Wherever farmers produced grain, it was milled, and whatever was not consumed as flour or meal was often distilled into whiskey. Milling and distilling developed in concert, both geographically and historically. These frontier businesses also began to move away from the economically limiting barter-exchange system to a system of debits and credits, which became the basis for the transition from a subsistence to a market economy in communities where these businesses prospered.[22]

Imprinting the Landscape

During the nineteenth century, distilling changed from a vernacular artisanal craft to a commercial industry, and that change resulted in pronounced alterations in operations and landscapes. Although the craft distillers' landscape was never static, adopting industrial techniques and technology led them to radically alter traditional procedures. Those alterations were sometimes nuanced, sometimes conspicuous, but they reflected the distillers' preferences for how their work should be done.[23] Distillers and kindred businesses, such as farming and milling, adopted new technologies and business practices: construction materials such as Portland cement and Pittsburgh iron; steam, electrical, and internal combustion power sources; farm machinery such as the corn planter and grain reaper; industrial machinery that facilitated grain handling and automated glass blowing; the automobile, truck, and tractor to move people, materials, and farm implements; and insurance to mitigate losses due to accidents, fires, and other hazards. Between 1810 and 1850, the number of distilleries in American declined by 90 percent, but the quantity of spirits produced more than doubled.[24] And all this was reflected in the changing distilling landscape.

The industrial transformation of Kentucky distilling took place between 1820 and 1860 and resulted primarily from the adoption of mechanization. Some aspects of agricultural production in the trans-Appalachian West were also mechanized.[25] Home food production, processing, and preservation had been present in most communities from the time of initial settlement, especially in the Middle West and adjacent Ohio Valley states. But during these four decades, farmers, mechanics, and artisans transformed the individual production of food and livestock into commercial-scale farming, milling, and butchering businesses. It took skill to manufacture new tools and implements, so the successful application of new technology was contingent on the development of new proficiencies. The industrialization of farming, milling, and distilling therefore proceeded in concert

Kentucky Distillery Census, 1810–2016

Year	Number of Distilleries
1810	2,200 (estimated; Fayette County had 139)
1840	889
1864	166
1870	141
1876	225
1880	242
1894	170
1919	183 (on the eve of Prohibition)
1920–1933	6 (licensed during Prohibition)
2012	6 (craft and industrial scale)
2015	31
2018	68 (craft and industrial scale)

Compiled from various sources.

with technical advances in manufacturing.[26] Farmers made harnesses and built wagons; cleared land and marketed sawtimber; invented and improved plows, harrows, drills, and reapers; and often became first-generation manufacturers. Inventors patented hundreds of new farm tools and implements.[27] Reapers replaced sickles, scythes, and rakes; threshers replaced forks and flails. Instead of planting grain by hand broadcasting, farmers planted seeds with drills and planters. Cutting grain with one of Cyrus McCormick's horse-drawn reapers gave farmers a five-to-one production advantage over a hand-swung scythe and cradle. By the end of the Civil War, farmers were planting and cultivating corn with machinery, and production increased three- to fourfold over the days of wooden plows and hoes.[28] After harvest, farmers could shell corn off the cob by machine rather than by hand. Importantly, farmers created the industries that processed their products: grain milling, cattle and hog butchering, lumber milling, brewing, and distilling.[29] Over the century from 1830 to 1930, mechanized grain production provided an advantage of roughly thirty-two to one over traditional manual labor practices. And transforming distilling from vernacular craft to mechanized industry was contingent on sizable increases in grain production.[30]

Commercial, industrial-scale distilleries gradually replaced farm stills, a process abetted by specialized machines that were efficient and productive but also required more space that offered protection from the elements. Distilleries could no longer function in simple lean-tos or single-room sheds; they required larger spaces, often configured as a series of connected rooms, each housing a different function. These compound distillery buildings sometimes gave the appearance of being cobbled together rather than purpose-built. Larger copper pot stills and new vertical column stills increased the volume of whiskey production but also required a change in distillery size and floor plan. Barrel storage warehouses evolved from low wooden sheds to large-capacity, multistory timber and brick structures. Some industrial distilleries added dedicated cooperage shops. Stationary steam engines provided unflagging power but required fuel, careful tending, and regular maintenance. Increased distilling capacity required a reliable supply of raw materials, necessitating the construction of grain bins and corncribs. The need for ready access by horse- and mule-drawn wagons obligated the distiller to give careful consideration to building placement and road access.

Although craft and early industrial bourbon distilling left distinct imprints on the landscape, the manufacturing process did not ravish the land. There was no "black country" in Kentucky like that created by the coal mines, coke ovens, and steel mills in southwestern Pennsylvania. Kentucky's small rural distilleries fit glove-like into the countryside. Antebellum industrial stills often operated in simple log or frame buildings that resembled farm barns and sheds. Adjacent sheds sheltered hogs or cattle that were fed on the distiller's spent grains or slop. Woodcutters and sawyers harvested trees from nearby woodland to provide fuel, and coopers drew wood from adjacent lumberyards. Neighboring farm fields produced grain for distilling. And wagons loaded with raw materials and barrels of whiskey moved along country roads, headed to markets or river ports.

Kentucky's distillers often encouraged or underwrote turnpike construction, and after the state's first railroad began operating in the 1830s, distillers lobbied rail companies to build lines into their counties. When a new rail network was developed after the 1850s, some distillers moved their works to cities, where they had direct access to railroads and factories in light industrial districts. Steam power enabled distillers to significantly increase the scale of their operations, which in turn stimulated a change in traditional business relationships with suppliers and customers. As distillers refashioned their industry during the nineteenth century, craft production gradually transformed into science-based manufacturing; the still moved from a log cabin into a post-and-plank shed or barn and, eventually, into a large brick, stone, and iron industrial-scale factory. As factory distilling increased in volume, distillers' imprint on the land was amplified. Related industries such as gristmills, lumberyards, and cooperage shops all contributed to the new industrial footprint, as did toll turnpikes and railroad yards and sidings. Some distillers prospered and built great houses, stores, and churches; others went bankrupt and lost their holdings to banks, lenders, or other distillers.

Locational Patterns in Kentucky Distilling

In 1810 more than 2,000 distilleries operated in Kentucky, although the county-by-county distribution was profoundly asymmetrical. This pattern was related to opportunities offered by benign topography and benevolent geology, but it was likely also influenced by transportation route quality and access to distilling grains and markets for surplus production.

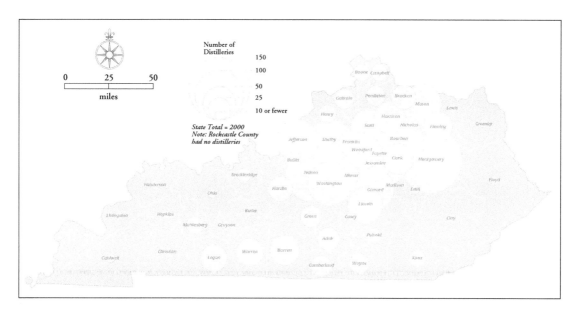

Kentucky's distilleries, 1810. (From US Census, 1810, "A Series of Tables of the Special Branches of American Manufacturers," 122–23)

Whiskey was produced at twenty-five or fewer distilleries in each of the eastern Appalachian mountain counties—or at least that was the number counted by census marshals. Correspondingly, few distillers could be found in the Western Coal Field or the far western counties bordering the Mississippi River. Each of the eastern Pennyroyal counties, such as Barren, Warren, and Hardin, had twenty or more distilleries in operation. The largest number of distilleries was clustered in the greater Bluegrass region, with 100 or more operating in several counties. More than 150 distilleries produced spirits in both Fayette and Montgomery Counties.[31]

The early stages of the transition from farmer-distiller craft production to commercial-scale production are reflected in distillery production capacity. Again, the overall pattern of distillery location centered in the Bluegrass region obtained. Distilleries with the largest capacity extended from Boone County on the Ohio River in the north to Lincoln County in the south, and from Mason County in the east to Jefferson County in the west. By comparison, the mountain and Western Coal Field distilleries were small in number and capacity. And, some important anomalies appeared. Harrison County had only about fifty distilleries in 1810, but total production approached 3,000 gallons per distillery. Nearby Montgomery County vied with Fayette County for the largest number of distilleries, but overall spirits production in Montgomery lagged well behind, indicating small works with limited capacity. Most dramatic, however, was the production pattern in the western Pennyroyal counties of Logan, Christian, and Hopkins. Fewer than ten distilleries operated in Hopkins County, yet each distillery produced nearly 4,000 gallons annually, the converse of the situation in Montgomery County.

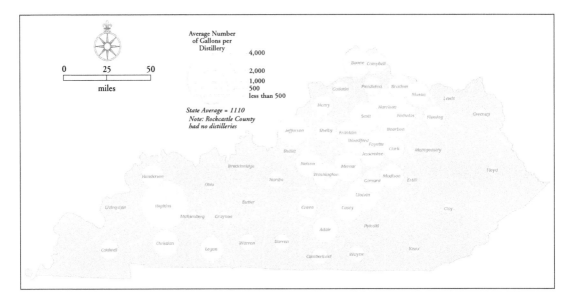

Distillery production, 1810. (From US Census, 1810, "A Series of Tables of the Special Branches of American Manufacturers," 122–23)

By 1830, the era of industrial distilling was under way, although many traditional distilleries continued to operate. Industrial-scale distillers supplied whiskey to local and regional markets, despite the limitations of primitive transportation. And working capital was checked by taxes imposed by a federal government anxious to pay its bills. Although the distilling process remained little changed until the mid-nineteenth century, successful

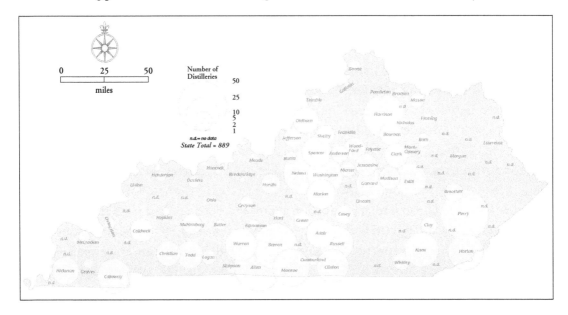

Kentucky's distilleries, 1840. (From US Census of Agriculture, 1840)

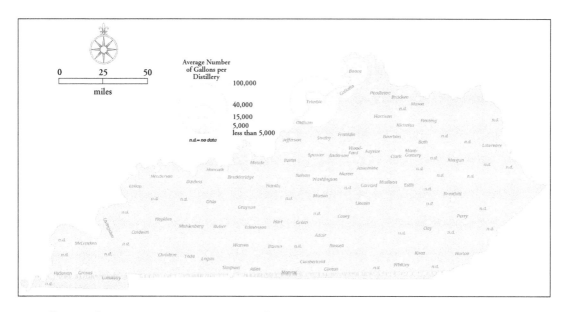

Distillery production, 1840. (From US Census of Agriculture, 1840)

distillers expanded their facilities and extended their geographic reach across the country-side to obtain grain, wood, and new and specialized mechanical equipment. Accordingly, farm fields, hardwood forests, distillery structures, mud tracks or stone-surfaced roads, and ancillary businesses became increasingly important elements in the distilling landscape.

By 1840, the total number of distilleries operating in the state had declined to 889. Although information is incomplete or missing for some counties, the overall pattern established by 1810 was still evident in 1840, with some notable exceptions. The southeastern mountain counties retained their distilleries or new works were established, especially in Perry and Harlan Counties. The eastern Pennyroyal counties maintained or increased the number of working distilleries, and new works appeared in the far western Jackson Purchase counties. In the greater Bluegrass, Fayette County lost a significant number of distilleries, as did Mercer and Franklin. By comparison, the number of distilleries increased in Harrison County as well as in the western Bluegrass counties of Nelson, Marion, Spencer, and Washington. After the Civil War, this latter group emerged as one of the core distilling areas. It survived Prohibition in the 1920s and 1930s and thereafter emerged as a major distilling center.

The impact of distillery industrialization and rapid improvements in river transportation introduced by the steamboat after 1820 is reflected in the distillery production capacity in 1840. Very few of the state's distilleries could manage to produce 5,000 gallons a year or more. The inland counties of Harrison, Nicholas, Bourbon, and Shelby reached this threshold likely because they had access to navigable streams, such as the Licking River and its larger tributaries, or because they were served by the state's first railroad

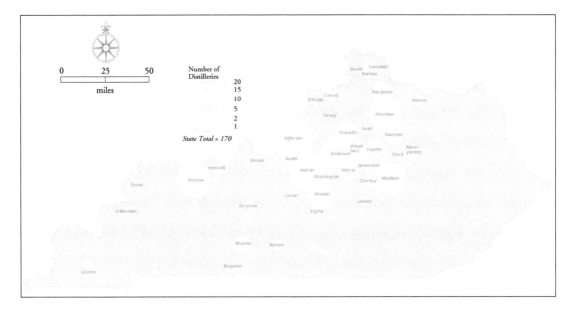

Kentucky's distilleries, 1894. (Compiled from *Sanborn's Surveys of the Whiskey Warehouses of Kentucky and Tennessee* [New York: Sanborn-Perris Map Company, 1894]; US Census of Agriculture, 1894)

line. The most dramatic production increases, however, occurred in selected Ohio River counties. Each of Henderson County's distilleries produced about 5,000 gallons; those in Gallatin exceeded 15,000 gallons, Boone's produced about 40,000 gallons each, and Trimble County's two distilleries averaged 100,000 gallons a year. By a considerable margin, the dominant works was William and John Snyder's distillery at Petersburg in Boone County. The Snyders increased production to 164,000 gallons in 1850 and surpassed 1 million gallons in 1860, becoming the exemplar of how industrial-scale technology and high-capacity river transportation could boost production.[32] Proximity to navigable water was not simply a convenience or an expedient for conveyance. Some distillers, and their customers, recognized that while awaiting the rivers' seasonal rise to accommodate safe navigation, barreled whiskey acquired some age, and some thought the motion of travel improved its taste.[33]

Prior to the 1840s, farmer-miller craft distilleries were generally distributed across the state. By 1894, the locus of industrial factory distilling had concentrated in the Inner and Outer Bluegrass, the eastern and central Pennyroyal, the Ohio River floodplain in the Western Coal Field near Owensboro and Henderson, and Louisville (Jefferson County). Industrial distillery sites were centered around special nodes that had links to local, regional, and national grain and coal supplies and access to distillery materials such as copper stills, cooperage, and specialized equipment and building supplies. Marketing distilled products became increasingly regional and national.

Anderson, Harrison, and Madison Counties had the largest number of distilleries in the Inner Bluegrass, and the early production center in Nelson and adjoining counties in the Outer Bluegrass continued to operate. Urban industrial distilleries at Owensboro (Daviess County) and Louisville (Jefferson County) sought sites with river and rail access and drew their labor force from the cities' large working-class populations, advantages that enabled these places to become major whiskey production centers.

Visiting a modern bourbon distillery is a useful exercise for learning how whiskey is produced, but it is not likely to provide a comprehensive appreciation of all the elements of the historical and contemporary distilling landscape; nor will it foster an understanding of how distilling evolved from a traditional agrarian industry into a large-scale modern commercial enterprise. This transition is of particular interest because, although distilling could be urbanized to take advantage of transportation facilities, industrial suppliers, and a concentrated labor force, whiskey production could also continue in the rural countryside where it originated. Urban distilleries often blended in with adjacent industrial plants, and their landscape was not immediately evident or distinguishable unless one paused to study the structures, watch the flow of commodities in and out of the buildings, and inhale the pungent aroma of fermenting mash. Close observation of any distillery, be it rural or urban, confirms that distillery structures are largely functional; they have an essential identity. Like most industrial architecture, early distilleries were designed to house the processing of raw materials into a consumer product, not to attract attention or declare values or status. In short, their architectural style could be thought of as vernacular industrial, comprising simple frame buildings or sheds whose sole purpose was to accommodate the various distilling functions and protect them from the elements.

After the Civil War, as distilling became increasingly industrialized and construction proceeded on a regional railroad system, large distilleries appeared, often housed in buildings designed by engineers or architects. Distillery design became considered and rational, a factory-like transformation into a formal industrial style, and the principles of aesthetics gradually joined with the principles of engineered efficiency, productivity, and safety. Eventually, some modern distilleries, especially their interiors, were designed or redesigned as showplaces, with large, gleaming copper or steel stills and polished and painted fittings and piping. From the modern distillery emerged products packaged in lustrous, distinctively shaped glass bottles and identified by colorful labels and brand names that elicited recognition almost anywhere in the country.

What is not apparent in the industry's modernization are the changing relationships among technology, economy, culture, and society that enabled the evolution of the production process, the structures erected to house it, and the methods of marketing and distributing the finished product. Importantly, one must recognize that industrial landscapes are closely tied to the people who build and work in them. The appreciation of construction, especially of historical buildings and industrial-related structures and facilities, is often limited to the vision and work of architects or engineers. While such recognition can be informative, it focuses our attention on the technical and the aesthetic. A richer interpretation of landscape extends to the historical precursors that alert us to important innovations and suggest a timeline of landscape change or adjustment. Further, although architects and engineers play a key role in the creation of industrial landscapes, it is the common person—the wage laborer or the salaried employee—who builds the structures and sets the entire operation into motion. Knowing something about the laborers' social and cultural worlds can expand and enrich one's interpretation of how industrial places work and how they relate to people's lives as well as the places they occupy. Limiting one's perspective on landscape construction to economic geography gives short shrift to the complex interweaving of social experiences and cultural influences that constitute the industry's geographic history and the full story of how whiskey is made.

Making Connections

Links to kindred industries such as machine tool manufacturing allowed whiskey makers to convert to machine-based production.[34] Distribution connections related to grain processing included the manufacture and dispersal of food products such as bread and cereals, as well as brewed beer and distilled spirits. Food processing created a demand for cooperage, which in turn supported the timber cutting, lumber milling, and woodworking industries. Lumbering required an investment in mills that produced building materials, barrel staves, and dimensional wood for boxes, furniture, wagons, carriages, and railroad ties. Agricultural-industrial development in the Ohio Valley and Middle West was stimulated in part by the availability of productive land and the regional demand for local and imported manufactured products. The industrialization of the Ohio Valley and the Middle West included traditional heavy industries, such as iron and steel manufacturing; large-scale metal fabrication; and the development of steam-powered machines such as riverboats, locomotives, and stationary power plants. Medium-scale industries such as grain and lumber milling, butchering and tanning, and brewing and distilling developed as well.[35] In addition to its primary reaper works in Chicago, the McCormick farm machinery company established a factory in Louisville in 1856, where it manufactured the Kentucky Harvester, suggesting that there was a demand for such machines by the state's grain producers.[36] J. B. McCormick of Woodford County, Kentucky, a cousin of Cyrus McCormick, became a sales agent for the company in 1845, selling reapers across the Ohio Valley and thereby facilitating increases in grain production.[37]

Nineteenth-century industry in America was also closely related to technology, cultural tradition, and social structure. When moving water was the primary industrial power source, manufacturers chose locations in the vicinity of stream rapids and falls, where the addition of dams and millraces could provide the necessary hydraulic head pressure. Because such advantageous sites were not ubiquitous, industries tended to concentrate at specific places along streams that offered this power capability. Productive agriculture requires fertile soils, so the most desirable land, though expensive, was settled, cleared, and planted before marginal land. The requisites for overland transport routes were shortest distance, lowest gradient, and driest ground. Water transport would thrive if harbors were sheltered from storms, docks could be constructed in deep water, and the waterway was free of obstructions. Raw materials, be they potable water for distilling, clay for bricks, iron for tools, or copper for containers, were generally found in specific places that were not always conveniently located near transport routes or population centers. Until the development of a systematic network of stone-paved turnpikes, beginning in the second and third decades of the nineteenth century, hauling bulky materials such as grain and lumber was slow and exceedingly expensive. Converting grains into flour exacerbated the transportation problem; although corn, wheat, rye, and barley were fairly durable if kept dry and free of vermin, flour and meal were perishable and required special containers and expedited handling.

Most industrial activity, past or present, utilizes extant technology to erect buildings to house the machines and tools required to make useful products. Industrial structures usually reside at important geographic focal points, such as sites that can supply raw materials, a labor source, a transportation node, or a market. A successful, long-lived industry may build structures at one focal point—because of the limited extent of a mineral deposit, for example—or it may operate at multiple sites over a broad area because the raw materials are widely available and the markets for the product are abundant. For example, during the nineteenth century, the production of fine ceramics in America tended to be localized at sites with high-quality clay deposits, such as those at Trenton, New Jersey, and East Liverpool, Ohio. Wagon and carriage making, in contrast, was common and widespread across the Northeast and Middle West, in part because hardwood lumber and iron were widely available and the market was ever present.[38]

Each industrial type requires specific raw materials and dedicated technologies; therefore, each industry requires different kinds of infrastructure, be it buildings for manufacturing and storage space or facilities for by-product disposal. In the aggregate, industrial structures contribute to a distinctive landscape signature or imprint. For those working in a particular industry or living nearby, the industrial landscape becomes central to their daily lives, to their sense of place. Eventually, an industry may adopt new technologies and change its infrastructure, or it may move and abandon a work site. The structures left behind also constitute a landscape, perhaps relict, that may continue to represent the region's industrial heritage.

Kentucky's distilleries contributed to the process of industrial development and landscape creation in the Ohio Valley and Middle West. Migrants established distilleries before Kentucky statehood in 1792, and the vocation evolved from subsistence-scale farms making corn whiskey and fruit brandy into modern, twenty-first-century commercial businesses that produce primarily bourbon on an industrial scale. Industrial distilling developed irregularly, change being contingent on the distiller's interests and financial wherewithal. Each increment of change was associated with a distinctive ensemble of landscape elements—structures and their placement relative to operant technology, water as a power source or transport medium, overland transport routes, raw material supply, labor availability, and regulation and market considerations.

Commercial industrial distilling was and is a complex process with scientific, technological, economic, social, and political dimensions. And the landscape formed by this multifaceted business is, necessarily, multidimensional. Of the more than 2,000 distilleries in operation at some time during the nineteenth century, many were dismantled. Others burned. A few remain as ruins, and only a small number remain in production. Interpreting and understanding the industry's geographic history requires familiarity with locational decision making; applicable technologies, inventions, and patents; state and federal regulations and revenue policies; and business linkages with associated industries.

2

Distilling's Backstory
The Prerequisites

Whiskey distilling in nineteenth-century Kentucky changed from a farm-based craft to a steam-powered industry. That change required distillers to engage with the physical environment, agriculture, technology, invention and innovation, transportation, workers, federal and state regulations, and social constraints. Successful distillery operation required insightful management of these elements individually and in concert. Corn, for example, was required as a starch source. But which corn varieties produced good yields and were also easy to mill? Livestock provided milk, meat, fiber, and motive power, but they also consumed grain and were therefore both supportive of and in competition with a farming-distilling operation. This chapter explores some of the interrelationships between distilling and the environment, farming, and milling and how those relationships changed as distillers industrialized their operations.

People relate to their natural environment in distinctive ways.[1] Understanding these relationships is difficult because it requires sorting through a crowded and disordered historical and geographic reality.[2] Agriculture, forestry, and mining are primary activities that yield useful raw materials and products and, in the process, create patterns of fields and farmsteads, cutover forests and logging trails, and opencast pits from which fuel and minerals are drawn. Products so obtained can be processed by manufacturing or by secondary economic activity, which is attached to work by a labor force, supply lines, and financial transactions. And all this takes place upon and within a physical environment that provides context but may present opportunities as well as impediments.

The technologies deployed in contemporary agriculture—labor-saving machinery, hybrid or disease-resistant seed, chemicals and fertilizers, irrigation, weather forecasting—greatly extend the farmer's ability to raise crops and livestock in accommodating environments, while also facilitating production in less hospitable places. Eighteenth- and nineteenth-century agricultural practices were radically different, of course. Two hundred years ago, Kentucky farmers lived not so much *on* the land as *in* the land. Following the furrow cut by a single-moldboard hand plow pulled by a mule put the farmer in intimate contact with every clod, every stone, every crease and irregularity in a field. Once a field's sod was turned or its trees and briers were cleared, the dirt often contained sufficient nutrients to produce plentifully. But the soil was also a storehouse of seeds dropped over decades by grasses, forbs, and other native plants, and working a field with a hand plow and harrow brought them to the surface, where they flourished and, if left untended, returned the field to sod.

Lore and experience taught that the sky was not innocent. Some clouds signaled fair weather; others produced hail and torrential rain. Clear skies for days on end could bring drought and heat sufficient to kill crops and livestock. In the early nineteenth century, the intrepid forecaster could do little better than depend on weather lore, which could be enlightening or misleading. "Red sky at night, sailors' delight" had some basis in fact. "Rain before seven, clear by eleven" rhymed but had little empirical validity. A successful harvest provided seed for the next season's planting, grain that the miller's burr stones turned into meal and flour, feed for livestock during the winter, and, if one's granary was built with ill-fitting logs, food for the neighborhood's vermin. Livestock might thrive or perish for no obvious reason. And while losing hogs or cattle to disease was costly, the loss of a draft horse or mule could be catastrophic. A farmer could till a garden with hand and hoe, but working a farm with plow and wagon required draft animals. Appreciating the intimate relationship between distillers and their physical world requires a basic familiarity with the vocabulary of nature: climate, geology, geomorphology, hydrology, soils, topography. These environmental elements are all co-influences, and for some distillers, co-determinants, of distilling's geographic patterns and processes.

In 1881 C. E. Bowman, Kentucky's commissioner of agriculture, made the bold assertion that the superior quality of Kentucky's bourbon whiskey was due to the state's soil and water, not the artful techniques employed by the state's distillers. Kentucky's "corn, as do its wheat and barley, and oats and grasses, partakes of the elements of the soil upon which it is raised, and of the water that percolates through them," he said. "The whiskies made in no other States have or can come in competition with [Kentucky's whiskey], . . . *because* the corn of which they are made and the water used in their distillation lack the essential qualities and ingredients possessed by Kentucky corn and Kentucky water. Herein lies the reason of it. Kentucky distillers possess *no art or skill or superior knowledge* above other distillers."[3] Bowman's rather maladroit and deterministic premise likely earned sharp reproof from the state's distillers. An effective rebuttal would be enhanced by a nuanced understanding of the multiplicity of environmental and human influences that shaped the industry and permitted distillers to produce a superior bourbon whiskey. Corn and water are key elements in the development of "fine" whiskey, but they are not the sole determining factors, as we shall see.

Water

Kentucky's frontier settlers were making, consuming, and selling whiskey by the 1780s. The belief that Kentucky whiskey's singular character was (and is) derived from "pure limestone water" is long-standing lore, but pioneer whiskey making was likely based on

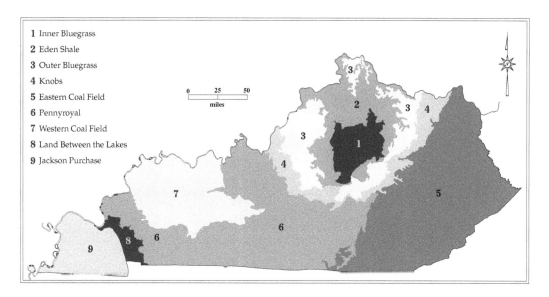

1 Inner Bluegrass
2 Eden Shale
3 Outer Bluegrass
4 Knobs
5 Eastern Coal Field
6 Pennyroyal
7 Western Coal Field
8 Land Between the Lakes
9 Jackson Purchase

Kentucky's physiographic regions.

pragmatic production requirements rather than romantic notions verging on environmental determinism. The frontier distiller required a source of sugar, be it from fruit or the starch in grains or potatoes, and a source of clean, fresh, cool water. Farmers provided the starch, and the water was easily located because central Kentucky's Bluegrass region is underlain by thick beds of water-bearing Ordovician-age limestone and shale.

The alluvial bottomland on the Ohio River's floodplain terraces—such as those at Maysville, Covington, Carrollton, and Louisville—was formed of Pleistocene glacial outwash sand and gravel, which proved to be productive aquifers when tapped by wells.[4] Precipitation, more than forty inches annually, falls as soft water. Some water runs off the surface by way of an extensive stream network. A substantial volume of precipitation percolates down into the soil and bedrock, where it can absorb minerals and metals and enter a groundwater system that is as intricate as the surface drainage network. In Kentucky's limestone country, groundwater feeds thousands of springs, which were favored sites for early settlements. Pioneers built Fort Harrod near Harrodsburg Spring, and Georgetown grew up beside Royal Spring—as did Elijah Craig's distillery, circa 1786—which has a flow rate of 400,000 gallons or more per day.[5] Early settlers preferred to situate their farmsteads at perennial or "never failing" springs that could supply water for their households and livestock. Village settlements on creeks and rivers could draw water directly from those watercourses. Ohio River towns drew water from the river and nearby springs. In time, wells would be bored into the Ohio floodplain's water-bearing gravel, yielding fresh water in volumes sufficient to support municipal and industrial consumers.

How pioneer settlers came to regard limestone groundwater as "pure" resides dimly in the lore of yesteryear, yet it is a staple of Kentucky's distilling origination story. Because

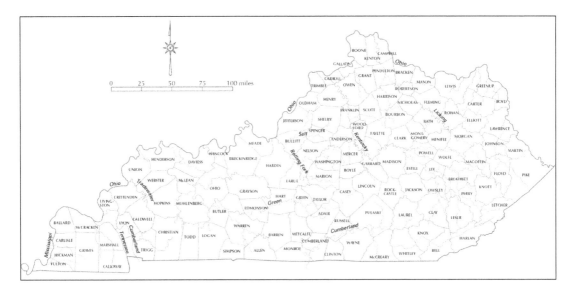

Kentucky's counties and major streams.

water is an effective solvent and readily takes up gases and minerals, pure water in nature is rare. Chemically pure water can be made by distilling it to remove soluble salts. But how would an eighteenth-century farmer-distiller analyze the chemistry of spring or creek water other than by its appearance, taste, and smell? Perhaps if the water was clear, not cloudy, and tasted fresh, not saline or sulfurous—as it did at Bullitt's Lick, Lower Blue Licks, Crab Orchard Springs, Drennon Spring, and Mayslick—it was deemed suitable for drinking and distilling. Certainly, the region had an expansive distribution of springs and surface streams, and sensory water "testing" sufficed until scientific chemical analysis became available. Early distillers also valued flow volume and reliability. Discovery of a new spring at the Frankfort Distillery was deemed sufficiently important to warrant a front-page announcement in the local newspaper. When blasting rock to create a pool for water storage, workers unexpectedly exposed "a stream of water as large as a man's leg, clear and pure and with a steady temperature of 56 degrees." The new spring was deemed "one of the finest in the State," and "the water is from a limestone formation and is absolutely pure. It flows with some force and shows no signs of diminution." The notice concluded: "As the water in Kentucky is what makes Kentucky whiskey different from any other whiskey the spring is invaluable."[6]

During the 1870s, E. H. Taylor Jr. operated three Frankfort distilleries: O.F.C. (Old Fire Copper), Carlisle, and J. S. Taylor. He published a publicity booklet in which he extolled the merits of the water issuing from a spring on the property. In it, he cited the recently published "Map of Kentucky" by John H. Procter, director of the Kentucky Geological Survey,[7] noting that the map shows "a small section of the state made famous by its fine sour-mash whiskeys, the rare-birds-eye limestone of the lowest stratum of the Lower Silurian formation." He continued: "The O.F.C. and other brands of the E. H. Taylor, Jr.,

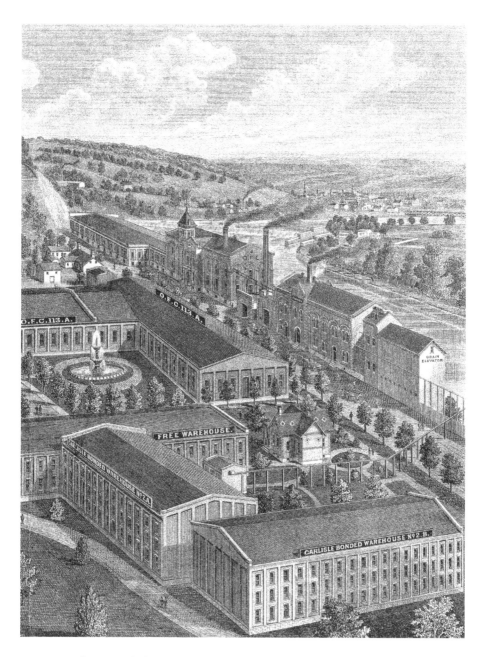

Engraving of E. H. Taylor's original O.F.C. and Carlisle Distilleries, 1869. (From E. H. Taylor Jr. Co., *Description of the O.F.C., Carlisle, and J. S. Taylor Distilleries* [Frankfort, KY: E. H. Taylor Jr. Co., ca. 1886], plate 1)

Co., are produced upon the depressed apex of this stratum, thus securing the best limestone drainage it can possibly afford. The result in fine whiskey is no doubt largely due to the water that, percolating through the limestone, becomes impregnated with its properties, and imparts them to the spirit during the process of manufacture."[8] An engraving of the spring shows it issuing from a hillside a few feet above the level of the Kentucky River.[9] The riverside distillery operates today as Buffalo Trace and is accessed by Wilkinson Boulevard–US 421.

Other distillers had different opinions about the importance of a water source for whiskey distillation. Captain Luther Van Hook, superintendent at the H. E. Shawhan Distillery near Cynthiana, in Harrison County, believed that "sulphur water" made the best whiskey. Such water kept the mash tubs "sweet," in his experience, and he ventured that the famous Blue Licks water made the best whiskey.[10] Since prehistoric times, the Lower Blue Licks spring near the Licking River in northern Nicholas County attracted bison and other animals to the site, where they licked the mineral accumulations in the soil. Indians hunted there, and early settlers established a salt-boiling operation nearby. By the mid-nineteenth century, the spring had become the focus of a large spa, where visitors came to drink and bathe in the "medicinal" waters. Dr. Robert Peter, professor of medical chemistry at the Kentucky School of Medicine and Transylvania University, published a paper on Blue Licks water in 1850. His analysis revealed that the water did indeed contain considerable amounts of sodium chloride, potassium, calcium, magnesium, and other minerals, and its "rotten egg" smell indicated the presence of hydrogen sulfide.[11] While it is unlikely that many other distillers shared Van Hook's opinion that water with a high sulfur and high sodium content was desirable for making bourbon, his contention suggests that there was broad latitude in determining acceptable water quality among distillers.

As long as distillers accessed their grain supplies and markets by overland tracks or trails, a distillery's location near a perennial spring or stream was economically viable. Transport by packhorse or wagon reinforced rather than challenged the decision to site a distillery by a spring or creek. But with the construction of hard-surfaced turnpikes and railroads in the mid to late nineteenth century, many distillers in central Kentucky abandoned springs and relocated their operations to the vicinity of railroad tracks. If "pure" limestone water was the critical element in the geography of distilling, then either pure water could be found wherever railroad tracks were located, or distillers could use any "clean" water source that was convenient to the transportation network, and water quality became a secondary consideration for distillery operation. Questions of appropriate distillery location were more complex for the miller-distiller. Many Bluegrass springs had flow rates of less than fifteen gallons per minute, sufficient for a farm household and a small distillery but inadequate for industrial-scale milling and distilling unless large storage tanks or catchment basins were available. A miller's primary consideration in mill location may have been sufficient water flow from a creek or spring to turn a mill wheel; supplying water to a nearby distillery was important but secondary.

Although distillers concentrated their production in the Bluegrass limestone country, nineteenth-century whiskey production extended across the state into nonlimestone topography. After the Civil War, commercial distilling increased in Daviess County in the

Western Coal Field country. Daviess County's bedrock geology and surface geomorphology are composed of two distinct sections, and neither features limestone. The hilly upland of the south consists of sandstone, shale, and coal measures, while the north features nearly level alluvial plains. Pleistocene glacial meltwater pooled here, creating a large periglacial lake that, when drained, left behind an extensive plain dotted with small hills. The plain lay atop 100 to 150 feet of alluvial gravel, sand, silt, and clay, closely akin to the alluvial plain in west Louisville.[12] Soils were deep, but, given the lack of gradient, natural drainage was sluggish at best. Much of the land between the Green and Ohio Rivers was forested swamp when pioneer settlers arrived. Distillers erecting new works in the late 1860s preferred accessible locations near the Ohio River's south bank, not in the low-lying swamps to the south. In the early 1870s J. W. M. Fields bought a distillery in Daviess County that he dismantled and moved about three miles east of Owensboro, where he reassembled it. The new location was likely along the railroad tracks at Pleasant Valley Road, about half a mile from the Ohio River.[13] Distilling began there in 1873. In 1882 Fields drilled a 1,000-foot well to obtain groundwater to enhance the distillery's water supply. Driller's notes logged the existence of several small coal seams and "impure" limestone, and at 765 feet, the well struck white sandstone, which produced a weak brine. At 900 feet, the well penetrated 70 feet of "coal-black" slate (likely shale). As the drill descended, "the water was growing less and less fit for the contemplated use." As noted by the Kentucky Geological Survey, the driller's log confirmed that the distillery stood atop the Western Coal Field's sandstone, shale, and coal, making further drilling futile.[14] Ohio River water was available, of course, but it was not pristine and required pumps and pipes to bring it to the distillery.

Modern industrial distilleries use potable water in two distinct ways. Potable water is mixed with milled grain to make fermentable mash at a rate of about twenty gallons per bushel of grain. Ideally, mash water should contain calcium sulfate to enhance the rapid conversion of starch to sugar, but it should also be low in iron, bicarbonate, and dissolved solids. The most desirable water is free of organic matter, bacteria, and fungi.[15] Bourbon whiskey is distilled at no more than 80 percent alcohol, or 160 proof. Potable water is also used to dilute barreled whiskey to reduce the alcohol content to no more than 62.5 percent, or 125 proof. Whiskey may be diluted with water again when bottled, bringing the final proof to 80 or higher. In addition, water is used to cool fermenting vats and for cleaning. Groundwater drawn from wells is used extensively for cooling because of its consistent temperature, which typically ranges from 56° to 59°F.[16]

To distillers, the most concerning chemicals found in surface water and groundwater are iron, calcium carbonate, and dissolved inorganic solids. Iron may leach into water from most types of rock and soil. The US Public Health Service recommends that the iron content in drinking water not exceed 0.3 parts per million (ppm); a higher level leaves a reddish brown stain on laundry.[17] Mildly acidic rainwater or groundwater dissolves limestone, producing calcium carbonate and hard water. Water containing calcium carbonate tends to reduce strong acids. A calcium concentration higher than 120 ppm is considered very hard water, and counts of 150 to 200 are cause for concern in the operation of steam boilers and water heaters. Groundwater can also dissolve some naturally occurring inorganic minerals, metals, and salt solids from bedrock. Examples include potassium, chloride, arsenic, chromium, lead, and mercury. The US Public Health Service recommends that domestic and industrial water contain no more than 500 ppm dissolved inorganic solids.[18]

Chemical analysis of spring and well water at a number of Bluegrass distillery sites found that its mineral and iron content was quite varied, and the groundwater was not consistently "pure."[19] Working on behalf of the Kentucky Geological Survey and the US Geological Survey, several geologists conducted a study of industrial water sources in forty-three Bluegrass region counties in the early 1950s. The researchers performed a complete chemical analysis of forty-nine industrial groundwater sources, including springs and wells used by several distilleries. Most distilleries drew their well water from Ordovician or Silurian limestones, and their readings for iron, bicarbonate, and dissolved solids varied significantly. Only a small number used water that contained less than 0.3 ppm iron. In the Inner Bluegrass, the Benson Creek Distillery in Franklin County, west of Frankfort, used about 144,000 gallons of water per day from a large spring and Benson Creek. The spring water contained 0.39 ppm iron, 245 ppm bicarbonate, and 302 ppm dissolved solids.[20] Several other distilleries used water with comparable chemistry values. Two distilleries used water that was exceptionally high in iron. The Carstairs Brothers Distillery at Lair, in Harrison County, pumped water from the Licking River and from a well. The well supplied water from limestone bedrock that contained 6.6 ppm iron, 316 ppm bicarbonate, and 345 ppm dissolved solids.[21] At Camp Nelson in Jessamine County, the Kentucky River Distillery drew water from two wells and the Kentucky River. The sampled well was sixty feet deep and pumped water from Ordovician limestone that contained 11.0 ppm iron, 306 ppm bicarbonate, and 307 ppm dissolved solids.[22] In the Outer Bluegrass at Deatsville, in Nelson County, the T. W. Samuels Distillery drew water from two wells. The sampled well water contained 3.3 ppm iron, 224 ppm bicarbonate, and 216 ppm dissolved solids.[23] Most of these distilleries used water that they, in effect, distilled by passing it through a commercial boiler.

A US Geological Survey analysis of groundwater drawn from wells throughout central Louisville's industrial and residential areas from the early 1940s through 1955 revealed, "Ground water in the Louisville area is very hard, very high in iron content, and generally of the calcium bicarbonate or calcium sulfate type."[24] The study included water drawn from seven distillery wells. Most samples contained concentrations of iron exceeding the 0.3 ppm standard, with values ranging from 0.23 to 5.6. Dissolved solids ranged from a low of 526 to a high of 1,270 ppm. Carbonate concentrations were exceptionally high, ranging from 327 to 619 ppm.[25]

In 1959 Edgar Bronfman of Seagram, one of Louisville's largest distilleries at the time, commented about the limestone water issue. "All of the famous old country distilleries used pond water," Bronfman said, "rain water most of it, the softest water imaginable."[26] Samuel Pollack, chief chemist for Schenley's Distillery, was equally skeptical of purity standards. "I've read volumes and volumes on water. But from a scientific point of view I have not reached a formula," he said, "so many grains of hardness, so much magnesium and so forth. Our water supply is analyzed twice a year, and it varies all over the lot." Pollack wrote a report on the relationship between water and whiskey quality. "Despite all the allegations in writing on the effects of water on the bouquet of whiskey," he said, "we must rely on fifty-four years of practical experience. Irrespective of any chemical or bacteriological analysis, there is no effect of water on whiskey." He concluded, "The only general rule is, if it is good enough for drinking purposes as water, it's good enough for distiller's purposes."[27]

Belief in the pure limestone water origination narrative seemed to depend on one's perspective and motivation. Small nineteenth-century countryside distillers embraced the narrative as part of their tradition and heritage. It was disdained as myth by modern industrial distillers, who were informed by science and empirical investigations and whose distilleries were sited to take advantage of transportation and labor pool access rather than proximity to a spring's "pure," unchanging water.[28]

Climate and Weather

Climatologists categorize Kentucky's climate as humid subtropical. Average temperatures from November through March exceed 32°F, so winters are comparatively short and mild. Prevailing westerly winds bring a succession of high- and low-pressure weather systems. Low-pressure systems produce clouds and precipitation in all seasons. High-pressure systems bring cool or cold, dry air from the north and northwest, often accompanied by clear skies. Summers are generally hot and humid, with a growing season that varies from 170 to 200 days. Precipitation varies from forty to fifty inches per year. About half of the annual precipitation falls from April to September, or during the growing season, which is optimal for agriculture. Summer droughts occur from time to time, as do periods of heavier than normal rainfall.[29]

In any era, weather can impose uncertainty and risk on farmers. Nineteenth-century farmers had limited options when it came to adjusting to weather variability. Before the development of disease-resistant crop varieties, hot, humid summers brought the likelihood of destructive rust and smut in grain crops. Heavy rains caused severe soil erosion before the development of winter cover crops, contour plowing, and sodded waterways. The farmers' intimate connection to the physical environment required anticipation and planning and a complex integration of diverse operations. If extraordinary weather events threatened agricultural production, they also inserted risk and uncertainty directly into the distilling industry and related businesses, including teamsters, coopers, lumber mills, hardware retailers, wholesale brokers, and banks.[30]

Seasonality

Ohio Valley farmers established a corn, wheat, and livestock economy in the six decades between 1800 and the beginning of the Civil War.[31] In Kentucky, farmers also produced hemp and tobacco. Grain production required concerted attention five months of the year. The total time expended on wheat could be less than one month, however, primarily at spring planting and again at harvest, which required one to two weeks of intensive work during midsummer. If planted by early May, corn required two or three cultivations before being "laid by" in June, when the plants had grown too large for further cultivation. The corn crop did not require workers again until the harvest in September or October, which involved the extended process of cutting, shocking, husking, and cribbing. Maintaining a herd of feeder cattle or hogs required daily attention year-round. Farmers raising tobacco followed a twelve-month calendar from seed selection and field preparation in late winter to barn curing, stripping, and marketing in late fall. Hemp production required labor for field preparation and spring planting, but the most intensive work occurred in the fall, with cutting, shocking, retting, breaking, cleaning, and storing.

Depending on the scale and type of farming practiced in a given area, rural laborers could rely on steady employment for half a year, and perhaps more on a tobacco farm. The remainder of the year, rural laborers found itinerant work cutting and splitting timber for shingles, fence rails, construction lumber, and fuelwood, as well as building and repairing fences and farm buildings. Day laborers might perform other farming jobs such as butchering hogs, salting meat, and digging potatoes.[32] Off-farm work might be available with turnpike contractors, gristmills, or distilleries. The nineteenth-century distilling season began in November or December and extended to May or June. Still house temperatures in the summer and early fall months were generally too warm for effective malting and fermentation.[33]

Site Selection and Development

Frontier farmers and millers erected mills and distilleries at favored sites utilizing local materials. Desirable site characteristics included a perennial spring or stream, abundant timber for fuel, productive farmland as a local source for grains, a local labor force, and waterway or road access. Millers generally built gristmills and companion distilleries at two types of sites: creek-side and upland. During the frontier decades, the most desirable mill and distillery sites lay along large-volume creeks, preferably with access to a navigable river. Creek-side mills were often of substantial capacity and remained operational until the mid-nineteenth century or later. Creek valleys in stream-dissected country with 200 to 400 feet of local relief were heavily wooded and difficult to access. Nevertheless, some creek-side sites were large enough to accommodate several dams, millraces, and mills along the valley bottom. Rock-ledge springs feeding the creeks were often used for water power, in addition to dammed pools on the main creek channel.

Lower Howard's Creek in Clark County, across the Kentucky River from Boonesborough, offered several potential creek-side industrial sites. Rising on the limestone upland south of Winchester, Lower Howard's Creek flows south to the Kentucky River, cutting a gorge through 400 feet of horizontally bedded limestone to river level. Mill construction and operation along Lower Howard's Creek began in the late 1700s, shortly after the founding of Boonesborough. The creek was not only one of Kentucky's first industrial centers but also one of the first large-scale industrial sites in the trans-Appalachian West, hosting fifteen gristmills and four distilleries, as well as sawmills, cooper shops, and leather tanneries.[34] Importantly, early mills and distilleries and their associated dams and millraces were often designed and built by skilled millwrights, carpenters, and stonemasons, assisted by common laborers.[35] Barrels of flour and whiskey produced at Lower Howard's Creek were moved down the valley to a landing on the Kentucky River, where laborers loaded them onto flatboats for the extended trip down the Kentucky River to the Ohio River and then, perhaps, on to Natchez, New Orleans, and other southern markets. Some mills and distilleries on Lower Howard's Creek stopped production during the Civil War. Others remained in production until the late 1800s.

The second type of preferred site for mill and distillery development was on the rolling upland sections of small streams in both the Inner and Outer Bluegrass country. In 1788 Bourbon County resident Isaac Ruddell built a dam on Hinkston Creek, near its junction with Stoner Creek, to impound water to power a gristmill and sawmill.[36] By 1790, carpenters had completed a bridge across Hinkston Creek, and five more mills stood at the site. The mill cluster attracted laborers and other businesses, and the settlement became known as Ruddles Mills.[37] By 1800, sixty-six mills operated in Bourbon County, many of them on Hinkston Creek and Stoner Creek.[38] Distillers built works at Ruddles Mills in the early nineteenth century, and some mills were converted into distilleries in the late 1860s and 1870s. Outer Bluegrass trunk streams in Nelson County, such as Beech Creek and Rolling Fork, and their tributaries, such as Knob Creek, accommodated numerous mills and distilleries.

Farmers, millers, and distillers also developed upland sites at or near large perennial springs, often surrounded by quality farmland but not oriented near a large creek or river. Upland mills and distilleries were likely smaller in scale than the early creek-side sites of the same period, and they were tethered to overland wagon tracks and packhorse trails. The oldest distillery at such a site in Bourbon County may have been the Jacob Spears Distillery on Route 1836 near Ewalts Crossroads. Spears built a stone house, a distillery, and a warehouse near an all-weather spring. In Washington County, in the Outer Bluegrass, a 500-acre farm four miles from Springfield was advertised for sale in 1839. The upland farm was "well adapted for a stock farm being well watered," the ad stated. "It is also well adapted for a distillery, having now an establishment for that purpose. It is well timbered, and all the land is good and lays well."[39] Farmers and millers viewed their upland properties as both agricultural and industrial enterprises and believed that a distillery or a mill increased a farm property's desirability. In June 1839 the *Franklin Farmer* carried an advertisement by Mr. B. Dougherty, who was offering his farm for purchase: "I have for sale, in Franklin county, a Farm containing about 200 acres situated about five miles from Frankfort on the Georgetown Turnpike road. Also, an Engine, Mill and Distillery. Apply on the premises."[40] Most such ads mentioned road access, which became increasingly important as mills and distilleries increased in size and production capacity. By 1850, Kentucky's residents included 742 millers and 224 millwrights.[41]

Eighteenth- and nineteenth-century farmers, millers, and distillers were bearers of traditional knowledge and practices that they used to inhabit their physical environments. Decisions about the locations of mills or distilleries were heavily influenced by people's perceptions and understandings of the environment available to them. Once they realized that some tactics worked better than others, their behavior became directed and intentional through informed decision making. Farmers, millers, and distillers accomplished much of their work by manual labor, and they repeated the day-to-day and season-to-season activities that proved effective. Yet their activities were often circumscribed by conditions and situations they could not fully address until the development of tools permitted them to establish dominion over their environments.[42]

Soils

Although distilleries operated in most sections of the state by 1810, the most attractive locations for large-scale rural distilling operations were the Bluegrass country and the Ohio River floodplain, where soils were fertile and farms productive. Three distinct physiographic zones or subregions make up the Bluegrass: the Inner Bluegrass, the Eden Shale Hills, and the Outer Bluegrass. Each subregion has a distinct bedrock geology and surface geomorphology, and the boundaries between them are visually demarcated by narrow transitions in bedrock and topography. Two major escarpments delineate the Bluegrass from bordering regions. The Pottsville Escarpment bounds the region on the east at the edge of the Appalachian Plateau, and Muldraugh Hill marks the region's southern and western boundary with the Pennyroyal.

With the exception of tributary valleys near the Kentucky River that are deeply dissected by streams, the Inner Bluegrass is a gently rolling upland that was formed on phosphate-rich Ordovician-age limestones. The soils are residual, having developed through weathering and erosion; they vary from shallow to deep and tend to be very fertile. Precipitation either runs off the surface in low-gradient streams or percolates through the soil into the soluble bedrock, where it erodes rock surfaces and creates fissures, often enlarging cracks into small passages and caves that may feed surface springs, creating a karst topography. The surface may be dimpled by saucer-shaped sinkholes, some of them hundreds of feet wide; surface streams may disappear into swallow holes and flow underground, often emerging miles away.

The annular Eden Shale Hills subregion forms an asymmetrical circle around the Inner Bluegrass. The foundation bedrock here is thinly bedded limestone, siltstone, and calcareous shale. The shale readily erodes, creating a sharply corrugated topography of narrow ridges connected to narrow valleys by high-angle slopes. Eden soils are thin. The slopes are heavily eroded, and their surfaces are often littered with stones. When cleared of the beech–black oak–hickory woodland that favors this area, farmers find the soils uninviting. The only sections suitable for field agriculture are the broader ridgetops and valley bottoms.

The Outer Bluegrass is also annular and asymmetrical and lies in a broad arc around the Eden Shale Hills—wide on the east and west, narrow on the north and south. The Outer Bluegrass surface is a gently rolling upland with deep, fertile soils that developed atop comparatively young Ordovician limestones. The eastern section of the Outer Bluegrass is traversed by the Licking and Kentucky Rivers and their tributaries. To the west, the Salt River, Beech Fork, and Rolling Fork flow in looping meanders across the low-gradient surface toward the Ohio River.

The outer perimeter of the Outer Bluegrass is set off from the fringing escarpments by the Knobs, a nearly horseshoe-shaped subregion that forms a three-quarter circle on the east, south, and west. Only a few miles in width, the Knobs' topography is punctuated by conical hills or knobs that rise 300 to 400 feet above the surrounding countryside and are capped by erosion-resistant conglomerate rocks. The Knobs' base material is shale, and the interstitial areas between the hills are underlain with shale and sandstone. The topographic surface is deeply dissected by streams, and the bedrock yields soils of modest fertility.[43]

To establish productive agriculture, eighteenth- and nineteenth-century Kentucky farmers had to adapt their practices to environments that often differed in complex ways over short distances.[44] Many farmers understood, at least in a general sense, the rudimentary differences in soil capability from one place to another.[45] And distillers and millers depended on neighborhood farmers to produce grains in ample amounts to yield a surplus to sell. Distillers and millers, therefore, had an interest in conducting their operations on or adjacent to land with good farming potential.

The relationship among environment, agricultural production, and the evolving geography of distilling begins with the soil's potential for grain production. Three county clusters in the greater Bluegrass region where distilling became a notable industry serve as illustrations.

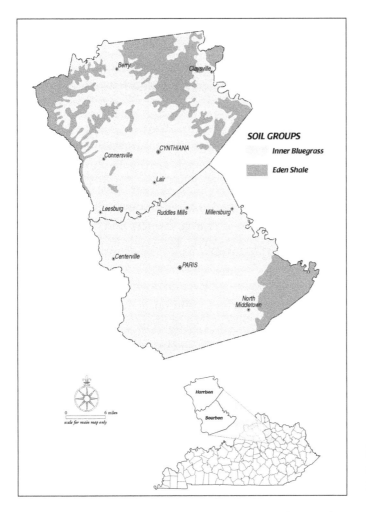

SOIL GROUPS

Inner Bluegrass

Eden Shale

Physiographic boundaries and soil associations: Bourbon and Harrison Counties.

Bourbon and Harrison Counties occupy the northeast corner of the Inner Bluegrass physiographic region. The stream-dissected Eden Shale Hills encroach in the north and southeast. The Maury-McAfee-Faywood soil association is highly desirable for agriculture and is representative of large sections of the Inner Bluegrass portions of these two counties.[46] The carbonate Lexington limestone parent material contains phosphate, some of which is imparted to deep, loamy, fertile soils.[47] The land surface is a rolling upland with broad karst sinkholes, and it supports intensive agriculture. In contrast, the Eden Shale Hills region offers only limited agricultural potential.

The northwest portion of the Inner Bluegrass, as represented by Anderson, Franklin, and Woodford Counties, is bisected by the Kentucky River palisades, a 300-foot-deep gorge with nearly vertical limestone cliffs. Land within four to five miles of the palisades is deeply dissected by tributary streams. The rolling upland surface is underlain by Lexington limestone and has a soil profile that closely resembles that of Bourbon and Harrison Counties. The surface is pocked with sinkholes in some areas, but the loamy soils are well

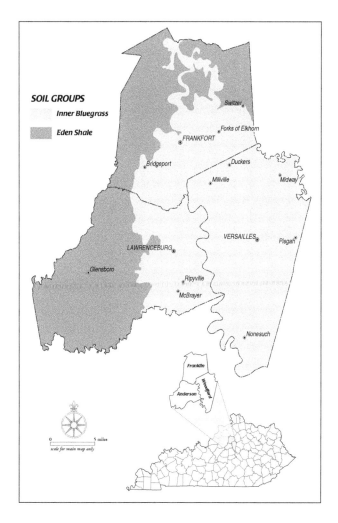

SOIL GROUPS
Inner Bluegrass
Eden Shale

Physiographic boundaries and soil associations: Anderson, Franklin, and Woodford Counties.

suited for intensive agriculture, and historically, they have been productive. The western half of Anderson County and the northern half of Franklin County are in the Eden Shale belt, where field agriculture has been largely confined to the valley bottoms.[48]

The western section of the Outer Bluegrass region is represented by Marion, Nelson, and Washington Counties. Karst and underground drainage is not as well developed as in some parts of the Inner Bluegrass. The surface drains west and north by way of the Chaplin River, Beech Fork, and Rolling Fork and their extensive tributary networks. Streams issue from the Eden Shale Hills to the east and cross the limestones of the Outer Bluegrass before entering the shales and sandstones of the Knobs region to the west. The Eden Shale Hills occupy the eastern half of Marion County and a small section of northeastern Nelson County. The topography and soils here are similar to those found in the Eden Shale sections of Anderson and Franklin Counties.

The Outer Bluegrass section is underlain by two different limestone formations. The

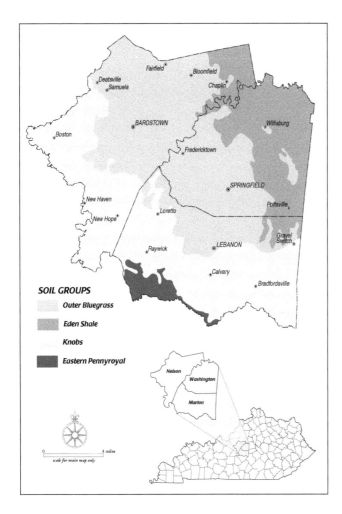

Physiographic boundaries and soil associations: Marion, Nelson, and Washington Counties.

Grant Lake limestone, which is interbedded with shale, occurs in a small section of northern Marion County and in significant portions of Washington and eastern Nelson Counties. A belt of Laurel dolomite extends northwest to southeast across the central section of Nelson County and extends into Washington County. On the Grant Lake limestone, soils are representative of the Lowell-Fairmount association; these soils occur on rolling land and are deep, finely textured, and of moderate fertility. The Pembroke association, weathered out of Laurel dolomite, has deep, loamy, fertile soils. The land surface ranges from nearly level to rolling and invites intensive agriculture.

The Knobs region covers the western quarter of Nelson County and the southern half of Marion County. Shale and sandstone parent materials yield soils represented by the Rockcastle-Colyer association. Rockcastle soils are found on heavily rolling to steep slopes; they are thin, do not readily retain moisture, and are only moderately fertile. Farmers cultivated the lower slopes but left much of the steeper land in woodland.[49]

Grains

Kentucky's nineteenth-century distilleries produced bourbon whiskey from a cooked and fermented mash of corn and small grains that included rye or wheat and malted barley. A common whiskey mash bill, or recipe, called for 30 percent small grains and 70 percent corn.[50] Until reliable roads allowed transport over significant distances, Kentucky distillers were acutely aware of the importance of locating their distilleries at sites that had access to large volumes of quality grains. Central Kentucky grain farmers often raised livestock as well. From the distiller's perspective, livestock production was both oppositional and complementary. It was oppositional because livestock were often fed grains, primarily corn, thus competing with distillers. But livestock production could also be complementary, in that hogs and cattle could be fed the distillery's spent grains, termed "slop," which provided a supplementary source of income for distillers while reducing the need to dispose of this otherwise nuisance by-product.

Corn and wheat were widely produced in the nineteenth century, but not always in sufficient amounts for home use, livestock feeding, and distilling. Some farmers also produced rye and barley, but in limited quantities. The editor of the *Cynthiana Democrat* offered this insight on the relationship between grain and distilling in 1869: "Farm lands are renting from $5 to $10 per acre. A great amount of sod land is being broken up; farmers are preparing to plant a large crop of corn. The distilling interests here amply justify the planting of a great breadth of land in this grain. They are but in their infancy and are as sure as the demand for whisky, which is as sure as the demand for bread."[51] Distillers deemed access to a reliable grain supply as important as access to a dependable spring or stream, and as distilling capacity increased, the expansive bluegrass pastures that had sustained the region's early cattle industry began to yield to the grain farmers' plows and harrows.

Corn or Maize

Indian corn (*Zea mays*) was Kentucky's frontier crop of choice and became the primary grain used for whiskey distilling. John F. D. Smyth, a British soldier who traveled extensively along America's Eastern Seaboard and through the trans-Appalachian West, was impressed by the versatility of Indian corn. The leaves could be cured for horse feed, and the tassels, stalks, and husks made fine fodder for cattle. The grain "supports the inhabitants themselves, both white and black, besides feeding their horses, and fattening their hogs," Smyth noted. More impressive, he thought, was corn's productivity when properly planted and cultivated. "A bushel of corn will plant near twenty acres; and on the richest lands twenty acres will produce two hundred and fifty barrels or one thousand two hundred and fifty bushels. A most astonishing increase indeed!"[52] In 1793 land speculator George Imlay published a glowing report of Kentucky's fecund Bluegrass and Green

River country. He observed that newly arrived settlers, equipped with only basic tools, could clear three acres of land, plant corn, and expect yields of thirty bushels per acre in their first year. Given the extraordinary productivity of crops and livestock, a farmer who cleared and improved two to three acres of land each year would be able to recoup his costs in three years.[53] By the 1880s, the Kentucky commissioner of the Bureau of Agriculture declared corn to be "our universal crop."[54]

Preceding statehood in 1792, Kentucky settlers pursued land claims based on private surveys or Virginia military warrants. According to Virginia law, settlers could claim title to land by surveying it and improving it, which meant building a house and planting a crop. The most valued claims lay in the Bluegrass country's limestone regions—lands that included perennial springs and may have been wooded or partially covered in cane (*Arundinaria gigantea*).[55] To claim their land, a farm family would clear the woodland or cane-brakes, build a house and a stable, split rails for fences, and plant a garden and crops.[56] Corn was usually the first crop planted by surveyors and settlers. Small single-family properties of 50 to 200 acres might have 1 to 3 acres of corn under cultivation by the second or third year of settlement. The fertile soils produced generous yields. Even desultory planting and weeding of an acre of corn produced 50 to 80 bushels. In rare instances, established farmers might produce more than 100 bushels per acre.[57] Corn became a staple crop; it was fed to livestock and consumed by the farm family at every meal. Within a few years, some Bluegrass farms were producing surplus corn well in excess of farm and household needs. Among farmstead structures, the corncrib was arguably second in importance only to the farmhouse itself.[58]

European settlers adopted several corn varieties grown by Native Americans. Indians in the Northeast grew a flint corn (*Zea mays* var. *indurate*) with thin ears and eight to ten rows of hard kernels. Mid-Atlantic Indians raised a number of varieties, including flint corns and a corn with thick ears and fourteen to thirty rows of soft kernels.[59] Indian corn grown in the South included southern big, small white flint, and Virginia white gourd-seed, which was widely planted by Anglo settlers moving from Virginia, Maryland, and the Carolinas to Kentucky and the Ohio Valley.[60] Because corn produces seed by open pollination, accidental crosses between flint and gourdseed varieties were common and produced a dent-type corn (*Zea mays* var. *indentata*) that was commonly grown in Tennessee and Kentucky, the country's top two corn-producing states by the 1820s.[61] A farmer in Boone County, Indiana, developed a deep-kernel dent variety in about 1874 that became known as Boone County white; it was favored for making meal for bread making and for distilling.

Managing a corn crop—planting, cutting, shocking, husking, and cribbing—was accomplished by manual labor and required months of effort. Distillers who wanted corn for their winter distilling season had to consider this schedule and sequence their purchases accordingly. This might have meant buying corn the previous year and storing it to ensure an adequate supply, although discriminating distillers preferred to use "fresh" corn harvested just weeks before milling and distilling.

By the early nineteenth century, corn was in demand for consumption as both a food grain (cornmeal) and a feed grain for livestock (ear corn or cracked kernels). It was also the basis for the distilling of spirits. Corn became a basic ingredient in the southern diet; wheat and rye flour were luxuries.[62] The price of wheat in 1820 was 75 cents to $1 per bushel, and milled wheat flour cost $3 per 100 pounds.[63] In comparison, rye was priced at 50 cents, while corn brought 37 to 50 cents. In the 1870s Ohio Valley distillers found that corn produced south of the Ohio River could be left in the field until it was fully ripe and dry, thus yielding more starch than corn produced in the short-growing-season Middle West. Knowing this, distillers were often willing to pay a premium of a few cents per bushel for corn grown in Kentucky and Tennessee.[64]

By the mid-nineteenth century, corn was the chief national agricultural commodity, bringing in nearly twice the gross revenue of any other crop. Farmers planted about 31 million acres of improved farmland in corn, and the average yield was about 18 bushels per acre. National corn production reached more than 592 million bushels. Beer brewers and spirituous liquor distillers consumed some 11 million bushels, or less than 2 percent of the national corn supply, in 1850.[65] Kentucky ranked second in corn harvested, producing about 59 million bushels, or nearly 10 percent of the total national production. By the late 1800s, Kentucky corn production had increased to more than 70 million bushels per year. Distillers who did not raise their own grain, especially those who built their distillery works in towns and cities, were compelled to compete directly with livestock feeders for grain. The Ashland Distillery in Lexington regularly advertised for grain. "Farmers will please understand," one ad stated, "we are *always* in the market [for corn], and willing to pay the highest cash price. We also want a few thousand bushels of No. 1 Rye."[66]

Kentucky's Corn Production and Distillery Consumption, 1880 and 1890

Year	Corn Produced (Bushels)	Corn Consumed by Distilleries (Bushels)	Percentage Consumed by Distilleries
1880*	72,852,263	1,685,440	2.3
1890	78,434,847	6,075,330	7.7

Sources: US Internal Revenue Service, *Report of the Commissioner of Internal Revenue, 1879* and *1890* (Washington, DC: GPO, 1879, 1890); US Census of Agriculture, 1880 and 1890.
* Because the IRS report for 1880 was unavailable, 1879 figures were substituted.

As distillers mechanized their operations and increased their production capacity in the 1870s, they rapidly drew down local grain supplies. Distillers used 2.3 percent of the total state corn production in 1880 and 7.7 percent in 1890. In Bourbon County, distillers purchased all their grain within the county until 1880–1881. Thereafter, most of their grain requirements had to be met by farmers elsewhere in Kentucky or by out-of-state sources. Those distillers who were unable to obtain "imported" corn were forced to curtail operations.[67] By the 1880s, corn cost 40 to 45 cents per bushel, which was still comparatively cheap, given that rye cost 75 to 80 cents. Assuming adequate transportation access, and discounting interest on loans, moderately priced grain permitted large, efficient distilleries—those that produced more than four gallons of distilled spirits per bushel of grain—to profit if their whiskey sold for 25 cents per gallon or more. By the first decade of the twentieth century, the expanding national railroad network allowed Kentucky's industrial distillers to obtain grain shipments from farms more than 1,000 miles away. Farmers on the northern Great Plains raised quality corn, wheat, rye, and barley, and some began to cater to the distilling industry.

Wheat

As a food grain, wheat (*Triticum aestivum*) provided sustenance. Colonial farmers found that although wheat did well in southeastern Pennsylvania and upstate New York, the grain did not thrive in the South, in part because the climate there was favorable to the development of blight, mildew, and a variety of other plant diseases. The region also harbored insects that attacked wheat plants. As settlement expanded west, the demand for wheat flour followed, and wheat acreage increased rapidly in the Ohio Valley frontier.[68] Corn was more widely planted initially, but wheat commanded a much higher price than corn by the 1840s.[69] The amount of wheat ground for flour and human consumption was estimated at more than four bushels per capita per year in the 1840s, and total consumption approached total production in several states. Given the demand for flour, wheat was often too expensive to be used as a primary distilling grain, other than in limited production.

Wheat cultivation west of the Appalachians increased in direct relationship to the extension and expansion of settlement, and grain milling tended to develop in tandem. "The miller's absence meant for the farm family a diet centered about home-pounded cornbread; his presence made possible white wheat bread and also furnished a market for flour."[70] Kentucky farmers planted several different wheat cultivars, although many preferred the Mediterranean and Lancaster varieties.[71] Bakers favored soft wheats for making flat bread, crackers, and pastries; millers found soft wheats easier to mill. Hard wheat had a higher gluten content and was used to make bread and as a general-purpose flour. The steel roller mill, invented in 1878, readily ground the hard wheat varieties and produced quality flour.

Grain production was more readily mechanized than corn production. Grain drills, available in the 1870s, placed seeds and fertilizers such as bone dust in the same furrow.

Some farmers reported that the addition of minerals increased yields by fivefold or more.[72] By the 1840s, wheat remained a subsistence crop in some areas, but farmers in the Ohio Valley who produced small surpluses sold the grain to millers and in general markets as a cash crop. Initially, wheat sales were largely local; the cost of transporting wheat any significant distance to a commercial market could approach 40 percent of its potential value. Corn remained the basic staple crop. In the Ohio Valley, average annual corn consumption equaled that of wheat; in the South, corn consumption exceeded wheat consumption by two or three times.[73] Certainly, the corn-wheat price differential did not encourage the use of wheat as a primary distilling grain, although some distillers used wheat as a secondary grain in place of rye, largely because it imparted a mellower flavor to whiskey. This was an important consideration when most whiskeys were given limited time to age before being sold.

Nineteenth-century rural communities were often served by small custom mills that ground farmers' grains in return for a portion of the grain as payment. Farmers loaded sacks of wheat onto a packhorse or a mule for delivery to the mill for grinding. As roadways improved and wheat acreage increased, merchant millers specialized in buying quantities of sacked grain delivered to the mill by wagon. The millers then shipped the grain or flour to wholesale and retail merchants. The system of shipping sacked wheat and other grains from farms to mills, then to warehouses and riverboats, and finally to wholesalers and retailers was widespread across the Ohio Valley and Middle West prior to the development of reliable railroads.[74]

Rye

Commonly grown as a winter- or spring-planted crop, rye (*Secale cereale*) flourished in cool climates. The grain was grown widely in the colonies from New England south to the Potomac River on those lands where wheat struggled. Colonists grew rye before they began to produce wheat, and rye flour and cornmeal were the primary ingredients in breadstuffs.[75] By the end of the Revolutionary War, farmers in western Pennsylvania were planting rye on the rough and stony uplands, where it became a staple grain. Surplus grain was not readily transportable to distant markets, so rye became the principal ingredient in farm whiskey distilling.[76] When the national government imposed a tax on whiskey to retire Revolutionary War debts, Pennsylvania farmer-distillers rebelled; many moved to the Ohio River Valley and Kentucky.

Rye production in the 1840s centered in New York and Pennsylvania, but acreage declined by one-third during that decade because of a decline in demand by distillers, "to which a large part of the crop is applied."[77] In 1850, out of a total US rye production of 14,188,600 bushels, 2,144,000 bushels, or 15 percent, was consumed in the manufacture of malt and spirituous liquors.[78] Rye acreage continued to decline in the eastern states as the crop followed the settlement of the frontier into the Upper Middle West and the eastern Great Plains.[79]

Rye varieties were less well developed than wheat varieties, the most common being winter, spring, black, white, and common.[80] By the 1830s, Kentucky farmers were planting rye in the fall on the stubble of harvested grain fields. The growing rye formed a dense mat that shaded and protected the soil from winter erosion. Some farmers turned cattle onto their rye fields to graze during the winter months, weather permitting. In early spring the rye revived from dormancy and continued to grow. When the field was dry enough to plow, the rye was plowed under to provide a green manure fertilizer before planting the field in corn or other crops.[81] That rye became a secondary distilling grain in Kentucky cannot be attributed to production surpluses or even purpose-grown crops. It is more likely related to traditional recipes and preferences brought by migrants from the Atlantic coast states and western Pennsylvania.

Malting Barley

Barley (*Hordeum vulgare*) has a wider ecological range than any other grain.[82] Malting barley is best grown in cool, humid climates, although the grain will tolerate higher temperatures and semiarid conditions. Dry, sunny weather in mid to late summer lowers the risk of mold or smut, which gives the grain a musty smell and makes it unacceptable for malting. Production of a quality crop requires well-drained loam soils; barley will not tolerate heavy clay. Much of the South, therefore, is not well suited to barley production. Barley was one of the first grains planted by New England colonists, and by 1611, the grain was under cultivation in pioneer settlements in Virginia, New Netherland, Nova Scotia, and Quebec. By 1648, barley production was widespread across the Middle and North Atlantic colonies, and barley's importance among grains was exceeded only by corn and wheat.[83]

From the beginning, colonists grew barley primarily to make malt for brewing rather than as a food or feed grain.[84] In 1850 total US barley production was 5,167,000 bushels; of this, 3,780,000 bushels, or more than 73 percent, was consumed in the production of malt and spirituous liquors, while much of the remainder was used as livestock feed.[85] In 1844 the Kentucky barley crop was estimated at 14,000 bushels, compared with 3.9 million bushels of wheat and 2.3 million bushels of rye.[86] From 1840 to 1850 New York's Mohawk Valley and Finger Lakes region led the nation in barley production. In 1860 New York's production was surpassed by farmers in California's Central Valley. By 1880, Kentucky's barley crop had increased to 20,000 acres producing 486,000 bushels, or 1.1 percent of the total national production.[87] From New York, barley production moved into the Middle West and central and northern Great Plains, where it flourished. By 1900, the Red River Valley of northwestern Minnesota and the eastern Dakotas, the high plains of western Kansas and Nebraska, and California's Central Valley had become the nation's three primary barley-producing areas.[88] Yields varied from thirty to fifty bushels per acre or more.

In the 1850s European and American farmers planted several barley varieties that maltsters preferred because of their disease resistance and because they produced a full kernel. As concerns about quality and production efficiency increased in the nineteenth century's latter decades, maltsters came to prefer the six-row Manchuria and Oderbrucker varieties because of their superior malting performance. Between 1870 and Prohibition in 1920, the distilling and brewing industry requirements for malting barley became more exacting. Malting-quality barley commanded a premium price, but typically three-fourths of the crop failed to meet malting standards. Contemporary maltsters select barley that has plump, mature kernels with fully developed proteins and starches, is free from disease or weather damage, and is clean and carefully threshed.[89]

The malting process converts barley into a distilling grain by converting its starch into sugar. Maltsters steep the grain in cold water and spread it on a dry malting floor to germinate. Chemical changes make the starch more soluble and readily extracted by water. The sprouting process is stopped by floor and kiln drying. The sprouts are removed, and the dried grain kernels are the malt.[90] Distiller's malt is generally germinated at relatively high moisture levels and dried in low heat to approximately 6 percent moisture; malts processed in this manner produce comparatively high enzyme activity.[91] Modern malting requirements are exacting, and the regional limitations on growing malting-quality barley are more restrictive than those imposed on barley produced to make flour or animal feed.[92]

Though malted barley is required for whiskey distilling, nineteenth-century Kentucky distillers often could not obtain locally produced malt. Some distillers were obliged to use malted rye—and perhaps oats or wheat—if acceptable malted barley was not available.[93] As regional railroad networks expanded into the Middle West and Great Plains after the Civil War, Cincinnati and Louisville brokers could purchase malted barley from distant suppliers. Because malt weighs less than unmalted barley, maltsters in the Dakotas and the Prairie Provinces of Canada could ship malt to Ohio Valley brokers at a comparatively low cost. By the mid-1880s, eighteen malting sales offices and three malt kilns operated in Cincinnati, in addition to the malt manufactured by the city's brewers for their own use. Cincinnati was thus a primary malt market for Kentucky's distillers.[94]

In the 1850s grains accounted for roughly 80 percent of the cost of distilling a gallon of whiskey.[95] In the second half of the nineteenth century, increased distilling capacity by a rapidly growing number of industrial distilleries pushed the demand for grains beyond the capacity of local farms. Long-distance grain shipping, abetted by a rapidly expanding railroad network, was required to ensure supplies. Trunk rail lines, distillery railroad sidings, and grain storage buildings had become an important part of the distiller's landscape.

Livestock

Livestock were ubiquitous on nineteenth-century Kentucky farms, where they provided meat (feeder cattle and hogs), milk (dairy cattle), wool (sheep), and motive power (horses, mules, and oxen). Subsistence farmers grew crops and raised livestock to support themselves. With the transition to commercial farming, crops were increasingly produced for livestock feed, and animals competed directly with distillers for farmers' excess grains. Farm distillers adapted by feeding their spent distilling grains, or slop, to cattle and hogs, with the happy result that the animals gained significant weight by eating a by-product the distiller otherwise would have discarded. But early farm distilleries used grains in relatively small quantities, and the slop they produced supported no more than a few hogs or cattle. As distilling became industrialized and production volume increased, some distillers established large feeding lots that they filled with livestock purchased from local farmers. Other distillers contracted with farmers or brokers to feed their stock on a per-animal or per-week basis.

Hogs

In the 1830s Kentucky hog farmers marketed their surplus hogs to local butchers but also drove them overland to markets in the Carolinas. Bird Smith, writing in the *Franklin Farmer* in 1838, reported that hogs raised in New England, where they were confined to barns and fed vegetables rather than being allowed to run in open pastures, produced pork that brought 10 cents per pound in Boston markets. Confinement of the hogs also allowed farmers to collect manure, which was worth $2 to $3 per load, or 25 percent of the total value of pork produced.[96] In contrast, pork prices in Louisville were only 5 cents per pound, and manure could not be collected and sold because hogs were not generally confined in Kentucky. Smith concluded that an extensive piggery would not be profitable in Kentucky unless it was connected with a distillery, where the confined hogs could be fed slop during the distilling season and put out to graze during the late spring and summer.

There was a convenient overlap in the seasonality of raising hogs and distilling. Distilling activity began in November and reached peak production during the winter and early spring. Given the dormancy of pasture grass and the limited availability of grain crops during the winter months, the demand for livestock feed was greatest during the same period that the supply of spent distillery grains peaked. As distillers industrialized and increased the scale of their operations after the Civil War, their demand for feeder stock, especially hogs, also increased. When a distillery on Elkhorn Creek in Scott County was put up for sale in 1870, the advertisement described the property as including "a Blacksmith Shop; Stone-House; Two new Corn Cribs that will hold Two Thousand barrels of corn; Hog Pens, capable of holding One Thousand Hogs; and situated on one of the best lots in the county, for slopping Cattle and Mules."[97] The phrase "best lots in the county" may have referred to the distillery property, or it may have referred to the exceptionally productive surrounding farmland, which could be a source of both distilling grain and feeder stock.

Cattle

Early settlers moving from Maryland, Virginia, and the Carolinas to claim land in Kentucky's Bluegrass region often drove their livestock on foot while carrying their belongings on pack animals. By the late 1700s, central Kentucky farms were producing feeder cattle for home consumption and local and regional markets. Farmers grazed their cattle on the region's natural woodland pastures and expansive stands of cane.[98] Farmers grew corn and, following Virginia custom, cut cornstalks and stacked them into shocks to cure. Two-year-old cattle were turned into the fields to feed on the ear corn and stalks over the winter. The following spring and summer, the cattle grazed in grass pastures. After the fall harvest, the cattle were again fed corn until February, when they were driven to distant markets.[99] Cattle breeding and feeding were sufficiently extensive in central Kentucky that, by 1800, the area had become the first of four major cattle feeding areas in the Ohio Valley. The typical Bluegrass farm might have thirty to fifty cattle, horses, hogs, sheep, and a still.[100]

Complementary Businesses

By the mid-nineteenth century, the beef cattle feeding industry was a long-standing tradition in central Kentucky. Distillery hog and cattle feedlots were part of that infrastructure and augmented the feeding industry's development. Distilling and livestock feeding continued as tandem businesses into the twentieth century. The Taylor & Williams Distillery near Fairfield, in Nelson County, was a medium-sized works with a cattle shed and a hay barn. A slop pipe likely carried spent grains to a nearby hog or cattle feedlot enclosed by a perimeter wood-slat fence.

Farming and distilling businesses were complementary in terms of the seasonality of grain production and consumption, as well as in the timing of labor use and availability. The agricultural production cycle ranged from four to six months for corn and small grains, six months to a year for the production of fat hogs, and three to five years for the breeding and fattening of cattle. Farmers were the distillers' primary source of distilling grains and feeder stock. At the beginning of a working year's cycle, farmers would either have to own breeding animals, feed, seed, and tools or have access to cash or credit to obtain them.[101] Distillers had to make periodic federal tax payments on their stored products after 1868, and if they did not have the cash on hand, they would have to borrow the funds. Thus, farmers and distillers required periodic access to financing and often sought credit from the same banks and other financial sources. In this way, farming and distilling were noncomplementary, in that both businesses competed for access to money from the same sources. Despite these tensions, grains and feeder stock continued to move from area farms to distilleries.

After the Civil War, many distilleries with railroad access industrialized and increased their

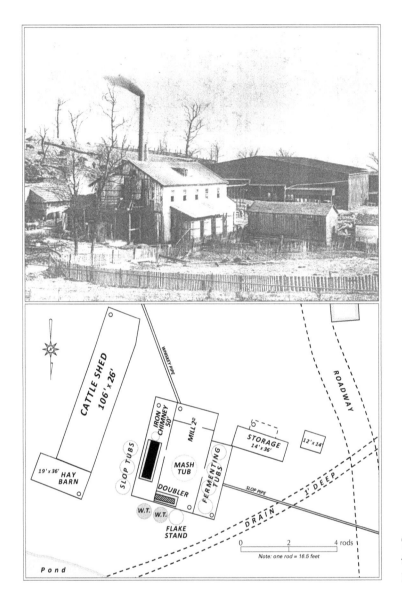

Taylor & Williams Distillery No. 240, Fairfield, Nelson County, ca. 1910.

production, thereby also increasing their demand for feedlot cattle and hogs to consume the slop produced. The railroad also facilitated the long-distance marketing of fattened livestock. By the 1890s, livestock feeding in the distilling counties had become a complex and productive business. Distillers contracted with local farmers for feeder stock and fed livestock owned by absentee brokers.[102] Distillers preferred to feed breeds that attained the most rapid weight gain, thereby reinforcing the transition from the casual production of common breeds of cattle to the focused management of purebred or crossbred stock.

3

Distillery Configurations

Kentucky's frontier settlers planted corn, and cornmeal became a dietary staple. But shelling ear corn by hand and pounding shelled corn into meal were burdensome. Both millers and distillers were among the state's frontier settlers, but the miller's equipment and skills were more important to easing life's labors and providing a food source if one's crops failed. Eighteenth-century farmers likely would have agreed that "a grist mill was regarded by some of the pioneers as a greater necessity than a store, a courthouse, or a professional physician."[1] Distillers also regarded gristmills as high-value neighbors. Following folk traditions, eighteenth-century farmer-distillers took their corn and grains to the nearest mill to be ground into mashing meal. As distillers increased in number and their processing capacity grew, they bought corn from neighbors if surpluses were available. And some millers became distillers if they were proficient at it and if corn and local grain production was sufficient.

Colonial farm stills were elementary: small, portable copper pots holding little more than a gallon of fermenting mash consisting of ground corn or rye, or larger three- to five-gallon cylindrical copper tanks set atop a stone-lined fire pit. A few wooden barrels provided fermenting containers and storage for the finished product; the whiskey was clear in color and, by contemporary standards, harsh in taste. Families and their neighbors consumed the spirits produced in this way, although limited amounts might have been marketed further afield. By the late 1700s, some distillers operated as part of a localized milling center erected beside a perennial stream. In 1801 farmer and hat manufacturer Montgomery Bell owned such a works on the upper reaches of a creek in Jessamine County, about five miles north of the Kentucky River. The complex included a distillery, a three-story merchant flour mill, a gristmill, a sawmill, and an equipped blacksmith shop. The large distillery building, measuring thirty-four by sixty feet, contained stills and boilers. Bell had planted fifty acres of his farm in winter wheat and wished to rent the land and the mills either separately or together. Also available for hire on the premises were "fifteen negroes; Men, Women, and Boys," likely enslaved people who worked Bell's farm and operated the mills.[2]

By 1810, mill and distillery works such as Bell's operated on several creeks that emptied into the Kentucky River and were the focus of local trails connecting to river landings and county seats. Such clusters also represented a craft or artisan stage of industrial development as distillers began to consciously improve their product by hiring experienced employees and purchasing better equipment. They catered to customer preferences, considered the quality of the ingredients they used, and situated themselves in a positive marketing position by recognizing competitors' products and trying to best them. Whether distilleries operated in rural isolation or in a mill-distillery cluster, they increased productivity and quality by adopting innovations and inventions in distilling and related processes.

Some early Kentucky distillers had distilling experience in Ireland, Scotland, and England, and others came from Maryland and Pennsylvania. They set up their businesses primarily at water power sites in rural areas or on the edges of emerging urban centers at river landings such as Maysville, Covington, Louisville, Owensboro, and Frankfort. Some distillers established operations at important inland crossroads such as Lexington. While rural Kentucky distillers could obtain grains from their own farms or those of neighbors, urban distillers lacked a local grain source.

In Scotland and England, eighteenth-century distilling was primarily an urban industry, with most large distilleries located in or on the outskirts of Edinburgh and London. Scottish and English brewers and distillers practiced the long-standing tradition of feeding spent grains to hogs and cattle penned in large sheds. Distillers bought feeder livestock at the onset of the distilling season and sold them to the slaughterhouse market after feeding them for fourteen to sixteen weeks.[3] Distillers did not enjoy complete production or market dominance for fattened hogs, however, because "country-fed" pork was deemed superior to "distillery pork." In some markets, the price of country-fed pork was nearly double that of distillery pork.[4] Kentucky distillers developed similar distilling and stock feeding relationships, although the process evolved over several decades before becoming fully organized by the mid-nineteenth century.

First-Generation Kentucky Distilleries: 1790s–1830s

Early Farm Stills

Frontier farm stills, be they legal or not, were modest in size and output and were housed in informal and idiosyncratic buildings; a small log barn or a simple lean-to or shed often sufficed. A farmer could produce whiskey with just a few small wooden vessels in which to combine water and grain meal and ferment the mixture with yeast; a copper pot or kettle served to boil off the alcohol, and a coiled copper condensing pipe reduced the vapor to liquid that, for those with fortitude, was ready for consumption.[5]

Farm structures and artisan craft buildings such as gristmills, sawmills, blacksmith shops, cooperages, barns, and sheds were shaped by common knowledge—part traditional, part practiced or professional.[6] When constructed of hewn timbers and sawn lumber, most such buildings followed basic forms and proportions that builders repeated from one building to the next. These structures were functional and required a minimal investment of time and effort. Some early Kentucky mills were basic vernacular structures;

Illicit Distillation, by A. W. Thompson, depicts an illegal still operating at night. Its component parts would have been similar to small-scale farm stills used in nineteenth-century Kentucky. An onion-shaped pot still, or alembic, presumably made of copper, sits atop a stone fire box. Two men tend the fire, while another carries a small wooden keg to a sled used to move heavy objects through hilly terrain. The lean-to roof on the right may cover the mash barrels. (*Harper's Weekly* 11, no. 571 [1867])

others built by accomplished millwrights and stonemasons exhibited clever engineering and aesthetic qualities. Millraces, dams, and foundations were often made of dimensional cut stone rather than rough-faced field rock. A mill's superstructure might be stone or, more commonly, heavy timber post-and-beam framing covered with vertical planks or horizontal clapboard siding.[7] A distillery was often built around an internal timber frame that followed a basic geometry of squares and rectangles, with a shingled shed or gable roof and similar siding. Because distilleries were designed to shelter machinery and heavy vats, they were usually more robust than livestock barns and utility buildings. Building size or scale was appropriate to its purpose, with little surplus internal space. Expanding production often necessitated the addition of sheds or lean-tos. First-generation distillery builders demonstrated little concern for artistry, never mind the picturesque or antiquarian values so popular with late-nineteenth-century Victorians. Traces of these concerns did appear in second-generation buildings.[8] Farm stills were comparatively isolated and consumed limited amounts of water, grain, and cooperage while producing small amounts of distilled whiskey. Whiskey markets were often local or, in time, regional.

Sites, Structures, Equipment, and Power

The transition from self-sufficient farm stills to commercial-industrial distilling was a gradual process that occurred over about four decades. Increased distilling capacity required larger structures, reliable power and heat sources, refined and dependable equipment, and ready access to raw materials in sustaining volumes. Early commercial distillers often paired their works with flour mills or gristmills. The mill-distillery structure might be designed and erected by a distiller, a millwright, or an experienced carpenter who selected horizontal plan dimensions and vertical cross-section configurations based on a repertoire of traditional forms, pragmatic experience, and astute reasoning.[9] As each new distillery began production, it became a demonstration model for builders and distillers, illustrating how effectively the structure served its intended purpose.

Eighteenth- and early-nineteenth-century mills and distilleries followed structural forms that were dictated in part by the power source available. Water-powered mill wheels ground grain; manual labor dipped water, lifted pails, and mashed these ingredients into a fermentable slurry. The primary concern in distillery site selection, therefore, was to enhance distilling operations—this meant ready access to moving water for power, potable water for mashing, a general water source for cooling, and an elevation change to permit the use of gravity to move grains and liquids. Selecting a site close to productive grain farms was important but secondary. In part, builders adapted a distillery's plan to its site, be it on a level river floodplain, on a low-angle hillside, or in a narrow, steep-sided valley. Leveling a large site with hand tools was impractical. A site at a spring on a south-facing hillside offered the advantage of a cool water source, an elevation change, and shelter from northerly winds during the winter distilling season. If a water-powered gristmill operated in conjunction with a distillery, millwrights deemed a waterfall of at least six feet necessary to create the gravity power required to turn a vertical overshot waterwheel and drive the millstones and pumps.[10] If only streams of low gradient or limited flow were available, millers could still capture that lower power potential by building a small mill with an impact-driven undershot waterwheel.[11] Mashing and fermentation required grain ground to a gritty or granular texture, not the exceptionally fine texture of milled and bolted flour. To grind distilling grains, a miller adjusted the millstones to produce a chopped or coarse grind—a medium texture for milled rye, and a fine texture for flint-type corn.[12]

Falling water powered most of Kentucky's first-generation mills and distilleries, although small steam engines were available for use by the 1830s. Operating under waterwheel or steam engine power required a building frame sturdy enough to hold the combined weight of the machinery, the filled mashing and fermenting vessels, and the charged still.[13] Early distilleries heated water and distilled alcohol with stone, brick, or iron fire boxes; wood was the predominant fuel. Because wood was heavy and difficult to move, the distiller required a timber source in close proximity and a wood yard for storage. Distillers preferred to use spring or creek water at a temperature of 60°F or lower to cool hot liquids and as a medium for mashing grain meal. By late spring, the surface water temperature of creeks or rivers had warmed, effectively limiting the distilling season to the period from late October to the end of May. A distillery not sited to take advantage of elevation required that water be moved vertically by hand. Hauling water to a distillery and carrying or pumping water by hand constituted a significant portion of the expense of operating a distillery and therefore limited distillery size and output.[14]

Some distillers made their own still equipment using basic tools. Others purchased equipment made locally or manufactured regionally by coopers, coppersmiths, and blacksmiths according to studied and practiced craft techniques.[15] The still apparatus, therefore, took many forms, with elements made from iron, copper, or wood. Fermented mash could be distilled by either direct heat—a fire directly under the still vessel—or indirect heat—a small iron fire box with a flue to direct heated air to the bottom of the still. Operational efficiency required low fuel consumption and high output of alcohol per unit of grain distilled. According to Michael Krafft, the most efficient copper still vessel had a broad concave bottom that was heated directly and short sides to maximize the volume of mash contents exposed to fire.[16] To attain these properties, a skilled coppersmith would fabricate an onion-shaped pot still, or alembic. The pot still was a batch still that had to be scalded clean after each charge, or batch. Ideally, the coiled copper condensation pipe, or worm, had a tapered diameter and was round in cross section. The section of coil that passed through the cooling water vessel, or flake stand, might measure up to forty feet in length. In the 1820s Scottish Lowland distillers began to use vertical continuous-flow column stills, following a design patented by John Haig and Robert Stein in 1826 and later modified by numerous refinements.[17] Column stills appeared in Kentucky when craft distilling began the transition to industrial-scale production.

Local coopers supplied mash tubs and fermenting vats made of wooden staves bound by wooden or iron strap hoops. The vats resembled the large hogsheads used to store and ship tobacco. Part of the distillery's interior space had to be shaped and sized to permit the tubs and vats to be positioned for ease of filling with milled grain and, according to the appropriate sequence, hot and cold water. Tubs and vats also had to be spaced to accommodate the workers who hand-stirred the water and grain mixture with wood-handled mash rakes and cleaned the vessels between batches. Fermentation produces carbon dioxide, so an enclosed fermentation room required venting by sidewall or clerestory windows. Some distillers placed their fermentation vats outside the distillery building under a shed roof.[18] The alcohol fermentation cycle varied from two to four days. Depending on their preferred strategy, distillers used at least one vat for each day of the cycle. Depending on the scale of operation and rate of production, distillers could be simultaneously mashing, fermenting, and distilling. Distillery structures had to be large enough to accommodate this attenuated production cycle. Increasing production required the building of additions or new structures.

Barrel-aging warehouses also varied in dimension, material, and design. Distillers operating small works might store filled barrels in an existing barn or outbuilding. Larger production favored discrete warehouses at the distillery site so that additional units could be built in a row, if the distillery was on a level upland site, or arranged along a floodplain, if the distillery occupied a riverside site. Some distillers built unheated and unvented warehouses that were fully enclosed except for the access doors. Others installed side windows to admit light and provide some measure of temperature control in the summer. The raised-gable monitor roof with clerestory windows and vents was a common configuration for American industrial buildings in the pre-electric nineteenth century, and several distilleries adapted this style for their warehouses to provide both light and ventilation.

Though farm distillery buildings were comparatively small, they were often accretive, evolving on the same site as buildings were added or attached to accommodate new technology or replace structures that had burned. Those farm distilleries that reached commercial scale often replaced old, undersized structures and adopted formal building plans like those used in general industrial buildings and manufacturing works. Instead of erecting basic multipurpose buildings, distillers built dedicated structures to house appropriate machinery and equipment, and these were laid out in a rational manner.[19] Similarly, millers often upgraded their gristmills to utilize elements of Oliver Evans's conveyor and gravity feed system and convert from waterwheel to steam power. If old mill buildings could not be economically retrofitted, a miller would construct new buildings of two or more stories.

Many commercial-scale distillers converted to steam engine power as technology and financing permitted. Installing a small steam engine in an existing distillery might require a new room or an attached shed with an external iron or brick chimney stack, in part to conserve interior space for distillery functions, and in part because a boiler explosion and ensuing fire could consume the entire works. Wood was the predominant engine fuel, and the transition from wood to coal required advances in transportation. Some distillers sited their new works adjacent to navigable rivers, where they could receive direct coal shipments. Inland distillers often awaited the railroad to reach them before converting from wood to coal.

Distilleries produced spent grains, or slop, in volumes proportional to the amount of grain processed and the quantity of water used for mashing. Feeding cattle and hogs on distillery slop was sometimes the most profitable part of the distilling business and was preferable to dumping the slop. Livestock feeding pens and barns were usually downslope and away from the distillery works. A hillside distillery might provide the elevation required to move slop by gravity from the still to the livestock pens. Alternatively, elevating the still floor or slop holding tanks allowed the distiller to use gravity to direct the slop into feeding troughs. Efficient distilleries could feed up to thirty hogs a day for every five bushels of grain processed.[20]

Early Distillery Function and Form

Late-eighteenth- and early-nineteenth-century whiskey distilling in Kentucky largely fol-lowed long-standing traditional practices. Adoption of new techniques and technology required confidence and foresight, as well as a willingness to accept a high but unknowable degree of risk. Failure could mean losing a season's production and the money invested in grain and livestock. Some farmer-distillers avoided risk by adhering to traditional prac-tices. Others embraced new technology and were early adopters. As businesses, distilleries operated within a larger and changing geographic context as the transport infrastructure expanded with the development and adoption of steam power and turnpike construction created durable roads, thus reducing transport times and costs. As individuals, distillers demonstrated different levels of experience and business acumen. But all operated within the context of volatile external influences—ranging from unpredictable weather truncat-ing their grain supply to a capricious economy closing off the market for their product. Generalizing such variations into meaningful periods or eras that reflect broad trends is not straightforward, but it can illustrate the process whereby the nineteenth-century dis-tilling landscape was constructed and maintained, or decommissioned and erased.

Early craft distillers followed vernacular traditions and developed their skills by ap-prenticing with experienced distillers and engaging in trial-and-error experimentation. Literate distillers may have encountered books on distilling techniques, such as those by Anthony Boucherie, Harrison Hall, and Michael Krafft.[21] Some distillers became aware of new science-based distilling techniques and may have adopted instruments such as the hydrometer to measure specific gravity, for example, but progress toward the scientific application of chemistry was ploddingly slow. Distillers took pride in using traditional methods to produce a traditional product. Nevertheless, some distillers began to adopt technology-assisted techniques, and as they did so, the distilling landscape changed. Dis-tillers added new buildings and remodeled or replaced others. Transport by packhorse and wagon along modest overland trails limited the distillers' grain supply to local producers. Yet the comparatively high value of their whiskey allowed them to seek out markets at greater distances if they had access to river ports. If distillers' grain requirements exceeded the capacity of their own farms, they could embrace new road construction technologies to extend their supply lines throughout their local neighborhoods and beyond.

In the aggregate, distillers who wished to industrialize were reliant on inventions in kindred or complementary manufacturing businesses that could be adapted to distilling or that increased the productivity of their suppliers, such as ceramics and glass, metal fab-rication, farm machinery, and power production.[22] Many distillers routinely invented and patented machinery and developed procedures that increased their production and the quality of their product. Such interdependencies suggest that early-nineteenth-century distillers could remain traditionalists if they wished, but they could also adopt new tech-nologies and techniques if they were interested and financially able to do so.

Second-Generation Kentucky Distilleries: 1830s–1880s

Miller-Distillers and the Industrial Transition

Collectively, the transition from craft to industrial distilling was not an abrupt revolution in structure and function but a gradual process of adjustment. For individual distilleries, gradual change was punctuated by the steam engine, new equipment, or railroad construction. Mechanization resulted in greater production volumes. The distiller remained an artisan, applying long-standing best practices, but this tradition also gave way to applied science. The transition to mechanized, high-capacity distilling required changes in complementary businesses, such as marketing, as well as access to capital; developing professional relationships with wholesalers and bankers became increasingly important.

The term "still" generally applied, individually and collectively, to the pot or column still fixture and to the assembly of tubs, vats, valves, coils, and pipes that moved grain and liquid. These mechanicals and the structure that housed them constituted the "distillery." Early distilleries were single-room buildings that accommodated all the equipment and activity. Over time, as new technologies developed, operational scale increased, and governmental regulations were put into place, the distillery structure was significantly enlarged and subdivided into enclosed rooms with different functions: mashing, fermenting, distilling, doubling, and so on. The distillery so modified became an outsized compound building. Distillers added powerhouses, storage warehouses, bottling plants, cisterns, and livestock pens, all tied together by in-ground or overhead pipes, walkways, and roads. The various elements operated in concert like a factory or manufacturing works. Distillery employees likely used specific building names or numbers while referring to the collective as the "distillery."

During the early decades of industrialization, distilleries did not adopt standard factory buildings, as did the textile mills of New England. Unlike the ranks of identical textile looms powered by water or steam and run off of precisely arranged pulley-and-shaft mill work, distilleries functioned in several different configurations with nonstandard equipment that was homemade or supplied by a variety of artisans and manufacturers.[23] Even though distilleries were engaged in product manufacturing and their aggregated buildings were often described as "works," distilleries were rarely referred to as factories. The term "factory" implied the production of standardized goods, and distillers, then as now, did not see their products as standardized. On the contrary, each distiller wished to portray his or her whiskey as different, if not unique, and as handmade, not the product of machines.

Distillers often moved into and out of the business. A farm-distillery might be abandoned and then salvaged or improved in small increments. A mill-distillery owner might sell the works to another operator who invested additional monies in equipment and buildings. As much landscape adjustment occurred through buying and selling as through gradual improvements made by a single owner. In June 1839 the following ad appeared in the *Franklin Farmer,* published in Frankfort: "I have for sale, in Franklin County, a Farm containing about 200 acres, situated about five miles from Frankfort on the Georgetown Turnpike road. Also, an Engine, Mill and Distillery, Wool Machinery, etc. which will be sold with the Farm . . . or separate. Apply on the premises. B. Dougherty."[24] Dougherty may have built this distillery or may have been its second or third owner. One sees here the beginnings of industrial-scale distilling, not in a town or a river port but in the countryside, on a farm, albeit one served by a turnpike. The term "engine" implies steam engine, which may have powered both the mill and the distillery, and although we cannot be certain, the mill was likely outfitted with continuous process elevating, grinding, and bolting equipment, which was in general use by this time.

Industrial distilling required specialized structures and equipment and adjustments in social arrangements. A distiller might operate a farm, a mill, and a distillery. The family occupied the farmhouse but frequently boarded employees there. Some distillers' households included farm laborers, distillery workers, coopers, and wood choppers who cleared the land of trees. The wood may have fired a mill and distillery steam engine as well as household stoves. Before mechanized personal transportation, employing farmhands or other laborers who lived more than a short walking distance from the works was impractical. And the small wages paid to young farmhands would likely not permit them to own and maintain a horse of their own.

Rural Distilleries and Industrialization

In 1840 Kentucky's distilleries were generally distributed across the state, with large clusters in the Bluegrass and eastern Pennyroyal regions, a small cluster in the southeastern mountains, and a thin distribution in the Western Coal Field and Jackson Purchase regions. The largest producers, or the first to reach industrial-scale production, were along the Ohio River in Boone, Gallatin, and Trimble Counties and a smaller cluster at creekside mill sites in the Licking River drainage in Harrison, Nicholas, and Bourbon Counties.

Achieving industrial-scale production required a reliable transportation network, be it water, road, or rail, to sustain high-volume grain and fuel delivery and provide access to product marketing outlets. Mechanized equipment minimized manual labor, but increased production volume, together with machine maintenance requirements, likely increased overall employment. The distilling process now aggregated discrete functions into an interconnected ensemble of high-capacity grain storage and milling, multiple mashing and fermenting vats, and one or more high-capacity stills, all integrated by elevators and gravity flow or pumps and pipes. Steam engines provided heat and horsepower but required a continuous flow of fuel, be it wood or coal.

Operations were no longer confined to a single modestly sized structure; they expanded to occupy clusters of integrated buildings. Distilleries also acquired second and third stories. This vertical expansion was necessary to accommodate gravity-flow

grain-handling equipment and the new vertical column still—twenty to forty feet tall—
if distillers chose to replace or supplement their traditional pot stills. Distillers operated
fewer one-off, purpose-built machines—perhaps made onsite by employees. Instead, they
purchased standardized equipment from local and regional manufacturers. Building design and configuration, however, remained idiosyncratic, in part because distillers had to
adapt structures to the verities of the site—spring location, creek frontage, slope, or road
or rail access. Industrial processing expanded a distillery's footprint. Distillery fires were
commonplace, and the growing size and number of distillery structures piqued insurance
companies' interest in "fireproof" construction, spurring the erection of new buildings
with brick walls and iron doors and window shutters.

Stationary Steam Engines

Until the steam engine allowed laborers to extract coal, iron ore, and limestone from the
earth in quantities sufficient to sustain the production of cheap iron and steel, America
was a wood- and water-dependent nation. Many eighteenth- and early-nineteenth-century
gristmills, flour mills, and sawmills were powered by direct-drive waterwheels.[25] Carpenters turned wood into buildings, tools, and utensils; woodcutters cleared trees from farm
fields and provided cordwood for fireplace cooking and heating. Wooden mill wheels and
windmills were prime movers, in that they converted natural power—moving water or
air—directly into mechanical power. Stationary steam engines were in very limited use
during the eighteenth century, but they pumped water from mines in New Jersey, powered
a cotton factory in Philadelphia, and, by the early 1790s, ran a small number of saw- and
gristmills in the trans-Appalachian West.

The conversion from water to steam power was the key element that enabled the
industrialization of distilling. Steam power was initially applied to distilling and other
manufacturing activities directly. That is, stationary steam engines converted heat and
reciprocating motion into rotational (turning) motion to directly operate belts, pulleys,
shafts, and gears connected to grain mills, mash mixing equipment, liquid pumps, and
other machinery. In the late nineteenth century, steam engines powered manufacturing
works indirectly by powering electricity generators, which in turn ran electric motors that
operated the same mechanical systems.

Philadelphia inventor and steam engine builder Oliver Evans opened a steam engine manufacturing shop in Pittsburgh in 1811. Within two decades, Pittsburgh and the
downstream Ohio River cities of Cincinnati and Louisville had become centers for steam
engine production.[26] By 1821, Louisville's Prentice and Bakewell foundry and other mechanical shops were building so many steamboat and stationary steam engines that they
were among the city's leading exports.[27] A large steam mill on the Cincinnati riverfront
powered a flour mill, a fulling mill, and a distillery in 1826.[28]

Skilled blacksmiths and machinists using hand tools built a limited number of basic stationary steam engines for use in mills. According to the US Treasury, 1837 was the earliest reported use of a stationary steam engine in a distillery and for corn milling.[29] Large-scale engine production was under way in New York by the mid-1840s, but the production of efficient and effective stationary engines in quantity awaited the development of machine tools and interchangeable parts, which became available in the 1850s.[30] Steam engine production in Middle West and Ohio Valley industrial cities was well established by the 1850s, and as the number of engines in use increased, so did the variety of applications to which they were put. Stationary engines tended to operate at low rotating speeds and moderate pressures of 30 to 60 pounds per square inch, less than half the pressure of steam-powered riverboats; these engines were also simpler to build and maintain. Whether refitting waterwheel mills or constructing new mills, potential customers were primarily concerned about engine effectiveness and efficiency. Engine effectiveness was a measure of reliability, frequency and difficulty of maintenance, and the overall cost of operation. Efficient engines delivered a high ratio of power per unit of fuel burned.

Louisville attorney W. S. Pilcher posted a notice in the *Louisville Daily Democrat* in September 1852 announcing the sale of a four-and-a-half-acre parcel of "limestone land" at Fisherville, about fifteen miles east of Louisville in Jefferson County. The property bordered Floyds Fork and included "a dwelling house, storehouse, other necessary buildings for a family; a large corn mill and distillery house, 3 stories high, 60 feet long by 30 feet wide, pens for 400 hogs, and a corn-crib nearly of the same size as the distillery building. It has a steam engine, and all distillery machinery complete."[31] Other businesses in the village included a second corn mill and distillery, a corn and sawmill, mechanic shops, retail stores, a Masons' Lodge, and, ironically, a Temperance Hall. Importantly, the Taylorsville and Louisville Turnpike passed through Fisherville, and a triweekly mail coach served the village. In addition to providing access to area grain suppliers and an outlet for marketing barreled whiskey, the turnpike permitted the delivery of heavy machinery such as steam engines.

Between the end of the Civil War and the great financial panic of 1873—and for several years thereafter—Kentucky's industries increased in scale, many converting from handcrafts to machine-assisted manufacturing. Many factories, especially in the riverfront cities of Covington-Newport, Louisville, and Owensboro, converted to steam power, and new works were purpose-built to operate on steam. Such was the case at Louisville's Grainger & Company's Phoenix Foundry, which had been making waterwheels and distillery and mill machinery since 1833. By 1868, the foundry had expanded into steam boiler and engine manufacturing.[32] Master mechanics also established machine shop businesses in county seats, thereby supporting those small-town and rural businesses that wished to convert from water power to steam. In 1883 the Macdonagh brothers, who had acquired proficiency during apprenticeships in England, opened a machine shop in Paris in Bourbon County; they offered repairs on steam engines and all forms of mill and distillery machinery.[33]

Power Sources and Workforces of Selected Kentucky Industries, 1870

Industry	Number of Establishments	Number of Waterwheels	Number of Steam Engines	Number of Workers	Number of Workers per Establishment (Average)
Cooperages	95	0	2	383	4.0
Flour mills and gristmills	696	321	314	1,686	2.4
Distilleries	141	6	95	1,033	7.3
Lumber mills	562	101	378	2,497	4.4
Steam engine and boiler manufacturers	10	0	9	2,238	223.8
Tin, copper, and sheet iron works	127	0	3	531	4.2
State totals	5,390	459	1,147	30,636	5.7

Source: US Census of Manufacturing, 1870.

Rural flour mills and gristmills continued to operate on a limited, seasonal basis, each employing only a few workers. Some mills converted from water to steam power, but by 1870, more than half of the state's 696 mills were still powered by waterwheels. By comparison, more than twice as many steam engines (1,147) as waterwheels (459) powered Kentucky's expanding catalog of urban- and transport-oriented industries. Mechanization proceeded apace in those businesses that adopted steam power. Those firms that made distillers' machinery, together with the ten works in the state that built steam engines and boilers, were the most technically advanced, being largely steam powered and employing an average of more than 220 workers per factory. Distillers and other distilling-related industries operated on a more modest scale. Ninety-five of the state's 141 distilleries were steam powered by 1870, and they employed, on average, about seven people. Cooperage remained a manual handcraft industry; only two of ninety-five establishments were steam powered, and they employed an average of four workers.

By 1880, the number of steam engine and boiler manufacturers in Kentucky had increased to fourteen. The construction and repair of steam engines and boilers used in steamboats were more exacting than the requirements for stationary land-based engines, so riverine industrial centers required skilled workers and acquired new machine tools as they became available. River cities therefore became important centers for engine and boiler manufacturing and repair. The steam engine manufacturing business became a pioneer industry, in the sense that the early firms established a nucleus of skilled labor and manufacturing facilities. When the mills and distilleries in Louisville's rural hinterland began to adopt small stationary steam engines, the pioneer factories were already in place

and expanded to produce not just steam engines but also a range of generic and proprietary machinery and hardware.[34]

Steam engines required fuel, of course, and the early engines were fired primarily by
wood.[35] Dry white oak, for example, produced about 6,750 BTUs per pound. But the logis-
tics of a reliable wood supply were awkward at best. Steam-powered distilleries employed
woodcutters or purchased cordwood from area farmers, who cut trees during the winter
months to clear their land. Periodic wood delivery required that teamsters contend with
difficult roads during the fall-winter-spring distilling season.

Conversion from wood to coal became possible when Ohio Valley mines opened and
shipped coal downriver via large barges. Bituminous coal produced roughly 12,000 BTUs
per pound, or about twice the heat value of dry, high-quality wood. Overland coal hauls
were simplified and transport costs were reduced when railroads extended their lines from
river city ports into the countryside. In the 1880s distillers along the Ohio River fueled
their steam engines with bituminous coal from southwestern Pennsylvania, whereas distillers with access to interior railroads used Kentucky coal.[36] Rail lines released millers
and distillers from the geographic imperative of stream-generated water power and gave
them the enviable option of vacating their isolated rural sites and moving to towns, where
turnpikes and railroads offered ready access to affordable coal and grain as well as market connections.[37] Some distillers preferred an alternative energy source; they purchased
well-dried ear corn and stored it in slat-sided cribs before shelling and milling. When thoroughly dry and shelled of kernels, corncobs were a good source of heat energy, producing
between 6,700 and 7,400 BTUs per pound, or approximately 56 to 62 percent of an equal
volume of coal and somewhat more heat value than white oak. In 1869 James Stone, owner
of the Elkhorn Distillery in Scott County, mixed corncobs with coal and may have burned
cobs exclusively when good-quality coal was unavailable.[38]

Distillers likely made gradual transitions to steam power, as suggested by the August 1870 inventory of the John R. Lair Distillery at Lair Station, south of Cynthiana in
Harrison County. The distillery stood on a low bluff adjacent to the Licking River near a
railroad station. The distillery property, which was being auctioned by the US marshal, included the following: "1 Frame Distillery Building about 120 by 25 feet; 1 Frame Warehouse
Building about 50 by 25 feet; 1 Portable Engine, complete, about 20 Horse Power; 1 Corn
Mill; 1 Corn Sheller; 2 Mash Kettles; 4 Large Copper Stills; 58 Fermenting Tubs; 5 Beer
Heaters; 1 Beer Pump; 1 Water Pump; Shafting; Belting; Hose; Pipe & etc."[39] That Lair's
steam engine was portable suggests that it was retrofitted into an existing distillery. The
miscellaneous collection of pumps, shafts, belting, and pipe suggests that water-power
equipment had been replaced, that the conversion to steam was not complete, or that Lair
had purchased too much equipment.

Not all distillers were early adopters of steam technology. When the Scott County
commissioner announced the sale of the Shawhan & Atkins Distillery in August 1870, the

notice described the large, year-old distillery as having a "capacity of Four Hundred Bushel per day. In addition to the latest Improvements and Conveniences, it has complete Water Power to Run all the Machinery."[40] Interestingly, those "latest Improvements" did not include a steam engine, and powering a new distillery with water in 1869 seems puzzling; perhaps the economies of location outweighed the impulse to modernize. Shawhan and Atkins built their distillery on North Elkhorn Creek at Lemmon's (also spelled Lemons) Mill Pike, the site of a mill, a mill dam, and a bridge. Roads to mills were often well traveled and of higher quality than farm roads. Moreover, had the distillery been powered by a coal-fired steam engine, the nearest railroad line on which coal might have been delivered was the Cincinnati & Southern Railroad, four miles away in Georgetown. The Frankfort & Cincinnati Railroad between Georgetown and Paris, known as the "Bourbon Railroad," would run three miles to the north but would not be completed until 1890.[41] Many traditional water-powered miller-distillers found, likely to their dismay, that their chosen sites were not readily adaptable to steam power. So they sold their distilleries for low prices, moved their usable equipment to new locations, or simply abandoned them to the elements.

Third-Generation Kentucky Distilleries: 1880s–1920

By 1894, Kentucky's distilleries had become concentrated in three areas that generally corresponded to the three different modes of distilling that had emerged. Small-scale rural distillers operated in an arc of Inner and Outer Bluegrass counties from Pendleton and Harrison in the northeast to Madison and Marion in the south. Large-scale rural distillers concentrated in the traditional centers of Anderson and Nelson Counties. And large-scale urban distilleries operated along the Ohio River in Kenton, Franklin, Jefferson, and Daviess Counties, and the Kentucky River in Franklin County.

The end of the 1890s marked the end of the turnpike–toll road era. Responding to vehement public protests, turnpike companies closed their tollhouses and sold their pikes to county and city governments to be operated as public roads.[42] Free roads reduced transportation costs for some rural distillers and grain farmers, but the rapid construction of overland rail lines and riverine navigational improvements ceded the advantage to those places with rail stations and river port connections.

Railroads became more efficient during the 1880s, consolidating lines and adding spurs that greatly extended access avenues. The American railroad network was national by 1871, with more than 60,000 miles of track; by 1890, the interlaced rail network had accrued more than 167,000 miles.[43] Some distillers moved their works trackside. Railroad companies accommodated new large-capacity distilleries with dedicated sidings and spurs. The spreading rail net permitted Kentucky distillers to market their product nationally and, with seaport connections through New York, Philadelphia, and Baltimore, internationally.

Many distillers achieved industrial-scale whiskey production so rapidly that by the late 1880s, industry leaders such as John Atherton believed that small producers hoping to open new distilleries could no longer compete with large established works.[44] In testimony before the US House Committee on Manufacturers in 1888, Atherton, a Larue County distiller, noted that Kentucky had only about 150 small distillers who mashed sixty bushels of grain or less per day and produced three or fewer barrels of whiskey. Small distillers continued to operate in conjunction with farms and mills, and distilling was not their sole business. They sold their product locally, often at the distillery itself, or regionally. Larger distillers who mashed 100 bushels per day or more were usually professional operatives with no other occupation. They bought their grain from regional markets and sold their whiskey to national and international markets. Atherton drew a further geographic distinction between traditional rural distillers and what he termed "Ohio River" distilleries—apparently referring to those operating in northern Kentucky and southwestern Ohio—which manufactured whiskey in high volume for sale to rectifiers, who added flavorings and sold the unaged product at low prices. According to Atherton, the "Ohio River" distillers were not engaged in making "fine Kentucky whiskey." He thereby informed the legislators that commercial distilling was actually differentiated into two distinct industries: one group of traditional Kentucky distillers who made "fine whiskey," and a second group concerned with large-volume production, expedience, and immediate sales at low prices. Kentucky distillers defined "fine whiskey" as that "made for ripening" or aging.[45]

W. H. Thomas, a wholesale whiskey dealer and former distiller from Louisville, saw the relationship between small traditional distillers and industrial-scale distilling quite differently. Small distillers were a competitive threat, he thought, and the federal internal revenue tax should be maintained and vigorously enforced to reduce their numbers, thereby allowing the industrial distillers to avoid unnecessary competition. In parsimonious testimony before the US House Committee on Manufacturers in 1888, the same committee Atherton addressed, Thomas complained that the small traditional distilleries would benefit unfairly if the internal revenue tax of 90 cents per gallon on whiskey were repealed, and the competition would ruin every person in Kentucky operating a large distillery. Large distillers invested a great deal of money in industrial distilling, and as he saw it, "if there was no tax upon the product there would be distilleries upon every farm in the United States that had a stream running through it." Small-scale whiskey production required much less money, and "any farmer in my State of Kentucky could make whiskey on a capital [investment] of $100." Substantial overproduction and falling prices would no doubt result.[46]

Distillers of fine spirits were confounded not just by large-volume producers but also by a cadre of secondary liquor manufacturers or rectifiers who compounded or blended whiskeys, cutting them with exotic ingredients to produce a cheap but profitable product for credulous mass consumption.[47] Rectified whiskey was made from undistinguished, mass-produced spirits manufactured by large distilleries such as those in St. Louis, Chicago, Cincinnati, and Peoria, Illinois. By the 1880s, rectified whiskey accounted for two-thirds to three-fourths of all spirits made in the country. Distillers used a high ratio of corn to rye and malted barley in making these whiskeys, as corn was cheaper than rye. Rectifiers or compounders then bought these whiskeys and blended them with flavorings and perhaps with some good, aged whiskey made in Kentucky or elsewhere. Rectified whiskeys usually contained "essential oils" and other additives such as sugar syrup sweeteners and herbs and spices. Iodine, caramel, or burnt sugar was often added to color the clear spirits, and prune juice softened young whiskeys, giving them "the appearance of older goods."[48] Rectified whiskeys were not made with the intention that they be aged.

To aid rectifiers in creating specific whiskey flavors, compounder Charles Cross sold a general "bourbon extract" and "essence," as well as five other bourbon essences that he identified as Cynthiana, Harrison County, Kentucky, Paris, and Sour Mash.[49] A rectifier could make forty-five gallons of "bourbon whiskey" from cheap spirits by adding one ounce of bead oil (a soap made with castor oil), "bourbon essence," and six ounces of brown sugar.[50] Bourbon essence could be formulated in various ways, but it often included rectified fusel oil (primarily amyl alcohol for flavor complexity), amyl acetate (scent of apples), pelargonic (rancid scent), orris (a perfume derived from iris plants), and acetic ether (fruitlike scent).[51] A few Kentucky distillers did produce bourbon, rye whiskey, and alcohol spirits for sale to large rectifying distilleries in northern Kentucky at Covington. During John Atherton's testimony before the House of Representatives, Henry Smith of Wisconsin asked him whether the cheap rectified whiskeys made principally by large-scale Middle West manufacturers had any redeeming qualities. Atherton responded in censorial fashion: "I have not been in the habit of drinking cheap whisky and I could not tell you that. You may know more about it than I do."[52]

Rectified whiskey producers had little direct business interaction with the distillers who produced fine whiskeys in Kentucky, Maryland, Pennsylvania, and Tennessee. The product that distillers referred to as "fine" was commonly known as "Kentucky whiskey," but it was also termed "bourbon whiskey," "family whiskey," or "table whiskey." Most of Kentucky's industrial-scale whiskey distillers aged their product for several years in charred white oak barrels, a process that produced a mellow, caramel-flavored red whiskey ready for drinking. And because fine whiskey was neither cut with additives nor blended with other whiskeys, it was also referred to as "straight whiskey." This type of whiskey was usually sold under a brand name and priced according to its age. Fine whiskey distillers reckoned the age of their product in terms of summers. A whiskey that had been in a barrel for three summers was said to be three years old and was ready for drinking. Most fine whiskeys, however, remained in barrel storage for four to seven years, improving in quality each year.[53] In 1908 the *Frankfort Weekly News and Roundabout* reported that straight Kentucky bourbon whiskey was in high demand because "the United States Government has begun to enforce strictly the proper branding of liquors under the last pure food law.

This law requires all liquor to be labeled according to what it really is, and the rectifiers and those who have been adulterating whiskey have been shoved into the background."[54]

A century-long timeline beginning in the 1790s and continuing through the 1890s would include most of the events, inventions, and innovations associated with the industrialization of Kentucky's distilling enterprise. Distillers began the period following craft traditions in operating their farms, mills, and distilleries; they ended it as professional industrialists who had adopted scientific methods and studied business practices. Distilleries that once operated in hand-built vernacular structures became, through the adoption of proprietary technology, modern industrial structures. The most advanced works were carefully designed and planned to operate at high capacity. Others were retrofitted with new equipment and otherwise reconfigured to increase production while also complying with federal law. Steam power was the most important technological change, but a host of other inventions in kindred industries were important elements in the century-long transition to industrialization.

By the 1880s, many distillers had converted their operations from water to steam power, thereby increasing the size of their operations and producing whiskey more efficiently and economically. The volume of spirits produced and stored in aging warehouses increased dramatically. Adopting steam power and expanding old still houses or building new ones radically altered the rural distillery's landscape imprint. In 1879 Congress passed the Carlisle Revenue Act, which revised the internal revenue tax code by extending from one year to three years the time distillers could store whiskey in bonded warehouses before paying production taxes.[55] In 1890 newly distilled whiskey sold for 35 to 50 cents per gallon, whereas whiskey aged for at least three years sold for five times that price. An unintended effect was that storing whiskey became as lucrative as making it.

4

Applying Technology

In 1883 engineer Robert Henry Thurston, the first president of the American Society of Mechanical Engineers, made the observation that inventions are never the work of one mind. This maxim is illustrated in the refinement of the whiskey still and the distilling process in Europe and America. Prior to the sixteenth century, distilling was a domestic practice in Celtic Ireland and Scotland. By the 1750s, spirits production was sufficient to both supply local markets and export substantial amounts to England. By the 1820s, with the development of dedicated technologies, distilling in Ireland and Scotland was evolving from a peasant craft to a factory industry.[1]

Inventions and Innovations

The Column Still

During the first two decades of the nineteenth century, several French, English, and Scottish inventors refined the distilling process by replacing the traditional onion-shaped pot still with cylindrical or column stills containing multiple distilling chambers in which the fermented mash was heated to evaporation temperature by rising steam rather than by the direct heat of an open fire. Early in the nineteenth century, French inventor Edward Adam developed a multichambered horizontal cylindrical still. The design's operational principles were refined by Laurent Solimani, M. Baglioni, M. Collier Blumenthal, and several others.[2] In 1822 English inventor Anthony Perrier patented an improved still in which the mash or wash passed continuously through a circular labyrinth of copper tubes arranged along a horizontal chamber or boiler that was fire-heated from below.[3]

French distiller Robert Winter patented a two-chambered still in 1824. Though mounted atop brick fire boxes, both chambers were housed inside larger water-bath containment vessels that provided indirect heat. The first chamber's temperature was maintained at 170°F, and the second at 140°F. The wash moved through the first chamber by way of small pipes. The liquid heated quickly and uniformly to evaporation temperature. The condensed liquid then entered the second chamber and passed through an arrangement of annular copper cylinders that created uniform evaporation of the remaining alcohol. The condensed spirit was high proof and free of contaminants.[4]

In 1828 Robert Stein of Scotland refined Perrier's still by creating a continuous-flow, steam-charged horizontal cylinder divided into eight chambers. Fermented mash containers were preheated by the circulation of spirit vapors and spent wash through the container jackets. The hot mash was then injected under pressure through small pipes into the still's chambers, creating a mist. Steam introduced into the chambers quickly and thoroughly vaporized the hot mash. The vapor then passed into a spiral-wound pipe or worm, where it condensed into a liquid. Stein's still produced more alcohol with less fuel than did pot stills, and it became the first commercially successful column still in the United Kingdom.[5]

Aeneas Coffey, an inventor born in France of Irish parents, patented an improved continuous-flow column still in 1830, based in part on Stein's 1828 design. Coffey's still had vertically stacked chambers divided by perforated copper plates. Fermented mash was introduced at the top of the still column; steam entered from the bottom, heating the plates and mash droplets and thereby evaporating the alcohol. This column still produced spirits of higher proof and at higher volumes—up to ten times the volume of traditional pot stills. The Coffey still was in commercial production and widely used by the 1840s.[6]

In America, the number of distilling inventions and patents increased after the Civil War. Patents for stills rarely represented full or radical departures from traditional designs or sequences; rather, they offered incremental improvements on established devices such as the Coffey still. The still patented by George Robson of Cincinnati, Ohio, and Melvin Hughes of Paris, Kentucky, in March 1869 is illustrative. The Robson and Hughes still was immersed in a steam-fed water jacket, with a tank in which mash or low wine was preheated before entering the second distillation stage, or doubler. Their design eliminated the risk of scorching the mash by direct heat.[7]

The still patented by William and George Robson was a more elaborate design.[8] It incorporated two brick furnaces or heating units, labeled A and M in the patent drawing, for continuous double distilling. Furnace A heated cylindrical steam boiler N. Fermented mash was pumped from vat B up into column still C. A pipe from the steam boiler introduced steam into the bottom of the still. Condensed alcohol vapor exited the top of the still through a pipe leading to a second still or doubler, labeled D. Vapor from the doubler then passed through pipe F into the flake stand, a vessel containing cool water, where the copper pipe coiled into a worm condenser. Spent mash exited the bottom of the still through pipe C, and low wine flowed from the flake stand into holding tank I. Pipe J emptied the low wine into the second still—a traditional copper pot still, labeled L—that was heated directly by a masonry fire box. The low wine in the pot still was also indirectly heated by coiled steam pipe N from the steam boiler. Vapor rose to the top of the pot still and entered horizontal drum K, which contained (as an option) removable colanders (depicted as small square boxes) into which flavoring elements such as juniper berries, coriander seeds, and peach pits could be added. The practice of flavoring alcohol was limited to whiskey rectifiers and would not have been employed by distillers of straight bourbon whiskey. Vapor, flavored or not, exited the drum by pipe P and entered the flake stand to

William and George Robson's improved alcohol still (patent no. 92,477, granted July 13, 1869). (W. and G. W. Robson, "Alcohol Still," US Patent and Trademark Office, http://www.uspto.gov)

condense into high wine—the clear, high-proof alcohol that was the still's final product. From the flake stand, the liquid drained into storage tank T. The inventors claimed that their still accomplished double distillation using both a steam-heated column still and a fire-heated copper pot still.

Distillers adopting new equipment had to consider whether it would fit into their existing buildings. If not, the works would have to be enlarged or torn down and replaced by a new structure of appropriate dimensions. Traditional pot stills, even the high-capacity renditions, were comparatively low profile, but the new vertical column stills required taller buildings, and their higher output led to the construction of additional aging warehouses and grain storage cribs and bins.

Many of Kentucky's industrial-scale distilleries installed large column stills in the 1870s and 1880s to increase production; distillers rarely claimed that the transformation also increased product quality. J. G. Mattingly installed and perfected a continuous-flow columnar or Coffey-type still in his West End Distillery in Louisville in 1888 to increase output.[9] Nearly two decades earlier, T. J. Megibben had built a new industrial-scale distillery in rural Harrison County. The *Cynthiana News* announced on March 4, 1869, that Mr.

Megibben and his brother had just completed construction of a new distillery near Lair's Station in southern Harrison County. "It is said to be the best in Kentucky," the newspaper declared. "Its capacity is about equal to fifteen hundred bushels per day, but we understand that not more than four hundred will be mashed."[10] The distillery building was seventy-nine feet long, forty feet wide, and three stories tall. The J. & E. Greenwald Company of Cincinnati installed the steam engine and related machinery. The Robson Company of Cincinnati built and installed the copper still equipment, likely the same William and George Robson whose still designs were patented that year. "The DeBus Company manufactured the mashing tubs which were said to be some of the largest in the world." The distillery also introduced "corn screens," which removed all corn dust and chaff from the mash, allowing the Megibben brothers to "make a pure article of Kentucky whiskey."[11] The Megibben distillery was something of a showcase for inventions. Both the distillery building and the equipment were outsized; the three-story height suggests that the distillery housed a column still and elevating grain milling equipment. Megibben did not build a dedicated cooperage but elected to purchase his whiskey barrels from the Andrew J. Oots & Sons cooperage in Lexington.[12]

Some small-volume distillers chose to continue to use traditional open-fire pot distilling and defended their choice of technologies. The Jacob Laval & Son Crystal Spring Distillery in Louisville made a sweet-mash "Pure Copper Whisky" in the 1860s; owner T. H. Sherley's advertisement in the *Louisville Daily Express* declared, "No steam used in the process of distillation."[13]

Slop Disposal

Distilling's primary by-product is a slurry of spent grains and water commonly called slop. A late-nineteenth-century whiskey distillery produced about forty-four gallons of slop for each bushel of grain mashed.[14] A medium-sized industrial distillery processing 300 bushels of grain per day produced about 13,200 gallons of slop that required some form of use or disposal. The Kentucky distiller's slop disposal problem was summarized by Howard, Barnes & Company, operators of the Montgomery Distillery near Mt. Sterling in Montgomery County. Their 1868 advertisement in the *Kentucky Sentinel* offered this plaint: "Having constantly on hand more Still Slop than we can profitably make use of, we have concluded to dispose of a portion of it to persons having stock of any kind to feed." The distiller suggested that farmers would find slop to be a superior feed for hogs, cows, and horses and the cheapest provender available. Slop could be purchased at the distillery for 25 cents per barrel, cash or monthly credit.[15]

Dumping slop into a stream, perhaps the same stream that supplied the distillery's fresh water, was a common disposal strategy employed by many early farm distillers. That same stream may have supplied "potable" water to downstream farms and towns. As the scale of distillery output increased, especially after the Civil War, dumping slop in streams became more common and drew complaints from neighbors, forcing distillers to come up with other solutions. Early on, many distillers adopted livestock feeding arrangements that not only addressed the slop disposal problem but also offered a second source of income as a hedge against the variable market demand for their whiskey. Distillers developed methods to feed their slop to cattle and hogs in large-scale, onsite feeding operations that required expanded management and considerable investment. These livestock feedlots had to be readily accessible. If a site had sufficient level land, distillers built large shelter sheds adjacent to the distilling works. Optimally, distillers pumped slop from the distillery by pipe into large wooden or metal tanks and then directed the fluid via gravity through overhead pipelines to feeding troughs. The scale of the operation related directly to the volume of grain processed each day. The Paris Distilling Company in Bourbon County produced eighty barrels of whiskey per day in 1904. The slop produced fed 800 cattle, which the company kept in "the latest imported cattle pens."[16] Distilleries fed livestock until they reached market weight or until the end of the distilling season, when they shipped the animals to area stockyards.

Cattle and Hogs Fed at Kentucky Distilleries, 1887

Collection District	Number of Cattle Fed	Number of Hogs Fed
2d	2,848	591
5th	13,215	2,694
6th	3,695	3,350
7th	2,066	1,770
8th	1,556	2,582
Total	23,380	10,987

Source: Tabulated from Joseph S. Miller, *Report of the Commissioner of Internal Revenue, 1887*, US Treasury Department document 1031, 2d ed. (Washington, DC: GPO, 1887).

Other distillers gave away or sold their daily slop output. J. H. Rogers's Limestone Distillery at Maysville invited "parties wishing to slop cattle [to] please call and get a bargain."[17] The Glenmore Distillery at Owensboro advertised its slop in area newspapers with the slogan: "Hog Raising Is the Poor Farmer's Fortune and the Rich Farmer's Protection." Each day during the distilling season, Glenmore sold 1,200 barrels of slop to Daviess County farmers, who waited in line at the distillery with their teams and tank wagons.[18]

Those rural counties with the largest number of distilleries also became centers of livestock production as farmers sought to take advantage of nearby distillery feedlots. For example, in the Fifth Internal Revenue Collection District, which included one of the state's largest distillery concentrations in Nelson, Marion, and Washington Counties, distillers fed nearly 16,000 cattle and hogs to market weight in 1887.

Farmers who arranged to feed their hogs at distilleries found the arrangement most effective if the distance between farm and distillery was minimal. In Anderson County, W. T. Bond's farm was only half a mile from the Bond & Lillard Distillery on Bailey Run, east of Lawrenceburg. Mr. Bond sent twenty-one hogs to the distillery to feed on slop. Several weeks later, the hogs weighed more than 500 pounds each. Bond found that the animals were so fat that they could hardly walk, and it would take two days to drive them back to his farm for slaughter.[19] Many believed that the Berkshire breed of hog, when fed on thick corn slop produced at a distillery, performed much better than other breeds in terms of weight gain and quality of pork produced when butchered.[20] Some livestock buyers were less than sanguine about the advantages of slop feeding and distinguished corn-fed hogs from those fed at distilleries and paid higher prices for corn-fed stock. In the late 1850s and early 1860s the national market price for distillery-fed pork was 10 to 15 percent lower than for corn-fed stock.[21]

Those distillers who fed their slop to onsite livestock instead of selling it to farmers or dumping it into adjacent creeks or sinkholes produced a secondary by-product: animal waste. Livestock fed in confinement at distillery pens produced large volumes of waste, and the manure-laden runoff from these feedlots flowed into nearby streams, polluting them. The State Board of Health conducted a meeting with distillers in July 1910 to consider the problem of manure accumulation and drainage at distillery livestock pens. The contaminated runoff, whether slop or animal waste, killed fish, snakes, turtles, and crayfish; the carnage invited buzzards to the creek banks to consume the carcasses. Livestock would not drink water from polluted creeks, and neighbors were offended by the stench.

A nuisance is a petty inconvenience, a niggling and tiresome irritation. In legal idiom, however, a nuisance is elevated to the level of a minor crime and misdemeanor. Common law gave citizens the right, without official authority, to seek the abatement of a public nuisance without first obtaining a formal legal injunction.[22] Distilleries discharging liquid slop or animal waste into a waterway were subject to a nuisance abatement regulation under section 1253 of the Kentucky Statutes. The statute prohibited people from putting any substance into a body of water that would sicken or kill fish, render the water unfit for use, or produce a stench. Such action was a misdemeanor offense punishable by a fine of not less than $10 or more than $100 and imprisonment for thirty days to six months for each offense.[23] Even though distilling was an economically important industry, in nuisance cases, the state courts apparently did not favor private business over the public interest. More broadly, prosecution of public nuisance cases proceeded across the country, as courts identified and sanctioned noxious trades and industries. Livery stables, swine yards, slaughterhouses, tanneries, bone-boiling plants, limekilns, blacksmith shops, brick-burning yards, soap and candle factories, and many other businesses were subject to the power of public complaint and sanitary regulation.[24]

Slop dumping was a serious matter for those situated downstream, and distilleries were often the subject of lawsuits and legal citations. The Paris Distillers Company in

Bourbon County did not have direct access to an all-season surface water supply. George G. White's 547-acre Gilt Edge Stock Farm was adjacent to the distillery and bounded, in part, by an extended frontage on Stoner Creek. For several years, the distillery paid White $300 a year for the privilege of pumping water from Stoner Creek, and another $300 a year for permission to deposit its cattle waste into natural karst sinkholes on White's farmland near the distillery.[25] The sinkholes functioned as surface receptacles, but the material drained through passages in the bedrock into a Stoner Creek tributary. The state brought a lawsuit against the distillery, claiming that "the waters of . . . Stoner creek were so corrupted and charged with filth, stenches, and smells as to be unfit for domestic uses."[26]

In May 1901 landowners along the Hinkston Creek south of Mt. Sterling in Montgomery County voiced complaints about water pollution caused by slop dumped into the creek by the McBrayer Distillery. "We could not help it," a distillery representative said, "for while we slept some despoiler of property cut our dam and let the slop out into the stream." The *Mt. Sterling Advocate* suggested that the distillery post guards at the dam and that the guilty parties be subjected to the full penalty of the law.[27] The McBrayer works was likely holding slop in a dammed pond next to the distillery, a common practice, to avoid the penalties associated with dumping the waste directly into Hinkston Creek. The following year, in April 1902, a *Mt. Sterling Advocate* editorial stated, "We are informed that distillery slop is being turned into Hinkston Creek at the distillery here, polluting the water so that stock refuse to drink and the smell of decaying matter is becoming past endurance."[28] The McBrayer Distillery, located about one mile south and upstream of Mt. Sterling, mashed more than 600 bushels of grain per day during the distilling season.[29] In November 1902 W. Gay & Company bought the slop from the distillery to feed 400 to 500 cattle onsite. The *Advocate* offered this anticipatory comment: "we may be sure that the offensive smell from the distillery will from this time on be a thing of the past."[30] Five years later, W. Gay & Company continued to slop cattle at the McBrayer Distillery. Although the cattle were apparently healthy, the smell and pollution likely continued; however, it seems that community criticism waned.[31]

Some distillers attempted to address the runoff problem by relocating their feedlots away from creeks. In the late 1890s E. H. Taylor Jr. & Sons' Old Taylor Distillery No. 51, near Millville on Glenns Creek south of Frankfort, fed more than 300 head of cattle. Neighbors raised "great complaint about the filth from the distillery running into the creek. Many fear that fever will follow unless there comes a big rain to wash the creek out."[32] Distillery operations continued, and in 1903 Old Taylor was mashing 300 bushels of grain per day; by 1906, the mashing volume had increased to 500 bushels per day. Cattle feeding operations also continued, although E. H. Taylor Jr. & Sons voiced concerns about "interference by the neighborhood in regard to slopping cattle." Apparently, Millville residents continued to express their displeasure about the outsized industrial operation in their midst.[33] Addressing their concerns, the distillery built new cattle pens "high above the valley and away from the creek."[34]

Slop Drying

Feeding slop to cattle or hogs was awkward at best. Hot liquid slop was difficult and dangerous to handle. Distillers ran pipes from the still house to slop storage tanks to their feedlots. Slop sold to farmers for livestock feed had to be moved from the distillery to the farm in barrels or special tank wagons. Although the cost of slop itself was usually low—or sometimes free—slop was heavy and expensive to move. Drying or dehydrating the slop would remove most of the moisture and allow distillers to ship the dried product in sacks—subtracting most of the weight and increasing storage life and transportability.

From 1790 to 1873 the US Patent Office issued 125 patents for grain and grain stillage dryers.[35] Inventors utilized various designs, including vertical or horizontal kilns or drums that circulated heated air or steam through flues or pipes onto the grain stillage.[36] Early dryers were intended primarily to dry high-moisture grain to prepare it for storage, but most operated poorly because of condensation and plugging. Direct-heat dryers scorched the grain and were susceptible to fires.[37]

Inventor John H. Turney established the Turney Drier Company in Louisville in August 1899. He patented a horizontal rotating cylinder grain dryer in 1903.[38] The following year, working with Charles E. Geiger, W. K. Koop, and G. W. Fisk, Turney patented an improved version of the dryer.[39] Turney's invention was an innovative departure from other dryer types. The dryer body was a double-walled horizontal cylinder set at a slight incline and supported by a wheeled cradle in which it rotated. Flues carrying heated air extended longitudinally through the cylinder's interior. An operator introduced wet material into one end. Vapor escaped the cylinder via a discharge tube, and the dried material exited the opposite end into a conveyor. As the cylinder rotated, the material was uniformly exposed to indirect radiant heat. Because the Turney dryer conducted heat through sealed flues, hot air did not come into direct contact with the material being dried, thereby reducing or eliminating the risk of scorching and fire. The dried material moved by grav-

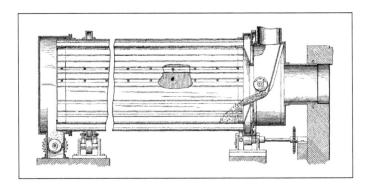

John E. Turney's rotary dryer (patent no. 774,859, granted November 15, 1904). (John E. Turney, "Rotary Drier," US Patent and Trademark Office, http://www.uspto.gov)

Stack-style brick warehouse (formerly Hillenmeyer's Nursery), Sandersville Road, Fayette County.

ity through the inclined cylinder in a continuous-flow process. Workers then bagged the dried grain solids for shipment to livestock feeders.[40] As distilleries adopted the practice of drying slop, the equipment necessitated a change in distillery form and the addition of drying rooms. The fully assembled Turney rotary dryer was more than thirty feet long and ten feet wide, and it required connections to a steam heating boiler; additional space was needed for weighing the grain and sewing shipping bags. The entire operation required a large enclosed room that would have to be built onto an existing works.[41]

Whiskey Aging Warehouses

The manufacture of fine Kentucky whiskey was not complete until it had aged in specially made white oak barrels. Traditional nineteenth-century aging warehouses were single-level frame buildings. Building larger, multifloor storage warehouses with load-bearing walls permitted the distiller to store barrels in a manner that reduced space requirements, conserved labor, and decreased the risk of damage and contamination. But such structures also required innovative ways of moving full barrels from ground level to the upper floors. Two types of inventions addressed these issues and, when perfected and implemented, radically changed whiskey warehousing methods and dramatically altered the distilling landscape: the hoist and the storage rack.

The Hoist.   Large industrial whiskey distilleries were capable of high-volume output and filled hundreds of barrels each day during the distilling season. Distillers generally stored their filled barrels near the distillery. Prior to the 1870s, most warehouses were one-story sheds with open floor plans commonly termed "stack" warehouses. Moving full whiskey barrels into and out of these warehouses was labor intensive. Workers had to lay the barrels on their sides, roll them into the building, and line them up on the floor in rows. Wooden chalks held the barrels in position in each row. Wooden planks on top of the first row of barrels supported a second row; if needed, a third or fourth tier might be added. This storage method was fraught with problems. Storing 400-pound barrels atop one another exerted considerable pressure on the bottom row of barrels, possibly causing them to leak or collapse. Whiskey evaporating from the white oak barrels introduced alcohol vapor into the air, which invited the growth of a black mold (*Baudoinia compniacensis*). Because air could not readily circulate through a vertical barrel stack, the mold lent a musty odor to the warehouse air and possibly even the whiskey. The oldest whiskey was contained in the first row of barrels, and removing those barrels from the bottom of a four-high vertical stack was arduous and dangerous.[42] Prior to the 1870s, and where topography permitted, some distillers built two-story warehouses into the sides of hills, with entrance doors on two levels. Others had two or three levels or floors connected by internal ramps. Both configurations required workers to roll or winch barrels to the upper floors. But most warehouses were configured as horizontal rather than vertical spaces and were therefore extravagant consumers of expensive property.

Hoisting devices have an ancient heritage, but the need to move minerals out of mine shafts and raw materials and finished products through multistory factory buildings in the industrial era stimulated systematic experimentation and development. Numerous hoist or elevator designs appeared in the late eighteenth and early nineteenth centuries. Steam and hydraulics powered large-capacity industrial elevators by the 1850s. Hand-operated traction elevators had practical applications in small factories and warehouses. These units were operated by ropes, pulleys, and counterweights that provided mechanical lifting power. Well-designed hoists had small space requirements but were capable of lifting 3,000 pounds or more without slippage. This capacity was sufficient to lift six or seven full whiskey barrels at a time. These hoists could be used to fill multifloor warehouses. What was still lacking was an efficient method of stacking barrels on each floor.

The Storage Rack.   Alsatian distiller Frederick Stitzel migrated to America in about 1848 and established a distillery in west Louisville by about 1870.[43] In 1879 Stitzel received a patent for "Improvement in Racks for Tiering Barrels."[44]

The Stitzel rack design was inspired. Deceptively simple in layout and materials, the rack was modular; it could be built and used singly or aligned in horizontal rows and stacked vertically. Carpenters set four stout wood posts (labeled E in the patent diagram)

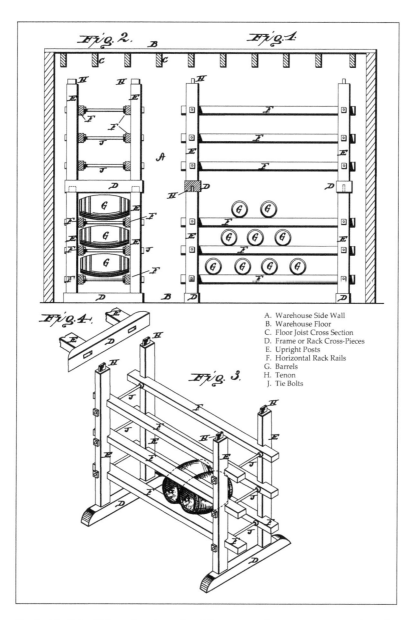

A. Warehouse Side Wall
B. Warehouse Floor
C. Floor Joist Cross Section
D. Frame or Rack Cross-Pieces
E. Upright Posts
F. Horizontal Rack Rails
G. Barrels
H. Tenon
J. Tie Bolts

Frederick Stitzel's bourbon barrel racking system (patent no. 9,175, reissued April 27, 1880). (Frederick Stitzel, "Rack for Tiering Barrels," US Patent and Trademark Office, http://www.uspto.gov)

vertically into horizontal base supports (D) with mortise and tenon joints (H). They set horizontal wood rails (F) into the vertical posts with square notches. Horizontal cross-bolts and nuts (J) passed through each post-and-rail junction, tying the open rack together. At each end, the rack's vertical support posts were spaced far enough apart to allow barrels (G) to be placed on the horizontal rails and rolled into position. Stitzel's rack permitted air

Maker's Mark warehouse at Loretto, Kentucky, under construction.

circulation between barrels, and workers could readily add or remove barrels from the bottom level without moving the barrels above. The rack became known as the "patent rack," and it was widely adopted by distillers; a version of this rack system is still being used to construct entire multistory warehouses as a single unified rack with access passageways.[45] When the interior rack system is completed to the desired height and width, the exterior cladding is attached like a curtain wall.

The Monitor Roof.   A third warehouse innovation, the clerestory-windowed monitor roof, admitted light and improved air circulation. Builders could address airflow problems in musty warehouses by raising a linear section of the roof along the ridge beam to form a monitor roofline. When fit with vent panels and windows, the monitor roof ventilated the building and admitted light to the upper floors. This warehouse form was used at several Kentucky distilleries and was very similar in design and function to early-nineteenth-century European engineering shops, New England textile mills, and Middle Atlantic industrial buildings.[46]

Mechanization and Landscape Transformation

Inventions and innovations do not stand alone; they have social, economic, political, and

T. J. Samuels Distillery warehouses with monitor roofs, Deatsville, Nelson County.

geographic implications. New processes and equipment, individually or in combination, foster landscape change—sometimes subtle, sometimes bold. The inventions distillers adopted to increase production or enhance product quality often developed incrementally, as a sequence of refinements. And each part of an invention-adoption sequence might require adjustments in the whiskey production process and, unavoidably, the built environment or landscape surrounding that process. Distillers increased the horizontal and vertical dimensions of their still houses to accommodate larger equipment; warehouses also climbed vertically, greatly increasing storage capacity. They often spliced new rooms onto existing structures or erected new stand-alone buildings to house specialized equipment. As distillery industrialization proceeded, the distillery proper and its attendant buildings came to resemble a modern manufacturing works, with specialized structures and transport connections that delivered raw materials and removed finished products.

Brick and Iron Industrial Distilleries

New technology requires accommodation. Conversion from animate to inanimate power increases productivity and changes the scale of operation, thereby requiring high-capacity infrastructure and high-volume transport access. Industrial distilleries became increasingly standardized, following the practice under way in other industrial sectors such as textile mills and metal fabrication and machine tool manufacturing plants.[47] Commercially manufactured building materials replaced farm-harvested logs and locally quarried stone. Distilleries transformed into large brick and iron buildings, often linear in form, and frequently combined new and existing structures into one functioning unit. Large buildings required long-span joists and load-carrying framework. When Covington, Kentucky, distiller N. J. Walsh decided to tear down an old distillery in Paris and replace it with a new works in 1897, building plans described "a brick structure four stories in height, 225 feet long and 154 feet wide. The front arches will be of iron and the floors cement. . . . The new distillery will use a process by which more whiskey can be distilled from a given amount of grain than is gotten by the process now in use."[48]

Whereas the small farm distillery may have obtained raw materials locally and otherwise functioned within the farm production unit or larger rural neighborhood, the industrial distillery became increasingly dependent on important links to other processes that might not be obvious at first. Somehow, a potable water source, steam engines and fuel, distilling grains, copper kettles, oak cooperage, and roadways and railroad tracks had to be combined with business knowledge and access to financing to produce a profitable product. Increased production obliged distillers to obtain more grain, perhaps outstripping the yield of their own farms and that of their neighbors. Hauling grain and fuelwood to a distillery required willing teamsters, healthy draft animals, sturdy wagons, and all-weather roads. Some riverfront distilleries at steamboat landings acquired railroad sidings and yards, giving them highly valued water-to-rail connections.[49] Rural distilleries sought connections to cross-country rail lines by building sidings and spurs. When clustered together in cities, distilleries integrated into industrial districts tethered to rail lines.

Steam power made the development of the modern industrial distillery possible. Adopting the stationary steam engine required distillers to adopt other related mechanical systems, thereby creating an engineered distillery. Resilient brick, ubiquitous but of variable quality, became the favored building material. Builders used fire-retardant iron for girders, beams, doors, and window shutters. Distilling with steam power required large, dedicated engine rooms—a powerhouse—and a reliable fuel source, which distillers secured by stockpiling wood or coal. Engine rooms or powerhouses required concrete engine mounts and brick or concrete floors. Smoke exited the fire box through large-diameter metal chimneys, which were in common use by the 1870s. Brick chimneys were more expensive to build but were installed at large-capacity distilleries, especially those operating in urban areas. Steam engines also powered liquid pumps and grain-handling equipment, and they piped steam-heated water to tanks and mash tubs. The high-capacity distillery incorporated large mash tubs and fermenting tanks, some exceeding 10,000 gallons in capacity. When filled, one tank could weigh in excess of 80,000 pounds. Large distilleries might use ten or more such tanks. Because basic timber or concrete floors would not support such weights, supplementary concrete footers were required for each tank. The adoption of steam power also abetted changes in operating costs. Craft farm distilleries often used their own or locally produced grain, fuel cut from their own woodlots, and barrels they made themselves or obtained from a local cooper. Industrial whiskey distilleries acquired external suppliers and sizable expenditures, with the costs of grain, fuel, and cooperage being the primary concerns.[50]

Distillers had been subject to federal taxation, episodically, since 1791. After the Civil War, taxation and regulation increased to pay war debts and underwrite the federal government's operating expenses. Accelerating tax rates paralleled, to some extent, industrial production increases, and distillers needed considerable business acumen. Consider the arcane wording of the federal excise tax law enacted in 1813:

> And for every boiler, however constructed, employed for the purpose of generating steam in those distilleries where wooden or other vessels are used instead of metal stills, and the action of steam is substituted to the immediate application of fire to the materials from which the spirituous liquors are distilled, for a license for the employment thereof, double the amount on each gallon of the capacity of the said boiler including the head thereof, which would be payable for the said license if granted for the same term and for the employment on the same materials of a still or stills to the contents of which, being the materials from whence the spirituous liquors are drawn, an immediate application of fire during the process of distillation is made.[51]

Though curiously convoluted, the statute specified that the fee to license an industrial steam-based still was double the fee imposed on a traditional fire-based distillery—per gallon of capacity. Perhaps this was based on the fact that steam systems were known to be more efficient and therefore more productive. Or perhaps legislators wanted to protect traditional craft distillers by handicapping those inclined to adopt industrial machinery.

Some distilling operations were not readily changed by new nineteenth-century technologies. Weather and climate still required distillers to adhere to a seasonal production schedule. The optimal temperature for yeast growth is about 80°F, and yeast cells die at temperatures above 140°F. Prior to the arrival of Willis Carrier's air-conditioning technology in 1902, distillers could control the temperatures required in the fermenting and distilling process only by operating during the coolest months of the year.

Changing Production, Changing Landscapes

Historically, Kentucky's distilling industry was centered on those sites with connections to both raw materials and markets. As industrial production capacity increased, distilleries were obligated to extend their search for raw materials beyond the local to regional or even national suppliers. Industrialization also led to the redistribution of distilleries from scattered rural farms to transport-oriented sites, some of them in urban areas. For distillers who wished to ship grain, fuel, lumber, barreled whiskey, or other materials, their best option in the last third of the nineteenth century was to select a site beside a navigable river, a hard-surfaced turnpike, or a railroad line. Relocation to sites in or adjacent to cities also provided distillers with direct access to banks and insurers. Early commercial stills were often family ventures that were either self-financed or funded by local or regional sources. By the 1880s, corporations with access to national and international financial markets owned many of Kentucky's large industrial distilleries.[52] When considered in the aggregate, commercial distilling created an industrial landscape comprising the distillery and its associated works, grain fields and bins, woodlots and sawmills, coopers' shops and wood yards, livestock barns and feedlots, and hardware manufacturers and suppliers.

Many of the processes and structures of the twenty-first-century distilling industry were developed between 1830 and 1910—an era of revolutionary, often problematic change for Kentucky distilling. The transition from farm to industrial distilling was uneven and fraught with doubt, risk, compromise, and failure.[53] Yet the contemporary retrospective view of that era is often one of idyllic nostalgia; it is seen as an idealized time when larger-than-life actors created the foundation of a modern industry. Some individuals achieved admirable business success, but their progress was neither linear nor unproblematic. Distilling's industrialization was not an inexorable sequence of grand accomplishments but a number of episodic, intersecting events: some of them random—a crop lost to bad weather or an unanticipated invention; some having a degree of actuarial probability—losses caused by fire or other catastrophes; and some of them certain—government-imposed taxes. Although the people involved only partially understood or perceived the larger social and economic milieu in which they operated, they managed to construct out of these idiosyncratic events one of Kentucky's quintessential industries and one of its most distinctive landscapes.

5

Complementary Industries

Nineteenth-century industrial distilling required the support of several complementary industries, among them cooperage and coppersmithing. Each of these industries was based on long-standing practical technologies applied within a context of confounding problems and constraints. Industrial productivity and product quality were often dependent on the experience and skills of individual craftspeople and were very difficult to improve. Innovation in process and mechanical production tended to be gradual and incremental. Key improvements often occurred not in the primary industry but in related or supporting industries, such as when a nail-making machine was patented in 1795 and refined in the early nineteenth century. What followed was a protracted transformation of practices related to the building of wooden structures.[1] High-capacity industrial distilling required innovation and mechanization, but technological advances in associated or complementary industries such as woodworking and metal fabrication were also essential. This chapter examines the cooperage and coppersmithing industries and reviews how they worked, how they changed, and how those changes affected Kentucky's distillers.

Cooperage

The safe and economical storage and shipment of bulk liquids and solids have long been concerns of producers, traders, and merchants. Ancient container technology was practical and elementary—people used baskets, bags, boxes, crates, and jars to store and transport a wide variety of goods. These common containers often lacked durability and were awkward to handle when heavily loaded. Terra-cotta amphorae, elongated clay jars with handles and cone-shaped bottoms, were used to transport liquids such as olive oil and wine throughout the Mediterranean region in Phoenician times. The winemakers of Georgia's Caucasus Mountains used barrel-shaped terra-cotta containers to store and ship wine some six millennia BC. The Celts may have invented wooden casks or barrels, likely starting with tapered wooden buckets; these were subsequently adopted by the Gauls and the Romans by about AD 300.[2] Celtic coopers made wooden casks or barrels out of staves they bent and planed to a convex cross section; they bound the round ends, or heads, together with wood or iron strapping. When properly made, Celtic barrels were strong, versatile, and easily moved.

Barrel making was physically demanding. The work required specialized tools and years of practice because the barrel's convex shape was difficult to fashion, especially if one desired a tight seal between staves. The shape proved advantageous, however, because barrels could be readily moved on flat or angled surfaces, such as riverboat gangplanks, or pivoted to change direction. The convex barrel was easier to roll than a cylindrical container and produced little friction. In contrast, moving boxes or crates required a deadlift or skid. An empty or lightweight barrel could be moved by tipping and rolling it on its top or bottom rim. A heavy filled barrel was best moved when laid on its side, resting on its narrow, wheel-like circumferential surface.

The modern wooden whiskey barrel's anatomy is straightforward. The body is composed of twenty-four to thirty-six staves—some wide (four to five inches), others narrow (two to three inches)—assembled alternately into a jig-like retaining hoop. Staves may be soaked in water or steamed to facilitate bending. In cross section, each stave is planed into an elliptical shape with chamfered or angled edges. Coopers notch, or croze, the staves about one and a half inches from each end. When the barrel is assembled, the stave crozes form an inside circumferential groove that receives the heads, or end covers. Circular barrel heads are made out of varying-width wood sections jointed or doweled together, with a beveled outer edge. When assembled with the staves, the head's beveled outer edge rests in the groove. Six to eight wooden or iron bands or hoops hold the staves in place. Traditionally, coopers made the wooden bands, and blacksmiths and iron foundries made the iron bands and retaining rivets. The cooper cuts a round hole in the center of one of the wide staves to allow filling and emptying. The hole is filled with a tight-fitting plug, or bung, often made of yellow poplar (*Liriodendron tulipifera*). When filled barrels are stored on their sides, the bung stave is positioned on top.

Coopering and joinery were exclusively skilled manual trades in the early 1800s. In Cincinnati, lumber mills began to mechanize by 1815, producing staves for cooperage. But skilled coopers made and finished barrel staves, heads, and hoops with hand tools until the various steps were mechanized, beginning in the 1840s.[3] Many Kentucky coopers learned their trade in Europe or by apprenticing to European coopers who had migrated to America. William Dorsey operated a cooperage on Main Street in Lexington at the turn of the nineteenth century. The "help wanted" ad he placed in the *Kentucky Gazette* in December 1801 suggests that the European method of training skilled craftsmen through apprenticeships was followed in Kentucky. Dorsey's ad stated: "Wanted Immediately, Two or Three JOURNEYMEN COOPERS, to whom good wages will be given—Also Two or Three APPRENTICES to the above business." The ad included an appeal for 8,000 to 10,000 staves.[4]

Barrels made to contain liquids—naval stores such as turpentine, brine containing pickles or sauerkraut, wine, whiskey, and potable water—were deemed "tight" and required exacting work to shape staves, joint heads, and assemble or "raise" the barrels. Tight barrels were usually made of oak. Solids such as sugar, flour, meal, tobacco, peanuts, smoked and salted meats, and metal goods such as hardware and nails were stored and shipped in "slack" barrels. A range of woods could be used to make slack barrels; species of elm, pine, gum, beech, basswood, and maple were most commonly used.[5]

From the first decades of European settlement through the mid-nineteenth century, America's material culture and economy were enabled by wood. It was the most important source of thermal energy and the primary construction material, whether for building houses, barns, mills, bridges, fences, or boats. Craftspeople converted wood into furniture, wagons, carriages, farm implements, hand tools, and, of course, containers. Conifer tree sap was the basis for a large naval stores industry, and wood could be burned to produce potash or processed and distilled into methanol.[6]

America's eastern old-growth forest extended from the Atlantic littoral to the eastern margin of the Great Plains. Frontier farmers gauged a property's soil productivity potential by the species of trees it supported. But trees were a nuisance to farmers, requiring heavy labor to clear them away before fields could be planted. At the same time, the demand for dimensional lumber fostered timber cutting and a sawmill industry that produced rough lumber—beams and boards, shingles and scantling. Simple wooden tubs and slack barrels could be made from cut logs with basic hand tools such as axes, augers, and froes. Tight barrels required seasoned, precisely cut wood; oak was preferable, in part because of its low permeability.[7] From the 1870s through the 1910s, Kentucky's rapidly developing timber industry harvested old-growth forest, especially in the eastern and southern counties, where a wide variety of hardwood tree species grew—opportunely predominated by white oak (*Quercus alba*). This venerated tree could adapt to a broad range of environmental conditions and grew vigorously in valleys and on north-facing hillsides. White oak was more widely distributed and more numerous than any other tree species in the region. In some areas, oaks accounted for 17 percent all forest growth—more than twice the hickories, three times the maples, and seventeen times the black walnuts.[8]

White oak lumber mills had multiple suitors. The timber was favored not only for general building, tools, furniture, and cooperage but also for wagon and steamboat construction. Cincinnati was one of the nation's primary manufacturing centers, and wagon factories there utilized large volumes of oak and other hardwoods. Two large shipyards operated in Jeffersonville, Indiana, across the Ohio River from Louisville, during the first half of the nineteenth century; one opened in 1819, the other in 1834. Both built boats through the early 1880s but were compelled to purchase their white oak from West Virginia lumber mills, 550 miles away, because by that time, the local supply had been nearly exhausted.[9]

Timber cutters and "bolters" judged the suitability of standing white oak trees for barrel wood. They placed the highest value on trees that were at least seventy-five years old, had large-diameter trunks, and were branchless from the base to twenty feet or more.[10] A superior oak tree had "two cuts of 'queen's pipe,' five cuts of whiskies and short 'splayed stock' clear to the limbs." "Queen's pipe" wood was straight grained, without imperfections, and yielded stave stock sixty-six inches long. "Whiskies" were staves with small flaws but suitable for whiskey barrels, and upper trunk "splayed stock" was used for small cone-shaped vessels.[11]

From the mid-1830s until the 1870s, lumbering in eastern and southern Kentucky was conducted almost entirely by itinerant laborers and farmers clearing their own land. Working with basic hand tools such as the broadax, froe, and maul, farmers also produced rough dimensional lumber, laths, fence rails, and stave billets.[12] Farmers worked their timber stands seasonally in a complementary farming–timber cutting cycle. Tree cutting began in late fall, after the crop harvest, and continued through the winter until field work and planting commenced again in March. Winter rains and early spring snowmelt filled creeks and rivers, permitting the cut logs to be floated to downstream sawmills. Timber cut close to the Ohio River was often sawn by sawmill boats.[13] Most timber was processed into dimensional lumber and used for a wide range of products such as planking, wheel spokes, and tool handles. Rough cut wood was transformed into shingles, fence posts and rails, railroad ties, and cordwood for fuel. Some farmers produced cooperage staves from their own woodland; others worked seasonally for lumber companies.[14]

Stave wood production usually began on farms along the lower reaches of accessible creek bottoms. Timber cutters started with the nearest white oak stands and gradually moved upstream toward the drainage basin's headwaters. Sawyers cut oak logs into stave-length bolts or billets. Bolters used a froe to hand-split the billets into staves, which were then roughly dressed with a drawknife. Riven staves so produced were acceptable for slack barrel construction. Farmers hauled their raw stave stock to the nearest railroad station, where they stacked the wood in large piles to await shipment to in-state cooperages or international customers.[15] By the 1870s, stave cutting crews were forgoing their hand tools in favor of steam-powered band and barrel saws and other mechanized equipment.[16]

In 1872 Lexington distillers William Tarr and James Thomas, together with Cynthiana distiller Thomas Megibben, incorporated the Kentucky Union Railroad. They planned to build a line into southeastern Kentucky to assure their distilleries a reliable supply of coal and staves. The rail line was completed from Winchester east to Clay City in 1885; an extension west from Winchester to Lexington opened in 1890. The rail line gave eastern Kentucky lumberyards an outlet that did not depend on high water in the Kentucky River, and by 1900, Clay City had become one of the largest stave shipment centers in the nation.[17]

By the 1880s, Kentucky and Indiana lumber mills were the primary suppliers of barrel staves to the American cooperage market.[18] From the 1880s through the 1910s, the extension of railroads into Appalachian Kentucky, Tennessee, and West Virginia supported the construction of stave mills in those regions. They produced staves in volume—1 million pieces annually—supplying not only American barrel makers but also whisky distilleries and breweries in Austria, Canada, Croatia, Ireland, and Scotland.[19] In 1900, 1,280 Kentucky sawmills cut more than 392 million board feet of white oak lumber.[20] Sawmills appeared in clusters along the rivers that drained the Appalachians, especially the Big Sandy, Little Sandy, Licking, and Kentucky. Seven saw and planing mills operated in Frankfort on the Kentucky River; most were situated near the mouth of Benson Creek.

In 1883 and 1884 the materials moving on the sixty-five miles of the lower Kentucky River between Frankfort and Carrollton included 130,000 saw logs and 500,000 staves worth $40 per 1,000. In July 1884, two years after completion of the four locks on the river's lower section, annual commerce was valued at more than $5 million; three years later, the value reached $10.8 million.[21] Cooperage materials cut by Kentucky sawmills in 1900 included more than 63 million staves and 3.5 million sets of barrel heads. In total value, Kentucky sawmills produced more than $21 million worth of cooperage materials—hoops, staves, and headings. Although cooperage wood made up only about 6 percent of all forest products, staves, heads, and hoops were more highly valued than basic dimensional lumber.[22] The market demand for tight barrels closely tracked distillery production, and stave mills operated at capacity when whiskey production surged.

Wood imparts flavors to a barrel's contents; more than 400 flavor congeners, including esters, carbonyls, lactones, and phenols, can be present in barrel-aged whiskey.[23] American white oak can taste of vanilla and coconut, although thorough drying reduces the intensity. White oak's cell structure evolved to resist invasion by pathogens, but it also blocks or slows the passage of liquids. Stave wood is usually air-dried in outdoor stacks for one to two years, or until the moisture content is reduced to 12 to 14 percent. Nineteenth-century cooperage shops were often surrounded by small lumberyards, where wood was stacked in piles or ricks under open-sided sheds or left uncovered.

Although they are initially sawn or split into straight lengths, barrel staves must be bowed. To facilitate bending, sawmills cut oak trunk wood to standard lengths or bolts; this is followed by quarter-sawing to achieve a desirable grain angle that resists cracking or breaking.[24] Coopers prefer quarter-sawn staves because they believe the sawing technique reduces barrel evaporation.[25] Filled whiskey barrels are "professional drinkers," in the sense that the wood absorbs liquid; alcohol and water evaporate through the wood, and the ambient air temperature determines which one vacates first. In addition, liquid may leak through the stave joints. Loss through evaporation or leakage is termed "outage."[26] In the 1880s well-constructed oak barrels could lose ten to twelve gallons during a three-year aging period.

The cooperage industry brought together raw materials—white oak and iron for whiskey barrels—and special tools used to make barrels, kegs, tubs, and hogsheads for a broad market. Accomplished coopers possessed a selection of axes, adzes, froes, planes, shaves, chamfer knives, hammers, and hoop drivers. Manufacturers of woodworking tools made specialized hand tools for coopers, and carriage and wagon makers began to manufacture specialized steam-powered machines that coopers adopted to modernize their factories. Planing and mortising machines were available by about 1830.[27] By 1900, toolmakers had invented, patented, and offered for sale more than 380 specialized cooperage machines. Some machines were powered by hand cranks or foot pedals; others turned by pulley and belt systems driven by steam engines. Straight oak slats that artisan coopers had laboriously but expertly transformed with hand tools into curved and chamfered staves could now be precisely shaped by machines at rates of more than 1,000 per hour. Some machines made barrel heads with grooved or crozed edges and curved metal hoops of different diameters. Other machines lashed staves together with power windlasses and drove hoops into position for riveting.[28]

Although cooper-crafted containers were in high demand, cooper shops did not necessarily operate in centralized manufacturing centers, as might iron foundries or textile mills. The cooper's stave material was widely available. Power requirements were minimal before mechanization, and thereafter, steam power could be adapted to a broad range of locations and building sites. The cooper's customer base encompassed the general public as well as manufacturers whose goods required wooden containers, including meat markets, flour mills, nail and bolt foundries, and distilleries. In 1850, 1,027 coopers worked in Kentucky in a variety of situations.[29]

Coopers working in small independent shops as owners or employees could supply diverse markets. They made extensive use of specialized hand tools and were slow to mechanize; nevertheless, these coopers were proficient and productive. Cooper shops often operated on a to-order basis, and demand slowed when distilleries shut down for the summer or started production late in response to sluggish markets. Coopers might produce slack barrels during these slow periods, although this diversification involved different raw materials, suppliers, and customers.[30]

A second type of cooperage shop was a larger commercial business that operated in an urban area with a dozen or more employees. The urban cooper might make his own staves and heads or buy finished staves, headings, bungs, and hoops; after assembly, the cooper sold the barrels to a variety of manufacturing, retail, wholesale, and private customers, including distilleries. The large-scale commercial cooperage likely adopted specialized machinery as soon as it became available, thereby enabling substantial increases in productivity. A completely mechanized cooperage shop might operate fifty or more different machines, each performing one specific function but integrated with other machines into an assembly line.[31]

A third type of cooperage was dedicated to one distillery or group of distilleries. These coopers might be distillery employees or operate the cooperage under contract. The C. B. Cook & Company Distillery in Harrison County, for example, operated a cooper shop with eight coopers as regular employees.[32] During the 1880s the Hermitage Distillery in Frankfort employed sixteen coopers. Each day the riverside works mashed about 1,000 bushels of grain, producing sufficient sour-mash bourbon to require forty "iron bound barrels."[33] The distillery cooperage often adopted mechanization early on and was capable of high-volume production. This type of cooperage likely purchased stave and head stock, perhaps preformed, and worked in tandem with a distillery blacksmith who produced iron barrel hoops and rivets. Given that whiskey barrels were not used twice, high-capacity distilleries used staves, barrel heads, and hoop iron in large quantities. Some distillers preferred to buy their hoop iron directly from foundries in Pittsburgh, Youngstown, and Cincinnati. Pittsburgh hoop iron was considered the best quality available.[34]

In the Ohio Valley, Cincinnati, a major woodworking center, had fifty-six cooperage establishments employing 1,270 people.[35] Three cooperages and five distilleries operated across the Ohio River in Covington. Owensboro had eight distilleries and three cooperages. In Evansville, Indiana, five cooperages employing 425 people used wood largely from southern Indiana to produce barrels for flour mills and distilleries in Kentucky and Illinois.[36] Louisville had twenty-three cooperages in 1886 producing $950,000 worth of products annually.[37] Kentucky's seventeen-county Fifth Whiskey District extended from Owen County in the north to Adair County in the south. In 1887 district distillers produced more than 35 million gallons of whiskey requiring some 165,000 barrels.[38]

Those industrial distilleries planning to increase their mashing and distilling capacity had to assure that their grain and coal suppliers could fill their orders and that their cooperage shops had sufficient white oak staves and skilled coopers available to supply the additional barrels required. The owners of Anderson County Distillery No. 418 at Tyrone, Kentucky, installed new machinery in 1899 and increased its mashing capacity to 4,000 bushels of grain per day, making it "the largest 'mash tub' distillery in the world" and creating a substantial demand for tight white oak barrels.[39] In 1903 many Kentucky distillers had to shut down production two months early, ending their distilling season in March because they were unable to procure enough barrels to continue operations.[40]

Andrew J. Oots and his sons operated an urban cooperage at 239 West Main Street in Lexington from the 1880s through the 1920s. The family resided in an adjacent building.[41] The Oots cooper shop manufactured both tight and slack barrels, including full-size forty-eight-gallon whisky barrels, forty-two-gallon tierce barrels used for salt pork and sausage, half and quarter barrels, five- and ten-gallon kegs, and tubs in various sizes.[42]

For Oots, production and sales followed a seasonal pattern. Slack barrel manufacturing predominated in the summer and fall months, with peak production in July. The timing likely correlated with the harvest of grains, fruits, and vegetables. Tight barrel production began in late September, reached 400 barrels per week in December, and increased progressively to 600 barrels per week in April, mirroring the annual distilling season. Tight and slack barrel production overlapped from September to mid-November, with the shop producing 100 to 200 barrels of different types each week.

Five to twenty-two coopers worked at the Oots cooperage during any given week, including Mr. Oots's three sons and other coopers from Ireland, Italy, and Hungary. Seven experienced coopers could produce 600 barrels per month, if sales warranted. Even though Oots did not sell any barrels during some weeks in the summer and early fall, his coopers worked steadily making and stockpiling them. The coopers also repaired barrels, often traveling to places as distant as the McBrayer Distillery at Mt. Sterling, in Mont-

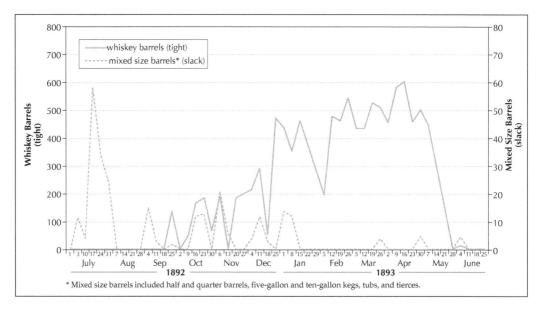

Cooperage sales of Andrew J. Oots & Sons, Lexington, July 1, 1892–June 30, 1893. (Compiled from Andrew J. Oots Cooper Shop Records, 1880–1926, Special Collections, University of Kentucky)

gomery County, to make repairs onsite. From January 1 to June 30, 1881, Oots's coopers visited the William Tarr Distillery in Lexington on twenty-seven different days and made more than $300 in repairs, including installing two slop cisterns, replacing barrel staves and heads, repairing yeast and mash tubs, and installing new tubs.

The Oots cooperage shop occupied the back half of a lot that extended from West Main Street to Water Street. The shop opened onto the Water Street railroad tracks.[43] Oots usually had stave wood shipped to his cooperage via railcar; about 7,400 staves made up a carload. Quality oak staves cost $40 per 1,000, and barrel heads cost about 30 cents for a set of two. Shipping costs in the early 1890s varied based on distance and commodity, but the freight cost for staves was commonly $23 to $29.50 per carload delivered to Lexington and more than $57 for one carload of barrel heads. Oots obtained iron barrel hoops from commercial suppliers in Covington, Kentucky; Youngstown, Ohio; and Allegheny County, Pennsylvania.

Oots paid his coopers 55 to 80 cents each to make barrels in the 1890s; he charged customers $1.95 to $2.35 for whiskey barrels, $1.30 to $1.60 for half barrels, and $1.75 to $2.15 for mash tubs. Ten-gallon kegs cost 75 cents. The cooperage shipped large barrel orders to customers via wagons and railroad freight cars. Oots charged a fee for local deliveries in or near Lexington. In June and July 1893, for example, he hauled 1,363 barrels from his cooperage on West Main Street to the J. E. Pepper Distillery on Manchester Street for $54.48. Delivery charges to distilleries beyond Lexington included turnpike toll fees, which were based on the size of the wagon and the width of its wheel rims.

The distilleries that were Oots's primary customers were subject to a capricious business environment, and the market demand for whiskey fluctuated from year to year. In the 1880s and 1890s distillers cycled into and out of the cooperage market. Some distillers sold their businesses to others who operated the works under different names or suspended operations to reduce overall production. All this had a dramatic effect on Oots's customer list. In 1881, for example, the William Tarr Distillery, a large, 400-bushel-per-day operation in Lexington, bought more than $12,000 worth of barrels from the Oots cooperage. Tarr's last transaction with Oots was in 1894, and Tarr went bankrupt three years later.[44] As distilleries suspended production or closed in the mid to late 1890s, Andrew Oots turned increasingly to producing tight and slack barrels and tubs of various sizes for the general commercial market for the storage of comestibles and hardware.

Coppersmithing

Copper, rather than aluminum, brass, iron, pewter, or tin, has long been the preferred material for making stills, condensation coils, and distillery pipes. Copper has several qualities that make it superior for distilling. The metal is malleable and can be readily worked into complex shapes without heavy dies and presses. Copper conducts and distributes heat evenly across a surface but also effectively extracts heat from vapor, thereby promoting condensation. The metal resists corrosion and is, to an extent, antimicrobial. When used in a whiskey still, copper is thought to react with the sulfur compounds, such as dimethyl trisulfide, produced by yeast fermentation. Exposing heated, fermented mash to copper still pots creates copper sulfate, which adheres to the copper vessel but is removed by post-fermentation cleaning.[45]

The process of obtaining refined and fabricated copper sheets, bars, and wire stock for use by American coppersmiths has been rife with complications, including the discovery of and access to sizable ore bodies, the development of suitable refining technologies, transportation difficulties, and international colonial and postcolonial trade policies and regulations. The principal sources of copper for the general world market during the first third of the nineteenth century were England, Ireland, Cuba, and Chile. England exported more than 1,400 tons to the United States in 1844, much of it purchased by East Coast metal fabricators and shipbuilders in port cities such as Boston and Baltimore.[46]

Copper was first commercially mined in colonial America at Simsbury, Connecticut, in 1709. Thereafter, North American copper mining focused on the uplands of eastern Canada, various sites on the Piedmont, and in the Appalachian ranges from Maine south to Tennessee and Alabama. Mines operated in eastern Pennsylvania by 1700 and in New Jersey by 1712.[47] The copper ore was mined, concentrated, and transported to England as part of a British colonial policy that required American raw materials to be shipped to England, where they were used in manufacturing—shipbuilding or military ordnance, for example—or turned into finished goods for export back to America.[48] The Piedmont copper deposits were exhausted by the beginning of the Revolutionary War.[49]

During the 1790s metal brokers and merchants in Philadelphia and Baltimore imported sheet copper from England, along with crocks, kettles, rivets, and stills ranging in size from 30 to 250 gallons. Paul Revere operated the country's first copper rolling mill in Canton, Massachusetts, in 1801 and supplied ship hull cladding to the US Navy. But American smiths working in the early nineteenth century lacked the technology to refine raw copper ore and resorted to fabricating copper by resmelting the metal salvaged from ships and rolling it into sheets for use in manufacturing. American copper miners exploited small ore bodies in Vermont (1809), Maine (1870s), Maryland (up to the 1850s), southeastern Tennessee (by the 1850s), and northern Alabama (1870s). But with few exceptions, mining operations were ephemeral, and production was trifling.

The largest deposit of Appalachian sulfide copper ore was discovered in the Toccoa-Ocoee River drainage of southeastern Tennessee at Copper Hill and Ducktown in 1847. After basic refining, processers shipped much of the ore to Baltimore. Refiners there had successfully adopted a Welsh concentration process, and Baltimore became an important processing and rolling mill center, producing quantities of copper sheeting. The industry grew rapidly, and the city became the most important copper refining center on the Atlantic coast. By the eve of the Civil War, Baltimore was one of the world's largest copper production centers.[50]

The extensive native copper deposits in Michigan's Keweenaw Peninsula on Lake Superior were commercially mined by the mid-1840s, and by the 1870s, Michigan accounted for more than 90 percent of America's copper production. The Keweenaw copper was pure, requiring only concentration, which made it much cheaper to produce than the sulfide coppers refined at Baltimore. By 1870, the Baltimore smelters had closed.[51]

As practiced in America, sulfide copper refining was not only costly but also environmentally destructive.[52] The development of an electrolytic copper refining process in Wales in 1869 revolutionized the practice. American refiners adopted the technology and established a new commercial refining plant in Newark, New Jersey, in 1883. By 1905, the United States had nine large copper refineries in operation, all of them employing high-capacity, low-voltage, direct-current electric dynamos.[53] The new electrolytic refining technology developed in tandem with the discovery of vast copper oxide deposits in Arizona, New Mexico, Montana, and Utah. The nation's rapidly expanding transcontinental railroad system provided an economical means of delivering refined ingots to fabrication and manufacturing centers in the Middle Western and East Coast cities of the Manufacturing Belt. By 1900, fabricated copper sheets and ingot stock were widely available at reasonable prices.

Nineteenth-century coppersmithing was largely a traditional craft that required significant handwork. Many smiths worked with hand tools that had been in use for generations or even centuries. Historically, coppersmithing in Kentucky followed two different forms: folk or traditional work, and professional work performed by experienced "mechanics."[54] Traditional smiths were largely self-taught craftspeople who made simple containers out of flat copper sheets that they rolled into cylinders and brazed or soldered together. (Brazing joins two metal parts with a molten third metal filler at 840°F or higher. Joining metals at temperatures less than 840°F is referred to as soldering.) For example, to make a basic still, the coppersmith cut a flat sheet of copper to the desired shape with hand shears, rolled the cut sheet into a cone, and bonded the seam. The smith then fitted the cone to the top of a similarly constructed cylinder, attached a flat copper circle to the bottom, and soldered or brazed all the seams, completing the basic still cooker. Pipes could be made of flat sheet material that was similarly rolled, soldered, and bent or coiled to form a condenser.

Professional coppersmithing was a demanding occupation that combined knowledge of metallurgy, an appreciation of artistic design, and an understanding of applied geometry, along with tactile skills and kinetic finesse.[55] Advanced skills were obtained through extended training or apprenticeship. The work's complexity resided not in the tools—a forge and a small selection of hand tools sufficed—but in the careful geometric calculations and measurements required to make precise patterns and cut and form flat sheets of copper into complex shapes. The smith also had to master the heat ranges and melting points of different copper, brass, and zinc alloys and the chemistry of fluxes when soldering and brazing. The shaping techniques required for coppersmithing were not readily mechanized, except for simple forms.

Although coppersmithing and coopering were important and complementary trades in the distilling industry, they were fundamentally different in organization and location. Skilled professional coppersmiths commanded high wages and usually made a variety of practical household utensils such as kettles, pots, and pans, as well as hardware—pipes, pumps, and scoops—and large, specialized tanks and stills. When E. H. Taylor Jr. rebuilt his O.F.C. Distillery in Frankfort in the 1880s, his construction crew lined the fermenting tanks with cement covered with copper sheeting. This impermeable surface, in Taylor's view, avoided the problem of acid saturation, which was common in wooden fermenting vats, and allowed thorough cleanup between batches.[56] Coppersmiths also supplied the brewing, marine, and railroad industries with various copper containers, boilers, pipes, and brass fittings.

Unlike coopers, skilled coppersmiths tended to work in large urban centers, not in small towns or rural settings. In the decade from 1860 to 1870, Nelson County, one of Kentucky's major distilling centers, had only one resident coppersmith. Most coppersmiths worked in larger towns and cities such as Louisville, Cincinnati, Lexington, and Owensboro.

Fishel & Gallatine, a copper- and tinsmith shop in Lexington, began operating on Main Street in the early nineteenth century. The shop made stills, kettles, and other copper and tin vessels. It was a place "where those who pleased to favor them with orders, may

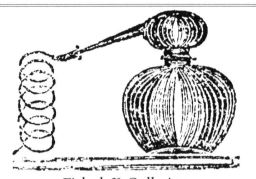

Fishel & Gallatine,
COPPER AND TIN SMITHS,
INFORM their friends and the public, they have now on hands, a variety of *STILLS* of the best quality, and having laid in an assortment of COPPER, and engaged Workmen of skill, can with satisfaction, complete any orders they may be favored with.
TIN WARE of every description, by whole-sale or retail; *Copper Boilers, Hatters' Kettles, Copper Tea Kettles, Brass and Copper Wash Kettles, &c. &c.*
☞ Tin Ware and Merchandize exchanged for old Copper, Brass and Pewter.
Lexington, 11th October, 1808.—tf

Advertisement for Fishel & Gallatine, Copper and Tin Smiths, Lexington. (*Kentucky Gazette,* February 27, 1809)

depend on their being strictly executed." The smiths announced that they had "received a fresh supply of thick copper," but they were also interested in purchasing old copper and pewter.[57] Most nineteenth-century coppersmiths bought scrap copper, brass, pewter, and tin, suggesting that these metals were in limited supply. Copper stock was expensive to buy and transport, but most accomplished smiths possessed the metallurgical knowledge and equipment required to repair old objects and to process scrap into sheet, bar, and wire material for reuse. Later in the century, illegal stills became another source of copper. When US marshals and revenue agents raided illegal moonshine stills, they demolished the equipment and confiscated the copper, which they then sold to coppersmiths—perhaps, ironically, to be transformed into new stills.[58] Brokers bought and sold copper by weight rather than by dimension.[59] In 1810, after Fishel and Gallatine liquidated their partnership, Fishel advised customers that his shop had received a "large assortment of COPPER & TIN, and ha[d] engaged from the Eastward, some of the first workmen in his line of business, from which circumstance he can with full confidence assure his friends and the public, that any work done by him will be executed in a *superior manner,* to any done in this *State heretofore.*"[60] Teamsters made regular trips from central Kentucky by road and river to Philadelphia and Baltimore to obtain goods for sale in local shops—including sheet copper. Carriage costs over that distance were estimated at $65 per ton, and a fully loaded

Conestoga-type freight wagon carried five tons.[61] The equivalent cost in present-day currency for one wagonload of goods would be roughly $6,500.

By the 1850s, more than twenty metal fabrication shops operated in Louisville and employed more than eighty smiths. Skilled smiths were in demand, as were shop boys or untrained assistants, who earned $5 to $7 per week. Louisville smiths produced whiskey stills, condensing coils, and related distillery equipment in significant amounts. They also fabricated equipment for brewers, steamboat builders, hotels, and hardware manufacturers.[62] Candle makers, such as Procter & Gamble in Cincinnati, converted tallow produced by slaughterhouses and butcher shops into a stearic fatty acid that they distilled into candle material. These candle makers initially obtained their large copper stills from Philadelphia, but by the 1850s, Louisville coppersmiths were able to fill their orders with acid-resistant equipment.[63]

Louisville metal fabrication shops tended to cluster together to take advantage of access to the Ohio River and primary roads. It was also convenient to have like businesses nearby as a source of raw materials, tools, or warehouse space.[64] Most of Louisville's metal fabrication shops operated along West Main Street from Third Street to Ninth Street or in that vicinity.[65] A Cincinnati copper and brass works, Hoffman, Ahlers & Company, established a successful branch shop in Louisville in 1879. Another family-related business, Hoffman & Company, opened a short-lived copper works at 725–729 East Main Street in the early 1900s. By about 1900, Hoffman, Ahlers & Company had become the Vendome Copper and Brass Works, operating at 625–627 East Main Street.[66] Vendome manufactured equipment for several industrial distilleries operating in the 1890s and 1910s, including Glenmore Distillery in Owensboro, E. H. Taylor Jr. & Sons near Frankfort, and J. T. S. Brown & Sons Company, which operated distilleries in several locations, including the Old Prentice Distillery south of Lawrenceburg. Vendome became, and remains, one of the nation's premier copper still manufacturers and serves a worldwide market.[67]

Without the inventions and innovations that enhanced the mechanization of the distilling process during the nineteenth century, industrial-scale production could not have been achieved. Moreover, the gradual mechanization of complementary enterprises such as power generation, agriculture, lumber processing, mining, and glassmaking also enabled and enhanced whiskey production. On the one hand, mechanization across the spectrum of American production was the product of inspired inventors; on the other hand, it was stimulated by greater market demand for finished goods that, up to that time, had been largely handmade. Mechanization had the effect of devaluing some traditional skills and discarding some of the specialized hand tools used by generations of craftspeople. It was a self-cannibalizing process in which new equipment replaced the old in the pursuit of higher, more efficient production. Specialized fabrication machines and tools enabled coopers to increase barrel production. Coppersmiths benefited from mechanical advances in smelting and metal processing, but they continued to rely on their traditional fabrication skills. The retreat of handcraft skills accompanied the mechanization of several trades that supported nineteenth-century distilling. Even so, bourbon distillers would long thereafter contend that their product was "handmade."

II

The Lands of Fine Whiskey Distilling

6

The Inner Bluegrass Region
Remnants and Contemporary Distillery Works

Traditional farmer-miller distilleries operated across the state in the first three decades of the nineteenth century. Thereafter, as distillers adopted steam power and mechanization, whiskey production increasingly focused on the Greater Bluegrass, especially the Inner and Outer Bluegrass subregions. These areas enjoyed the mutual advantages of fertile soils and productive farms, a near ubiquitous distribution of cool-water springs and perennial streams, and hard-surface turnpikes and railroad trunk and branch lines to transport raw materials and finished products. Within the Inner Bluegrass, distilleries clustered in several areas that were particularly favorable.

Bourbon and Harrison Counties

Sometime between 1774 and 1777, Joseph Bowman of Frederick County, Virginia, at the northern end of the Shenandoah Valley, was among a group of colonists who moved to Kentucky's frontier settlement at Harrodsburg. Another Shenandoah Valley resident, twenty-year-old Jacob Spears from Rockingham County, served as a captain in Bowman's group.[1] Spears eventually settled in Bourbon County and established a farm north of Paris, the county seat. Many pioneers from Maryland and Virginia brought enslaved people with them to Kentucky. Evidence that Jacob Spears was a slaveholder is indirect, but in 1790, on the Spears farm on Clay-Kiser Road north of Paris, two black men (either slaves or employees) felled trees and cut them into logs, which they then hauled to the Spears farmstead. Spears hewed and notched the logs to shape and positioned them on a fieldstone foundation near a small flowing spring, building one of the first distilleries in the county. The output of the Spears farm distillery was small, less than two barrels per day. Several years later, a local stonemason, Thomas Metcalfe, built a large stone house on the property; he also may have built a stone storage warehouse–malt house that fronts the road near the distillery site. The log distillery building stood only a few years, but the warehouse remains in good condition and is used to store livestock feed.

Mr. Spears and his wife Elizabeth had six children, including Noah and Solomon. As adults, these two young men shipped the family's whiskey to New Orleans by flatboat. Nearby Stoner Creek and the South Branch of the Licking River proved too shallow for flatboating, so the Spears brothers likely hauled their cargo southwest to the Kentucky

Jacob Spears house, Bourbon County.

River for shipment to the Ohio River at Carrollton.[2] Jacob Spears died in 1825, and his family's experience offers a sketch of how Kentucky's early farm-distillery industry began. Spears possessed practical skills such as woodworking, construction, farm management, and distilling. Slaves or African American employees constituted at least part of the labor pool and worked split seasons on the farm and at the distillery.[3]

As farm, mill, and distillery mechanization and industrialization increased after the Civil War, operational capacities grew, requiring additional labor. Two large distilling works in Bourbon County provide examples. George G. White employed thirty-five hands to mash 400 bushels each day, while also feeding 500 cattle and 800 hogs at his Chicken Cock Distillery on the Maysville Road on the north side of Paris. H. C. Bowen employed twenty hands at a wage of $2 a day to mash more than 400 bushels at his distillery at Ruddles Mills, near the junction of Hinkston Creek and Stoner Creek, north of Paris. Bowen also had a large cooper shop that produced thirty-five to forty barrels per day.[4] In addition to routine day-to-day distilling work, with its comparatively stable labor demand, distillers hired extra hands for special projects, such as filling large whiskey orders, which involved retrieving, gauging, and moving barrels to railroad loading docks or other shipping facilities.

Distilleries and mills inhabited the banks of Stoner Creek and the South Fork of the Licking River at opportune sites in a rough alignment from Paris to Ruddles Mills

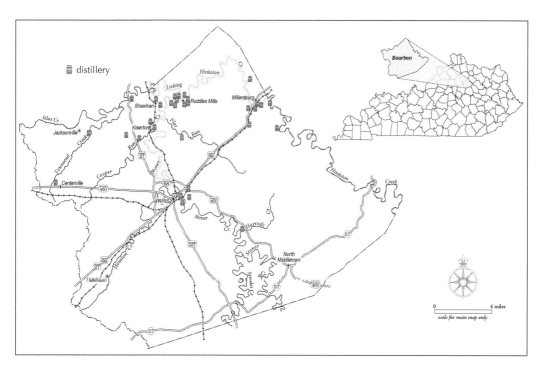

Bourbon County distilleries, ca. 1790–1950. Distillery site locations are approximate. Some distilleries were short-lived, while others were in production for decades. (Compiled from *Atlas of Bourbon, Clark, Fayette and Woodford Counties, Kentucky* [Philadelphia: D. G. Beers, 1877]; Chester Zoeller, *Bourbon in Kentucky: A History of Distilleries in Kentucky,* 2d ed. [Louisville, KY: Butler Books, 2010])

and extending to points north of Cynthiana, the Harrison County seat. Distiller, farmer, horseman, entrepreneur, and politician Thomas Jefferson Megibben worked at, owned, or had a financial interest in six Inner Bluegrass distilleries from about 1849 until his death in 1890. Two of his distilleries, Excelsior and Edgewater, operated about four miles south of Cynthiana near Lair's Station. The *Cynthiana News* announced in March 1869 that Mr. Megibben and his brother had just completed construction of a new industrial-scale distillery near the station. "It is said to be the best in Kentucky," the newspaper declared. "Its capacity is about equal to fifteen hundred bushels per day, but we understand that not more than four hundred will be mashed."[5] The distillery building was seventy-nine feet long, forty feet wide, and three stories tall. The J. & E. Greenwald Company of Cincinnati installed the steam engine and related machinery. The Robson Company of Cincinnati built and installed the copper column still. "The DeBus Company manufactured the mashing tubs which were said to be some of the largest in the world."[6] Megibben's distillery was something of a showcase for new inventions. The distillery building and equipment were outsized; the three-story height accommodated the tall column still and the elevated milling equipment. Megibben may have operated a dedicated cooperage, but he also purchased whiskey barrels from Andrew J. Oots & Sons in Lexington.[7]

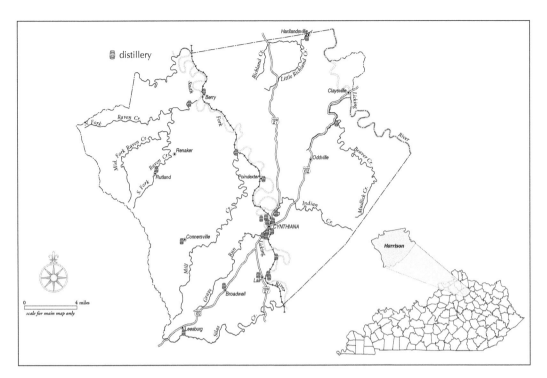

Harrison County distilleries, ca. 1790–1950. Distillery site locations are approximate. Some distilleries were short-lived, while others were in production for decades. (Compiled from *Map of Harrison County, Kentucky* [Philadelphia: D. G. Beers, 1877]; Chester Zoeller, *Bourbon in Kentucky: A History of Distilleries in Kentucky,* 2d ed. [Louisville, KY: Butler Books, 2010])

Mr. Megibben built a palatial home on a ninety-acre hilltop property overlooking Cynthiana in 1883. He called the $300,000 mansion Monticello. Samuel Hannaford & Sons of Cincinnati, one of the nation's leading architectural firms at the time, designed the eclectic brick and stone structure. The outsized house included multiple Victorian gables and a wrap-around porch built of turned posts and spindles with a wrought iron balustrade. Amenities included a second-floor music room and a third-floor ballroom. The exterior brick was imported from England, as were the woods used in the lavish and elaborate interior.[8] Although Megibben's house earned a place in the National Register of Historic Places in 1974, the building has since been razed.[9] The carriage house is the only remaining structure on the property, and it serves as a church.

Lexington and Fayette County

Near the center of the Inner Bluegrass Ordovician limestone plain, the land surface is 900 to 1,000 feet above sea level, and surface water drains primarily northwest toward the Kentucky River by way of the Elkhorn Creek watershed's North, Middle, and South Forks. Precipitation runoff also drains by way of underground channels whose direction and vol-

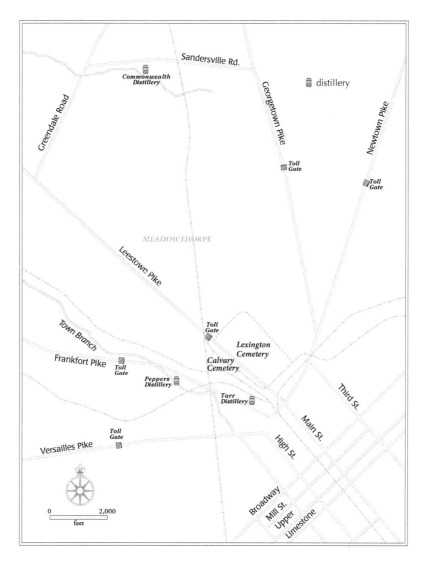

Lexington distilleries, ca. 1891. (Compiled from W. R. Wallis, *Maps: Fayette County, Kentucky*, 1891, Library of Congress)

ume of flow are not yet fully understood; they are evident in hillside springs and valley swallet holes that capture surface streams and direct them underground. In the early 1790s Lexington surveyors drew up a street plat on which Main Street paralleled Middle Fork, a tributary of South Elkhorn Creek that was later renamed Town Branch. In dry weather, the branch was sluggish and meandering, but with heavy rains it became a torrent. Despite flow variability and a potential flooding hazard, several industrial works—tan yards and water-powered mills of various types—operated along or near Town Branch by 1802. A gunpowder mill was likely in operation at McConnell Springs near the branch by 1813.[10] Shallow wells and water pumped from springs through underground log pipes supplied water to distilleries. By 1810, the city's 4,300 residents obtained their domestic water large-ly from wells.[11]

Physician and Transylvania University professor of chemistry Robert Peter was con-cerned about Lexington's water quality, and he wrote a report describing the water drawn from two wells bored through limestone rock. In 1852 a druggist drilled a well to a depth of forty feet at Cheapside on the courthouse square. The well yielded water that contained "hard masses of iron pyrites, and the water was such a strong chalybeate, sparkling with carbonic acid gas, depositing oxide of iron on exposure to the air, and containing quite a variety of saline ingredients, that it soon became quite popular as mineral water." Upon exposure to the air, however, the odor of the water became offensive. Dr. Peter deemed the water to be impure and found that water from every well in the Town Branch watershed contained nitrate salts and hydrogen sulfide. The source of the groundwater's contamina-tion, he concluded, was drainage from backyard privies, bathhouses, and laundries.[12]

As the basis for a land claim, William McConnell built a station, or fortified house, between Old Frankfort Pike and Town Branch near the site of a large "sinking spring," lat-er named McConnell Springs. The spring was near the Headley Distillery, also known as the Henry Clay Distillery, built in 1858 by the Headley & Farra Company.[13] The distillery burned in about 1873. The Blue Grass Pork House packing plant operated on the site from 1875 to 1879. The James E. Pepper Company purchased the packing plant and in 1880 erect-ed a new brick and stone industrial-scale distillery with three corncribs and shed space for 500 feeder cattle. Wedged between Town Branch and Manchester Street, the forty-eight-acre site had access to creek water, the road network, and the railroad. Powered by two steam engines, Mr. Pepper's works consumed 250 bushels of coal and mashed some 500 bushels of grain per day. The distillery included twenty-one mash tubs, a cooper shop, a bottling works, and five aging warehouses with a capacity of more than 40,000 barrels.[14] Pepper elected not to use water from Town Branch or a well on the distillery site; instead, he contracted with John and Laura Wilson, owners of Wilson's Spring (aka McConnell Springs), to pipe water some 3,000 feet from the spring to the distillery. In 1894 Pepper lived in a two-story Greek Revival house at Meadowthorpe, a large stock farm in what is now north Lexington, about half a mile from the distillery. The property became the city's first airport in the 1920s and was split up in 1949 to create the Meadowthorpe subdivision.

In about 1866, Turner, Clay & Company established the Ashland Distillery some 2,500 feet east of the Henry Clay–James Pepper Distillery. The eleven-acre site on Man-chester Street, near Cox Street, Town Branch, and the railroad tracks, had once been a lead works and thereafter a pork packing plant.[15] William Tarr & Company purchased the distillery in 1871 and operated it until it burned in 1879, whereupon the company rebuilt the distillery on the same site. The distillery's three steam engines burned 160 bushels of coal per day, likely delivered via the Louisville, Cincinnati & Lexington Railroad. Distill-ery laborers mashed between 420 and 1,000 bushels of corn, rye, and malted barley each day and fed the slop, supplemented with hay, to cattle tethered in a large pen beside Town Branch. The works fed about 500 cattle to market weight each year. Two warehouses beside Manchester Street stored the aging whiskey. A cooper shop operated just north—downstream—near the Red River Lumber Yard and a railroad siding. Rather than draw water from Town Branch or a bored well, the company leased spring water from nearby Ater Spring, using some 200,000 gallons per day.[16]

Four large distilleries operated in rural Fayette County during the second half of the nineteenth century.[17] One began as a five-story brick and stone building used as a cotton spinning and weaving mill, purchased by Stoll, Hamilton & Company in 1880. The company converted the steam-powered mill into a distillery; it stood adjacent to Sandersville Road, three miles north of Lexington, and was near Boiling Spring and Hillenmeyer Spring, whose water quality was deemed excellent.[18] A 40,000-bushel crib supplied 300 bushels of corn and 150 bushels of rye and malted barley for each day's mashing. An extended trough delivered slop directly to cattle pens situated downstream from the distillery. The works also fed 1,000 hogs. The Cincinnati & Southern Railroad tracks were about 2,000 feet distant, and wagons moved grain from the tracks to the distillery, and whiskey from the distillery to the warehouse.[19]

Woodford County

Woodford County borders the Kentucky River on the east. The river's proximity yields two radically different topographies—a gently rolling and astonishingly fertile upland to the east, and a rough, stream-cut area to the west. The river flows in a 300-foot-deep palisaded gorge, and small tributary creeks flow west down that gradient, incising deep ravines into the limestone upland. Each creek valley offers potential water-power sites, and by the late eighteenth century, these were being developed by millers and distillers. Woodford County distillers also built works on the uplands, especially in Versailles, the county seat, and in the railroad town of Midway.

Glenns Creek rises near Versailles and flows northwest, incising a 300-foot-deep valley to its juncture with the Kentucky River, about two miles south of Frankfort. The stream gradient was sufficiently steep to attract nineteenth-century water-powered industries and between 1811 and 1830, Isaac Miles, Roderick Perry, and Randolph Darnell built gristmills and sawmills along the creek. Small distilleries also operated there among the mills. These industries attracted laborers, who erected houses, churches, and stores, creating a mile-long string town named Millville.[20] This lower section of Glenns Creek was also known as Crow Valley.[21] Small farms along the valley's wider sections produced crops and livestock. The valley's most successful distilleries included Oscar Pepper (1812), John Shields (1844), Old Taylor (1850s), and Old Crow (1860). Each was sold, purchased, upgraded, expanded, reorganized, and resold several times during the nineteenth century. Today, the McCracken Pike provides access to the valley.

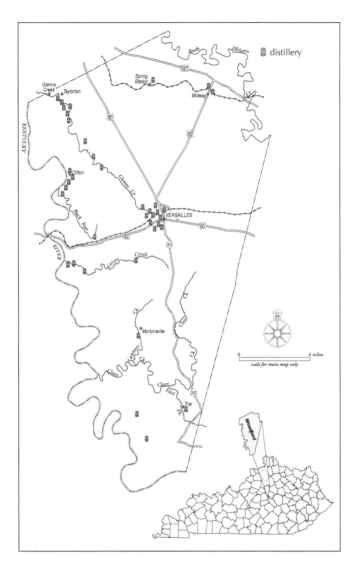

Woodford County distilleries, ca. 1790–1950. Distillery site locations are approximate. Some distilleries were short-lived, while others were in production for decades. (Compiled from *Atlas of Bourbon, Clark, Fayette and Woodford Counties, Kentucky* [Philadelphia: D. G. Beers, 1877]; Chester Zoeller, *Bourbon in Kentucky: A History of Distilleries in Kentucky,* 2d ed. [Louisville, KY: Butler Books, 2010])

Labrot & Graham Distillery

Elijah Culpepper of Culpepper County, Virginia, settled in Woodford County in about 1780 and soon thereafter started operating a distillery in Versailles. Mr. Culpepper changed his name to Pepper at some point, and in 1812 he built a small distillery on the middle reaches of Glenns Creek; after 1825, the distillery was operated by his son, Oscar Pepper.[22] In 1833 Oscar Pepper hired Scottish physician and chemist James C. Crow as distiller. Mr. Crow applied scientific methods to the distilling process and produced a highly regarded bourbon whiskey.[23] Oscar Pepper died in 1865, and his son, James E. Pepper, directed distillery operations. The works were sold to Leopold Labrot and James Graham, who continued to produce bourbon whiskey under the name "Old Oscar Pepper Distillery, Woodford Coun-

Labrot & Graham Distillery site.

ty, Ky."[24] As noted earlier, in 1879 James Pepper purchased a distillery on Town Branch in northwest Lexington near the Louisville, Cincinnati & Lexington Railroad tracks (later the Louisville & Nashville Railroad).

Additional ownership and management changes occurred, but operations terminated with Prohibition in 1920. Production began again in 1935. The Brown-Forman Corporation bought the Labrot & Graham Distillery site in 1940 and operated it until 1973, when it was sold. Brown-Forman repurchased the property in 1994 and spent $7 million to restore the works, part of which dated from 1838.[25] Speaking to the restoration strategy, Bill Creason of Brown-Forman said, "The site is the most historically important place in bourbon distilling." Kentucky has thirty places designated by the US secretary of the interior as National Landmark Sites, and three are distilleries: Burks Spring Distillery (Maker's Mark), George T. Stagg (Buffalo Trace), and Labrot & Graham (Woodford Reserve). The distillery is presently best known for its primary bourbon product, Woodford Reserve.[26]

Old Taylor and Old Crow

In about 1850 J. Swigert Taylor built a distillery on the lower section of Glenns Creek, about one and a half miles from the creek's confluence with the Kentucky River. Taylor appointed his nephew, E. H. Taylor Jr., as manager. Oscar Pepper's distillery on Glenns

Creek, near Millville, produced Old Crow whiskey. In the late 1870s W. A. Gaines & Company bought the Old Crow Distillery, and the works was soon mashing some 500 bushels (twelve wagonloads) of grain per day.[27] Although Glenns Creek offered bountiful water-power potential, access was awkward and cumbersome. To avoid driving wagons along the narrow creek bottom, laborers hewed a narrow road into the base of the limestone bluff. In 1907 Mr. Gaines oversaw the extensive expansion and remodeling of the old distillery works, increasing the mashing capacity to 1,800 bushels per day.[28] The project likely included substantial stonework on the main building so that it resembled the Old Taylor building just to the south. Gaines also contemplated building a five-mile branch railroad from the Old Crow works to Jett's Station on the Louisville & Nashville line. The Jett's Station site is presently about one-quarter mile north of the US 60 and I-64 interchange southeast of Frankfort. The *Frankfort Roundabout* opined, "The road will only be about five miles long, and will be of immense advantage to this big distillery as they do an immense amount of shipping, both of grain into the distillery, and of the finished product of their stills from the distillery."[29] The Kentucky Highlands Railroad Company completed the new rail spur connecting to the Louisville & Nashville line in December 1907.[30] The spur not only provided the high-capacity access required to operate an industrial-scale distillery but also permitted E. H. Taylor Jr. to open his distillery to visitors. The line also meant that distillery employees living in Frankfort could commute to work via the railroad; the one-way fare was 30 cents.[31] In 1911 laborers completed a rail line extension from Millville southeast eight miles to Versailles, including a spur line to the whiskey warehouses at the Labrot & Graham Distillery.

The relict remains of the Old Crow Distillery and E. H. Taylor Jr.'s Old Taylor Distillery stand in close proximity just above the Glenns Creek floodplain, four miles north of the Labrot & Graham Distillery site.

In May 2014 investors purchased the 113-acre Old Taylor property, which had been abandoned since 1972. They planned to spend $6 million to refurbish the works and put it back into production as Castle & Key Distillery. By 2016, when the property was nominated for the National Park Service's National Register of Historic Places, the expansive site retained more than forty architecturally distinctive buildings, most of them constructed of stone or brick. Building conditions ranged from relict to good. Reconstruction included reconditioning some of the old equipment, as well as installing new gear where needed. After the repeal of Prohibition in the early 1930s, National Distillers Products reopened the distillery and installed new high-capacity steel fermenting vats: six 22,000-gallon tanks and fifteen 11,000-gallon units. The steel tanks that replaced Mr. Taylor's original wooden vats still stand. Six have been refurbished, cleaned, and relined. The old still was replaced with a new fifty-foot copper column still, manufactured by the Vendome Copper and Brass Works in Louisville, for distilling bourbon and a forty-foot stainless steel column still for making gin and vodka.

Old Taylor Distillery site.

Warehouse B was built of brick, with stone quoins at the corners. At four stories tall and more than 530 feet long, it is thought to be the largest whiskey aging warehouse of its type in the world. The turreted castle-style still house was constructed of Tyrone limestone, sometimes referred to as Kentucky River marble; with the passage of time, the stone has weathered to a bright white. This iconic building not only housed the distilling apparatus but also came to represent E. H. Taylor's distillery and appeared in publicity photographs and postcards. A large sunken garden, built in 1906 and central to the site, has been reclaimed from overgrowth. Artisans restored the peristyle spring house or pergola that, together with the garden, were places favored by early twentieth-century visitors. When fully operational, the renovated works will be capable of producing about 12,000 barrels of spirits per year.[32]

Midway

At Midway, one is reminded that while distilleries offered seasonal employment and markets for grain farmers, they were also potential hazards. In the early 1880s Thomas Edwards built a new distillery near the Southern Railroad tracks in Midway. S. J. Greenbaum purchased the distillery, and when Mr. Greenbaum died in 1897, his family continued to operate the distillery under his name.[33] The distillery fed cattle in pens downslope near a creek, Lee's Branch. This led to complaints, and in November 1887 the Woodford Circuit Court fined the Greenbaum distillery for "suffering still slops and offal from [the] distillery and cattle pens to run into a branch near by."[34] To partially address the slop dumping problem, the distiller installed a new slop dryer. But in January 1904 the dryer and boiler room caught fire, causing some $25,000 in damage.

Four years later, in August 1908, an arsonist set fire to the distillery's six bonded warehouses, which contained 47,500 barrels of whiskey. As the blazing warehouses collapsed, burning whiskey poured from smashed barrels and ran downhill into Lee's Branch, incinerating the homes of several African American residents. When the liquid fire reached the creek, it ignited the Southern Railroad trestle and two county bridges. For a time, the fire threatened the entire northern section of town. The Midway fire company, possessing only one fire engine, was able to save the distillery works and offices, the superintendent's home, and the bottling house; the Southern Railroad depot; and the Cogar Company grain elevator, all adjacent to and uphill from the burning warehouses.[35] When the burning whiskey in Lee's Branch reached South Elkhorn Creek, it set the creek afire for several miles, burning a number of houses along the banks. Burning whiskey stained the creek water a dark brown and killed thousands of fish and waterbirds.[36] The downstream collateral damage included a "water famine" for creek-side residents, who were unable to fill their cisterns because whiskey contaminated the water for an extended period.[37] The loss of the warehouses and the whiskey was estimated at nearly $1 million, for which the Greenbaum family had insurance coverage. The distillery was rebuilt and reorganized by new owners but went bankrupt in 1915. It remained closed during Prohibition. New owners reopened the works in the 1930s, but bankruptcy again forced closure. Another set of new owners operated the works until 1959, when it closed for the last time. Most of the distillery buildings have been razed; the Cogar grain elevator still stands and is now occupied by a popular restaurant. Warehouse A has been converted to apartments.

Anderson County

Three miles east of Lawrenceburg, the Kentucky River flows north between near-vertical limestone palisades forming Anderson County's eastern boundary. Several small streams have cut steep valleys into the palisades' western face, including Bailey Run and its northern branch, Cedar Brook Run.

Before flowing into the Kentucky River, Bailey Run (called Bailey's or Baileys Run at one time) flows across a limestone terrace that lies some thirty feet above the Kentucky River. The terrace is 1,000 feet wide and about 6,500 feet long, a rare bit of nearly level topography that is adjacent to central Kentucky's primary navigable river and was bisected by a short rail line between Lawrenceburg and Versailles, in neighboring Woodford County. Rafts and steamboats frequented the south- to north-flowing river, and the mouth of Bailey Run provided river access and a suitable place for a boat landing. W. H. Dawson

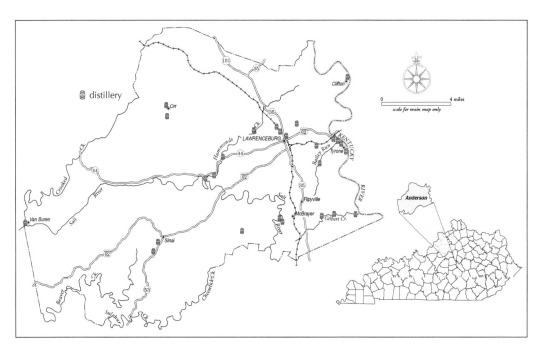

Anderson County distilleries, ca. 1790–1950. Distillery site locations are approximate. Some distilleries were short-lived, while others were in production for decades. (Compiled from Ripy Family Papers, 1888–1963, Special Collections, University of Kentucky; Chester Zoeller, *Bourbon in Kentucky: A History of Distilleries in Kentucky*, 2d ed. [Louisville, KY: Butler Books, 2010])

and Joel Boggess built a wharf house at the landing in 1850, and the people working the riverboats called the small cluster of houses near the landing Steamville. Nineteenth-century distillers established large-scale industrial distilleries on elevated river terraces and smaller works along the tributary creeks. As distillery employment increased, Steamville became the village of Tyrone. Contemporary visitors can reach the village from US 62 by turning south on Tyrone Road (KY 1510).

Tyrone and Peanickle

The valley cut by Bailey Run and Cedar Brook Run offered water-power potential, and the river terrace below offered transport access that was not found elsewhere in this section of the Kentucky palisades. Millers and distillers were attracted to the area early on, and Samuel P. Martin established the first distillery there in the 1860s. In July 1869 business partners S. P. Martin, Monroe Walker, and James Ripy sold the distillery, whiskey aging warehouses, and a house and lot to William H. McBrayer and Thomas B. Ripy (James Ripy's son) for $13,000.[38] The three-acre property was situated just upstream from the mouth of Bailey Run, and the distillery operated under the name Walker, Martin & Company.

James Ripy was born in 1809 in Tyrone, Ulster, Northern Ireland. He migrated to the United States and settled in Lawrenceburg in 1839, where he worked as a merchant and a wholesale liquor dealer. Mr. Ripy and his wife Artimesa had two daughters, Ema and Beebe, and two sons, James P. and Thomas B.[39] The Ripy family moved to a farm north of Lawrenceburg in about 1855. In 1860 James Ripy's real estate holdings were valued at more than $28,000 and his personal estate at $12,000. By 1870, the value of his personal estate had increased to $30,000, and he was one of the wealthiest farmers in the county. James Ripy also owned eight slaves in 1860: five men aged twelve to thirty-eight, two women ages ten and thirty, and one child.

William McBrayer, like his business partner Thomas Ripy, was a descendant of Scots-Irish immigrants. McBrayer was a Lawrenceburg dry goods merchant and livestock broker, and he established a small distillery on Cedar Brook Run east of Lawrenceburg in about 1847. McBrayer owned six slaves: two men, a woman, and three children. Newton Brown, a white man, was McBrayer's distiller for many years. At the time, distillers were paid $300 to $400 per year.[40] In 1876 McBrayer's Cedar Brook whiskey apparently won a medal at the Philadelphia Centennial International Exhibition.[41] For his efforts, McBrayer gave Brown a gold watch.[42]

Turnpikers completed the connecting road between Lawrenceburg and Versailles in 1857. The stone-covered macadam pike descended the bluff to the Kentucky River near the mouth of Bailey Run and then ran the length of the Tyrone terrace to a ferry landing. Thomas Ripy's Clover Bottom Distillery and warehouses stood beside the pike. Distillery slop flowed through troughs to elevated slop tubs at two cattle sheds positioned on the terrace north of, or downstream from, the distillery. The roofed sheds covered almost two and a half acres and housed 2,500 cattle when filled to capacity.[43] Livestock broker Charles Byrne shipped to market some 300 boxcars of cattle that had been slop-fed at Tyrone at the end of the 1891 distilling season. In late June 1892 the distillery sent 76 carloads of cattle, some 1,500 head, to eastern markets over the Louisville Southern Railroad. At the time, that consignment was thought to be the largest single shipment of cattle made from Kentucky. Ripy's distillery also fed hogs.[44]

Freight companies operated wagon lines from Frankfort to Lawrenceburg with connections to Tyrone, but when the water level in the river was sufficient to permit steamboat traffic, packet boats, including Thomas Ripy's *Little Dora,* made daily trips hauling goods between Tyrone and Frankfort in the 1880s. High water in late winter and early spring brought rafted timber from southeastern Kentucky's forests downriver to sawmills at High Bridge and Frankfort. Ripy ordered steam coal, which usually arrived by river in three-barge lots.[45] In April 1895 two 150-foot-long log rafts outfitted with large plank boxes landed at Tyrone. Loggers had filled the boxes with eastern Kentucky coal for delivery to the Ripy distillery. Lumber mills in south-central Kentucky supplied the Tyrone works with staves for the distillery cooperage—100,000 or more staves in a shipment. These arrived by water or by railroad when the Louisville Southern line opened.[46]

Distillery workers, including distillers and coopers, lived in the village of Tyrone and its attached neighborhood, Peanickle. A high proportion of Peanickle's population was African American, and the neighborhood originated as a post–Civil War settlement.[47] By 1910, Tyrone and Peanickle Village were home to 61 of the county's 143 distillery workers. Seventeen residents, all women, worked in the distillery bottling shops. Tyrone was not formally planned or platted as a town; rather, as the distillery expanded and its work-force grew, the demand for homes and services spurred the development of residential lots, streets, and shops.[48]

Two distillery partners, John Dowling and Edward Murphy, bought small lots in Ty-rone in 1880.[49] In 1881, the same year Tyrone was incorporated, Thomas Ripy partnered with William Waterfill and Edward and John Dowling to build the Clover Bottom Distill-ery at Tyrone; they incorporated their company as Waterfill Dowling & Company.[50] The incorporation papers stated that the company "shall be distilling hand made sour-mash whiskey and conducting and operating in the same place a cooper shop and saw mill."[51] Ripy later bought out his partners and expanded production in both of his distilleries, which were mashing more than 1,500 bushels per day and employing about 145 people in the 1890s.[52]

By 1900, Tyrone's population exceeded 500, with 150 children enrolled in the school built by S. P. Martin two decades earlier; a decade later, the village had nearly 600 resi-dents. Benevolent citizens built several town buildings, including two churches; distillers T. B. Ripy and S. P. Martin built a Methodist church in 1880, and store owners built a Christian church in 1890.[53] The town also had an Odd Fellows Hall, a large general store, several retail shops, a barbershop, machine and blacksmith shops, a doctor, a courthouse, and a jail. The Tyrone Dramatic Club presented plays and musical performances.[54] Ty-rone was a "dry" town, with no liquor sales—a profound irony, given its dependence on distilleries for employment. In 1906 residents voted to go "wet."[55]

In 1888 J. P. Ripy bought a distillery atop the bluff above Tyrone and, after rebuilding, operated it as the Old Hickory Spring Distillery.[56] That same year, the Louisville South-ern Railroad Company, whose primary rail line ran from Louisville to Lawrenceburg and Harrodsburg, began to build a new branch to connect Lawrenceburg to Versailles and Lex-ington. The line required a new railroad bridge across the Kentucky River palisades near Tyrone. Completed in August 1889, the trussed cantilever deck bridge had a 550-foot cen-tral span, the longest of any bridge in the nation at the time, and it stood more than 280 feet above the water. Named the Young Bridge, after railroad company president William Bennett Young, the span and its new rail line bolstered the bluff-top distillery opera-tions. J. P. Ripy's distillery stood beside the tracks.[57] Following the repeal of Prohibition, the works was rebuilt, and its descendant continues to operate in the twenty-first century as the Wild Turkey Distillery.

In 1900 Tyrone was the state's leading whiskey manufacturing center outside of Lou-isville. Operations continued until Prohibition, when the works were closed and dismantled, thereby truncating the town's livelihood.[58] Residents and businesses moved away. Fires and tear-downs removed many of the abandoned buildings. In the twenty-first century a few houses, trailers, and church buildings remain, but the town is now quiescent; its concrete sidewalks cross grassy open space, and driveways end at vacant lots.

Lawrenceburg

Several Anderson County distillers built large homes in Lawrenceburg, the county seat, William B. Saffell, John Dowling, and Thomas B. Ripy among them. Saffell owned 500 acres of farmland on the south side of town, where today a street and a school are named for him. He may have initiated real estate development on Lawrenceburg's South Main Street when he sold land to distillers and others who wished to build houses fronting the thoroughfare. In 1880 Saffell was superintendent of the Cedar Brook Distillery near Tyrone and served as vice president of Lawrenceburg National Bank. In 1889 he built the W. B. Saffell Distillery along the Southern Railroad tracks north of Lawrenceburg, near Alton.[59] Saffell's two-story brick Queen Anne–style house on South Main Street was constructed circa 1900. The 7,000-square-foot structure had a circular turret at the right front corner and a wraparound porch. The paneled front door was inset with a large beveled-glass panel and surrounded by circular stained-glass sidelights. Capable carpenters and other artisans finished the interior with cherry and walnut woodwork, including full-length window shutters and hand-carved fireplace mantels. Gas lighting illuminated crystal chandeliers.

John Dowling migrated from Ireland during the Great Famine of the 1840s. In the early 1870s he opened a cooper shop in Lawrenceburg and, with partner Thomas Ripy, operated a distillery east of Lawrenceburg in Tyrone. In 1886 Dowling completed construction of a two-and-a-half-story brick Italianate-style home at 321 South Main Street. The front door is set with beveled glass and opens into the base of a prominent three-story pavilion that is centered on and extends out from the front façade. Brick quoins accentuate the pavilion's front corners; a metal mansard roof caps the entire assembly. Dentils and large paired brackets are suspended below the roof cornice, and paneled and corbeled chimneys extend well above the roofline. The interior includes marble fireplace mantels, doorways with stained-glass sidelights, and paneled wainscoting and door jams. A carriage house stands at the rear.[60]

Across the street from the John Dowling house, Thomas B. Ripy purchased a ten-acre residential lot from farmer-distiller William Saffell for $7,500 in August 1885. The *Anderson News* announced that Ripy intended to build a residence on the lot and observed, "there will be a building there that would be an ornament to any city." It noted, "you may be sure that [the house] will be done in a style proportionate with the cost of the grounds" and "will be something worth going to see."[61] In September of that year Ripy bought an adjoining ninety-acre tract from distiller W. H. McBrayer for $125 per acre. A large force of workmen began foundation work during the spring of 1886, and in April the *Anderson*

John Dowling house, Lawrenceburg.

Thomas Ripy house, Lawrenceburg.

News triumphantly pronounced, "Lawrenceburg will soon have more palatial residences within its borders than any town of its size in the state."[62] Artisans completed Ripy's outsized Queen Anne–style home in 1888; it had thirty rooms and approximately 11,000 square feet of interior space.[63]

The façade of Ripy's mansion is finished in brown brick, with a limestone water table and stone belt courses above and below the windows on each floor. A projecting gabled porch supported with square, fluted wooden pillars covers the front entrance. The porch connects to a veranda that wraps around the right (north) wall. The polychrome slate roof has a small street-facing gabled dormer and two tall brick and stone gables. At the left (south) corner, a three-story octagonal tower extends above the roofline. At the third story, the tower has a mansard roof with five small gabled dormers capped by a small enclosed "widow's watch." The interior stairs, doors, and wainscoting are mahogany and walnut. Several doorways have arched transoms with stained glass. The fireplaces are finished with marbleized cast-iron mantels stenciled in gold leaf. Elaborate moldings crown the fourteen-foot ceilings, and chandeliers illuminate the largest rooms. The Ripy house is undergoing restoration.

About four miles south of Lawrenceburg's Whiskey Row, old US 127, or South Main Street, merges with the multilane US 127 Bypass. Some 600 feet south, toward the Bluegrass Parkway, Bonds Mill Pike heads west to the Salt River. In a short half mile, the pike crosses railroad tracks at the former site of McBrayer Depot. It descends a low-angle slope into the Salt River Valley and enters a repository of milling and distilling heritage. Three-fourths of a mile west of the depot, Four Roses Distillery stands on a hillside north of the road. Three aging warehouses clad in tinned sheet iron stand on the hillside to the south; two more stand downslope near the river. A bridge spans the river just downstream from an old mill dam. And across the river to the left, a concrete slab and scattered debris mark the site of another old distillery—likely built in 1935 by the Bonds Mill Distilling Company. The works produced Bonds Mill bourbon and, later, J. T. S. Brown whiskey.[64]

By 1891, J. M. Waterfill & Company was operating a wood-frame distillery on the narrow creek-bottom flats beside the Bonds Mill Pike and across the road from the present-day Four Roses works. J. T. S. Brown & Sons of Louisville bought the works in 1894 and changed the name to Old Prentice Distillery. By 1910, the works mashed about 200 bushels of grain per day. A coal-fired steam engine provided power and heated water; mash was fermented in eight large tubs. Pipes directed some slop to a hog feeding yard; the remainder flowed to a slop dryer behind the distillery. A pump pushed sour-mash whiskey by pipeline up the south hill to a cistern and warehouse, where the spirits were barreled and stored; or they were moved along a barrel run to a barrel-head branding room and a second warehouse to the east.[65] Little remains of the original Old Prentice works, although the warehouses on the south hill may be the same structures that were there in 1910. One of J. T. S. Brown's sons built a new distillery across Bonds Mill Road in 1910 or 1911. That works also operated as the Old Prentice Distillery for a time. The main building was designed by respected Frankfort architect Leo Oberwarth and is considered the best example of Spanish Mission architecture in Kentucky. The exterior walls are beige stucco-covered brick. The low-angle red tile roof extends to broad, overhanding eaves supported by large brackets. The end walls are finished in large curved baroque gables. A curved bell gable arches over the front door.[66] The distillery closed during Prohibition and reopened in the 1930s as the Old Joe Distillery. Louisville whiskey broker Paul Jones and his business partners owned the Frankfort Distillery, which made several whiskies, including the popular Four Roses brand. Their Frankfort Distilling Company bought the Old Joe works sometime in the 1930s. The works was acquired by Canadian distilling company Seagram & Son in 1946 and operated under several names, most recently as Four Roses.[67]

Frankfort and Franklin County

The Kentucky River flows northwest across the Greater Bluegrass country to join the Ohio River at Carrollton. Frankfort's site on the Kentucky River is sixty-five miles upstream from that confluence; it also marks the irregular splice between the Inner Bluegrass Middle Ordovician limestones and the Upper Ordovician limestones and shales of the Eden Shale Hills. South of Frankfort, the river's meanders have sliced a narrow, palisaded gorge into the Middle Ordovician basement rocks. The gorge widens to accommodate elevated river terraces in only a few places, such as at Tyrone in Anderson County, east of Lawrenceburg. Tributary creeks have dissected steep valleys into the adjoining uplands, giving the river corridor a rugged, ribbed character; it is difficult to cross, even at points where the tributary valleys on the east correspond with valleys across the river on the west side. Near Frankfort, the Kentucky River exits the palisades and begins a transition into the Eden Shale Hills. The river flows across the competent limestones there, but it readily erodes laterally into the compliant shales, widening the valley.[68] The hillsides rake back at low angles, and the valley widens, providing ready access to the river along several tributary creek valleys.

The river has changed course over the millennia, leaving behind cutoff meander loop terraces with nearly level floors. One of these loops is horseshoe shaped, with its open end attached to the Kentucky River on the southwest. The meander's northwest arm is the site of Frankfort's first settlement at Leestown, the point where a buffalo trace and Indian trail, Alanant-O-Wamiowee, crossed the river. The meander's southeast arm was the site of the first capitol, early residential development, and a small business district.

Before engineers completed river improvements and dam construction on the lower river at and below Frankfort, numerous shoals and rapids hampered river navigation; even small craft had to be carried or pulled through some sections during low water.[69] Construction crews completed the first five dams between the river's confluence with the

Ohio at Carrollton and Lawrenceburg by 1842. Thereafter, steamboats could readily traverse the slack-water pools between dams during most of the year.

In the nineteenth century, people and freight wagons moving overland toward Frankfort from the east could gain access to the river by following a broad, tapering ridge down to river level. This was the route most likely followed by English traveler Fortesque Cuming in 1807 and is similar to that followed in the 1880s by the Frankfort and Georgetown Turnpike and, presently, by US Highways 60, 421, and 460.[70] This was the most direct route west from where the North and South Forks of Elkhorn Creek join about three and a half miles from Frankfort. The creeks flowed northwest from the Lexington area and, during the nineteenth century, were intensively developed by millers.[71] Approaching from the west, wagons could descend the low-gradient valley cut through the hills by Big Benson Creek to its confluence with the Kentucky River. Railroad surveyors used the Big Benson Creek valley as a route west toward Louisville. The Lexington & Ohio Railroad gave Frankfort its first rail connection to Lexington in 1830, but a reliable, high-capacity rail line to Louisville and the Ohio River was not completed until 1851.

In addition to being the state capital, Frankfort's nineteenth-century population growth was stimulated by river-related commerce. The city became a nineteenth-century sawmill center, processing logs floated downriver from eastern Kentucky. But Frankfort also became a major distilling center. Small distilleries operated in Franklin County by the early nineteenth century. A distillery site adjacent to the river at Leestown was developed by a series of owner-distillers. Edmond H. Taylor Jr. modernized the distillery in 1869 and operated it for a time as the Old Fire Copper (O.F.C.) Distillery. Taylor added the Carlisle Distillery on adjacent land in about 1880. When the O.F.C. Distillery burned in 1882, Taylor had it rebuilt to resemble a two-story brick and stone Victorian mansion with a three-story tower and Greek Revival and Romanesque architectural details. Beer from copper-lined fermenting vats traveled by copper pipe to a copper beer well, where it was heated before arriving at the copper stills and doublers.

Taylor regarded Franklin County as a choice distilling site because the area's "waters, climate, and special facilities have long caused it to be known as the almost exclusive locality for the manufacture of pure, old-style, sour-mash whiskey."[72] The O.F.C. Distillery drew water from a riverside spring, and a 4,600-foot-long pipe brought water from a reservoir to the east. A coal-fired steam engine powered the works, which mashed 500 bushels of grain per day. An elevated, gravity-flow slop pipe carried spent grains to distant cattle and hog feedlots. Barreled O.F.C. whiskey was aged in four warehouses with an aggregate storage capacity of 35,680 barrels. The adjacent Carlisle Distillery was located beside the river and stood end to end with the O.F.C. works. The Carlisle had a large riverfront grain elevator, mashed 500 bushels per day, and aged whiskey in three brick warehouses with a combined 28,760-barrel capacity. The Leestown Turnpike passed through the distillery property, but by 1886, neither the Carlisle nor the O.F.C. Distillery was served by a railroad.

During the 1870s, E. H. Taylor Jr. operated three Frankfort distilleries: O.F.C., Carl-isle, and J. S. Taylor. He published a publicity booklet in which he extolled the merits of the water issuing from a spring on the property and cited the recently published "Map of Kentucky" by John H. Procter, director of the Kentucky Geological Survey.[73] Taylor embraced what he considered the science represented by the map, noting that it "shows that a small section of the state made famous by its fine sour-mash whiskeys, the rare-birds-eye limestone of the lowest stratum of the Lower Silurian formation alone [sic] outcrops." He continued: "The O.F.C. and other brands of the E. H. Taylor, Jr., Co., are produced upon the depressed apex of this stratum, thus securing the best limestone drainage it can possibly afford. The result in fine whiskey is no doubt largely due to the water that, percolating through the limestone, becomes impregnated with its properties, and imparts them to the spirit during the process of manufacture. Opinions and assertions are debatable—a geological fact, stereotyped in and reflected from the earth's crystallized strata, is as solid and immovable as the everlasting hills."[74] Taylor's booklet included references to "distinguished chemists," including a Professor Barnum of Louisville, who stated, "The water is of wonderful purity, and of peculiar adaptedness for the manufacture of whiskey. Your water contains very appreciable quantities of phosphate of lime, which would have the same effect in promoting the growth of the yeast plant that a dressing of bone phosphate would on a wheat field."[75] An engraving of the spring shows it issuing from the side of a hill a few feet above the level of the Kentucky River.[76]

By 1877, the O.F.C. Distillery had been acquired by George T. Stagg and others, who conducted business as Stagg, Hume, & Company. In 1894 the distillery's water supply still included Taylor's spring, carried to the works by a three-and-a-half-inch pipe. Insurance maps published that year, however, show that the O.F.C. Distillery used two force pumps to draw water directly from the Kentucky River via two pipes of different diameters—one eight inches, the other three and a half. Moreover, as depicted on the maps, the pipe drawing water from the spring was likely spliced directly into the river pipe of the same diameter, so it appears that the spring water was mixed with river water before it entered the distillery.[77] The works operates today as Buffalo Trace Distillery.

W. A. Gaines & Company, financed by investors from Kentucky and New York, built the industrial-scale Hermitage Distillery in 1868 on a terrace some fifty feet above the Kentucky River in South Frankfort. By 1886, the large wooden distillery mashed more than 900 bushels per day using water from two wells and the river, apparently not sharing Taylor's passion for "pure spring water." The Hermitage aged whiskey in eight brick warehouses with a combined storage capacity of 50,300 barrels. The distillery management operated a large dedicated cooper shop, presumably using staves and barrel heads provided by local mills. Wood and coal fueled the distillery's steam engine. A large shed adjacent to the warehouses sheltered slop-fed cattle. The distillery had no railroad connection and was dependent on wagons and river barges. Barge deliveries arrived at a river landing and reached the distillery via a steep driveway up the bluff face. Management compensated for irregular grain deliveries by building two large wooden "corn houses" adjacent to the distillery.[78] Laborers and artisans completed construction of Kentucky's new limestone, granite, and marble state capitol building in 1910 on property south of the river. The distance between the capitol grounds and the distillery site was less than half a mile.[79] Today, an early 1950s and 1960s subdivision of brick houses occupies the distillery site, bisected, appropriately, by Hermitage Drive.

Four other small distilleries operated in Frankfort, and four large industrial distilleries operated in rural Franklin County, including the Baker Brothers' works, which became the Old Grand-Dad Distillery in 1940.[80]

Frontier distillers found the Inner Bluegrass a hospitable environment in which to practice their craft. Perennial streams and springs provided water to power mills and operate stills. Fertile soils produced sufficient grains not only to provide subsistence for farm families and their livestock but also to supply a substantial number of small distilleries. The conversion from craft to industrial distilling was abetted by infrastructure improvements, such as overland turnpikes and railroads, and river navigational enhancements that included channel clearing and locks and dams. The region's economy was supported by productive agriculture and numerous manufacturers of products such as hemp, cotton, and timber. Banks and private investors provided the financial wherewithal to foster distillery expansion and mechanization. All of this invited innovation, and in addition to extending basic distilling to an industrial scale, some of the state's most creative distillers promoted their products through a variety of marketing tactics, such as representation at World's Fairs or hosting social events at their distilleries. Although the distilling economy was enhanced by such advantages, the Inner Bluegrass was not as idyllic as it was sometimes portrayed. Weather might be benign or threatening; groundwater could be sweet and iron free or bitter with salt and sulfur; and the whiskey market might be lucrative or an accomplice to insolvency. But, considered as a whole, Inner Bluegrass distillers advanced their business during the nineteenth century, some with remarkable success.

7

The Outer Bluegrass Region

Railroads and the Transition to Industrial Distilling

The western section of the Outer Bluegrass region is represented by Marion, Nelson, and Washington Counties. Surface waters drain west and north by way of the Chaplin River, Beech Fork, and Rolling Fork, and their extensive tributary networks accommodated numerous mills and distilleries during the nineteenth century. Streams issue from the Eden Shale Hills to the east and cross the limestones of the Outer Bluegrass before entering the shales and sandstones of the Knobs region to the west. Groundwaters move through karstic channels, but such systems are not as well developed here as they are in some parts of the Inner Bluegrass. The Eden Shale Hills occupy the eastern half of Marion County and a small section of northeastern Nelson County. The topography and soils here are similar to those found in the Eden Shale sections of Anderson and Franklin Counties.

Two different limestone formations provide the bedrock basement for the Outer Bluegrass. Grant Lake limestone, which is interbedded with shale, occurs in a small section of northern Marion County and significant portions of Washington and eastern Nelson Counties. A belt of Laurel dolomite extends northwest to southeast across the central section of Nelson County, with an extension into Washington County. The Grant Lake limestones yield soils in the Lowell-Fairmount association that occur on rolling land and are deep, finely textured, and moderately fertile. Laurel dolomite weathers into Pembroke soils, which tend to be deep, loamy, and fertile. Extensive sections of the land surface are nearly level to rolling and invite intensive agriculture.

The Knobs region tracks across the western quarter of Nelson County and the southern half of Marion County. Shale and sandstone parent materials yield soils in the Rockcastle-Colyer association. Rockcastle soils reside on heavily rolling to steep slopes; they are thin, do not readily retain moisture, and are only moderately fertile. Farmers may plow and plant the lower slopes, but woodland dominates the steeper land.[1]

Northern Nelson County—Fairfield

Rural, open-country distilleries operated across the Outer Bluegrass by the mid-nineteenth century. Water requirements prompted distillers to site their works at large springs or along perennial streams. The McKenna Distillery at Fairfield provides an example of how these businesses functioned.

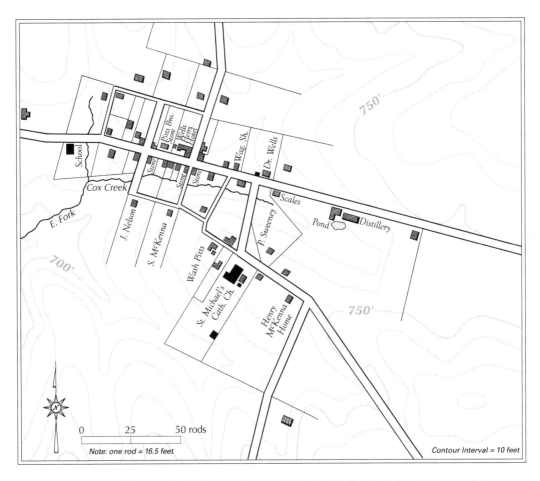

Henry McKenna Distillery, Fairfield, Nelson County. (After D. J. Lake, *An Atlas of Nelson and Spencer Counties, Kentucky* [Philadelphia, 1882])

Henry McKenna was born in 1813 in Draperstown, County Londonderry, Northern Ireland. He migrated to Philadelphia in 1838 and in 1851 moved to Fairfield, a village established by Catholic migrants from Maryland. He worked for several years as a turnpike contractor and reportedly built the Bloomfield-Fairfield Turnpike in the early 1850s.[2] That pike, present-day KY 48, connected with the Bardstown-Louisville Turnpike at the crossroads settlement of Cox Creek to the southwest. McKenna and carpenter Richard Constantine bought an acre of property in Fairfield bordering the road and situated at the head of the East Fork of Cox Creek. The two men built a gristmill and added a distillery about a year later.[3] Henry McKenna's 1855 distillery was likely a simple timber-framed structure covered in clapboards. That structure was replaced by a brick building in 1883; by 1912, it had evolved into a modern plant with seventy mash tubs, a column still, a traditional pot still doubler, and external flake stands or condensers.

A wood-fired steam engine powered both the mill and the distillery.[4] Initially, the simple wooden still house produced only twenty gallons, or half a barrel, of whiskey per day. McKenna dammed the creek to create a small holding pond, from which he could draw water for cooling purposes and for his penned livestock. The establishment of McKenna's mill and distillery preceded the railroad's extension of branch lines into Nelson County, and the site was never directly connected to the railroad. However, after 1860, when the Louisville & Nashville (L & N) Railroad line reached Bardstown, McKenna's teamsters hauled goods on the Fairfield–Samuels Depot Turnpike ten miles south to the T. W. Samuels Depot. They also moved goods on the Bloomfield-Fairfield Turnpike to the L & N depot in Bloomfield after that branch line opened in 1880.

Irishman Patrick Sweeney boarded with Henry and Elizabeth McKenna and their five children. Sweeney started work as a laborer and eventually became McKenna's distiller. McKenna's son John worked at the mill; son Daniel worked on the family farm and was managing the distillery by 1881. Sometime before 1882, McKenna's family built him a large brick house near St. Michael's Church on a low hill overlooking the mill and distillery. When Daniel McKenna died in 1918, his brothers James S. and Stafford E. managed the distillery until Prohibition and resumed doing so after repeal. In 1933 James and Stafford incorporated the business as H. McKenna Incorporated.[5]

Initially, Henry McKenna's primary income was from milling farmers' grains into flour, meal, and bran. He operated the mill as needed and was especially busy after grain harvest in July and August and corn harvest in October and November. The distillery operated during the winter and early spring months. McKenna marketed his whiskey as "Old McKenna Sour Mash Whiskey," the brand he originated in 1855.

After the Civil War, McKenna gradually expanded and improved the distillery. He

Henry McKenna Distillery, Fairfield, Nelson, County, 1886.

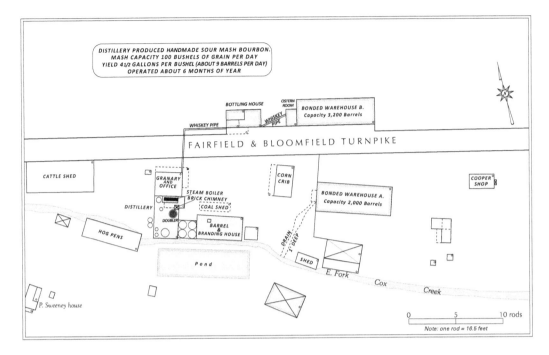

DISTILLERY PRODUCED HANDMADE SOUR MASH BOURBON.
MASH CAPACITY 100 BUSHELS OF GRAIN PER DAY
YIELD 4½ GALLONS PER BUSHEL (ABOUT 9 BARRELS PER DAY)
OPERATED ABOUT 6 MONTHS OF YEAR

Henry McKenna Registered Distillery No. 111, Fairfield, Nelson County, ca. 1910.

built a new still house in 1883 and increased his mashing capacity to about three barrels per day. A cooper shop stood to the east, flanked by piles of staves. The livestock feeding shed stood to the west, downstream from the distillery. The works eventually mashed 100 bushels per day before Prohibition suspended operations.[6] Federal regulators designated the works Kentucky Registered Distillery No. 111.

By 1910, the distillery works included a still house, a mill and granary, two bonded warehouses, a bottling house, a cooper shop and woodworking shop, an icehouse, a corn-crib, a coal bin, dwellings, a cattle shed, and a hog pen. An overhead pipe carried distilled whiskey over the turnpike to the bottling house. Relict distillery buildings still stand on both sides of the highway in Fairfield.[7]

Henry McKenna died in 1893. His legacy included an integrated farm, mill, and distillery, as well as a kind of general store and a community "bank" that served more than 350 local customers' credit accounts. Tradition was important to McKenna's style of business, and although he did not adopt mass production methods and new technology, he did develop an extensive mail-order customer base. He was a pioneer in advertising, running ads in public circulars and medical and other professional journals. Federal tax policies stifled other distillers, but McKenna paid his whiskey taxes, perhaps with income from his mill and farm. He held his tax-paid, or "free," whiskey in warehouses for extended periods— some barrel-aged as long as sixteen years. This not only increased the prices he could get but also enhanced his reputation as a producer of high-quality whiskey. His neighbors and

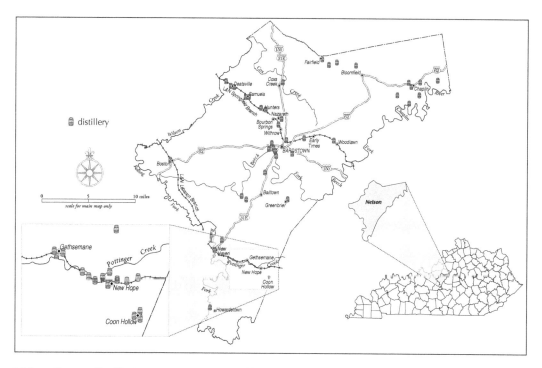

Nelson County distilleries, ca. 1790–1950. Distillery site locations are approximate. Some distilleries were short-lived, while others were in production for decades. (Compiled from D. J. Lake, *An Atlas of Nelson and Spencer Counties, Kentucky* [Philadelphia, 1882])

patrons deemed him personable and kindly.[8] Today, the H. McKenna brand is owned by Heaven Hill Distilleries of Bardstown and continues in production as a ten-year-old sour-mash bourbon. Henry McKenna's home and the home of his distiller, Patrick Sweeney, still stand.

Central and Southern Nelson County—Bardstown and Environs

In 1851 Louisville & Nashville Railroad executives announced that monetary subscriptions by local communities would determine the main line's southbound route. Two routes held promise in terms of profitability for the railroad. The first, an upper or "air-line" route, projected a track through Bardstown near the center of Nelson County before turning south to New Haven and then extending south and west to Larue, Hart, Barren, and Allen Counties. Bardstown's residents had long advocated for the line, but Nelson County officials rejected a proposed $300,000 bond issue that would have met the railroad's subscription expectations and underwritten the costs of construction.[9] Instead, the railroad chose the second route—a lower or southern route through Hardin, Warren, and Simpson Counties. The L & N's main line to Nashville opened in 1860.

In 1850 the Kentucky legislature had chartered an L & N branch from the main line at Lebanon Junction near Rolling Fork, east thirty-seven miles to the Marion County seat at Lebanon. The Lebanon branch crossed Nelson County well south of Bardstown, passing through Boston, New Haven, Gethsemane, and New Hope. Completed in about 1857, Nelson County's section of the Lebanon branch soon attracted distillers. Edward Miles built a new distillery at New Hope beside the L & N tracks soon after the line opened; finding the location favorable, he enlarged production capacity in 1875.[10] J. Bernard Dant began operations at a new distillery near Gethsemane Station on the Lebanon branch in about 1865.[11] And in 1870 Richard Cummins opened a new distilling works at the Coon Hollow Station.[12]

The L & N Railroad completed the first section of the Springfield branch to the Early Times Station just east of Bardstown in 1860. Sometime before then, David Beam built a new distillery about three miles east of Bardstown. When laborers completed the L & N's Bardstown-Springfield branch in 1860, the tracks ran directly in front of the distillery; one dedicated siding delivered coal and grain to the distillery, and another shipped barreled whiskey to market.[13] Sam Lancaster built a small distillery on Plum Run Road north of Bardstown in 1850. Lancaster relocated his works to a site on the L & N tracks in 1881.[14]

Bardstown

Approaching Bardstown from the south on US 31E, the New Haven Road, one is welcomed by a roadside sign offering two messages: "Bardstown, Bourbon Capital of the World," and "Named Most Beautiful Small Town in America." Rand McNally/*USA Today* awarded the "most beautiful" designation in 2012. The town's standing as "bourbon capital" is self-proclaimed. Depending on the period of interest and where one draws Bardstown's political boundary, at least ten distillers operated works within a few miles of the town over the years from 1790 to 1950. At present, three large distilleries still produce or bottle bourbon there: Tom Moore-Old Barton, Heaven Hill, and Willett. New works are under construction.

Thomas Moore established a distillery about two-thirds of a mile southwest of the Nelson County courthouse in 1879. He chose the location in part because the 196-acre site fronted one of the area's principal turnpikes, but also because the property included limestone bluffs from which several perennial springs issued; the largest of these became known as Tom Moore Spring and is today marked with a commemorative plaque.[15] The spring feeds a small creek that flows south into Beech Fork, the area's trunk stream. Moore made sour-mash bourbon and bottled whiskey for private brands sold by wholesalers and taverns. In 1905 the original single-story limestone still building was expanded by adding a second story made of yellow brick. The works closed during Prohibition, and much of the equipment was salvaged, although some buildings remained intact. Moore's son, Con Moore, rebuilt the works to industrial scale after Prohibition and resumed production. In 1943 Oscar Getz bought the distillery and changed the name to Barton. During World War II the distillery made industrial alcohol for use in the manufacture of military materiel. In

1946 Getz modernized the works with an extensive red brick addition, natural gas boilers, and new grain milling, mashing, and fermenting equipment. The distillery was sold again in 1982, and the name was changed to Barton Brands Ltd. The Sazerac Company of New Orleans bought Barton in 2009; Sazerac also owns Buffalo Trace in Frankfort. Today, water from the hillside springs is directed into a small lake from which the distillery draws its water supply. The Vendome column still processes nine truckloads of corn, rye, and malted barley per day (a load of corn is typically 1,000 bushels). Slop is dried, and the distilled grain product is sold to local beef and dairy farms as a high-protein feed supplement.

Two years after the repeal of Prohibition, members of the Shapira family and other investors built the Heaven Hill Distillery on a farm about one mile south of the Nelson County courthouse. After making manufacturing spirits during World War II, the family-owned distillery converted back to whiskey production and installed new high-volume processing equipment. Mashing capacity increased to more than 2,000 bushels a day, producing enough bourbon to require additional warehouse storage capacity. A catastrophic fire started in one of the storage warehouses on November 7, 1996. Although the storage buildings were separated by 400 feet or more, high winds carried the flames to other structures, destroying seven large storage warehouses and more than 90,000 barrels of aging bourbon. As the buildings collapsed, smashed barrels released a torrent of burning whiskey that flowed downhill toward Rowan Creek, where it set the distillery works ablaze, destroying that as well. Remnants still stand along US 31, just north of the Willett Distillery, which commands the high south bluff of Rowan Creek. Heaven Hill did not resume distilling operations at the Bardstown works, but the company operates the Bernheim Distillery on West Breckinridge Street in Louisville, one block east of the Brown-Forman Distillery. That complex includes seven large brick aging warehouses. In Bardstown, Heaven Hill's postfire campus contains some twenty-two rebuilt aging warehouses and a bottling plant. Its Bourbon Heritage Center includes a museum and gives tours to visitors. The center's architectural design echoes a structural feature used in traditional aging warehouses—a monitor roof with clerestory windows to enhance interior lighting and ventilation. The best local example of this classic industrial design is at the former T. W. Samuels Distillery in Deatsville, on KY 245 northwest of Bardstown.

After the repeal of Prohibition, Thompson Willett founded the Willett Distilling Company in the mid-1930s on a hilltop farm just south of Bardstown, overlooking Rowan Creek and Heaven Hill Distillery. The independent, family-owned works produced bourbon until the 1980s, when it was converted to an ethanol plant that subsequently failed.[16] The distillery has since undergone extensive reconstruction and remodeling, and the result is a modern works that follows the accretive forms found in nineteenth-century distilleries, such as attached rooms of various sizes and ceiling heights and low-angled shed-like roofs. Spirits issue from three stills—a column still, a copper doubler, and a copper pot still. Clerestory windows and stone-faced exterior walls add to the historical nature of the building. Storage capacity includes eight onsite warehouses that are less than half the size of warehouses found at most modern industrial distilleries. The distiller follows traditional family recipes, some more than a century old, to produce about 1,000 gallons of rye and bourbon each day during the distilling season. A signature product, Willett Copper Pot Still Reserve bourbon, is sold in a bottle whose award-winning design is a miniature of the distillery's primary still, which resembles the venerable pot stills used in Ireland and Scotland.

New Hope

Small farm distilleries produced whiskey in the Pottinger Creek valley, east of New Haven in southeastern Nelson County, by the 1790s. In 1857 construction crews built the Lebanon branch of the Louisville & Nashville Railroad—later renamed the Knoxville branch—following the creek toward Lebanon, the county seat of Marion County.[17] Just north of the height-of-land divide between Pottinger Creek and Sulphur Lick Creek, five miles east of New Haven, the L & N built a station and a railroad siding that became known as New Hope Depot.

Henry Miles, a member of a group of Scots-Irish Catholics who migrated from Maryland, operated a distillery in the valley in 1796.[18] His son, Edward L. Miles, also operated a small distillery and actively invested in valley real estate. Edward Miles bought 172 acres in the area in 1849.[19] In 1853 he bought a twelve-acre parcel on Pottinger Creek beside the Springfield Road, apparently anticipating the alignment of the L & N branch that would be completed four years later.[20] Miles continued to acquire land in the vicinity of his distillery and the depot, and in June 1865 his mother, Ann Miles, bought 1,140 acres in the area between Pottinger Creek and the headwaters of Sulphur Lick Creek that likely included the developing settlement of New Hope.[21]

Together with several other land developers, Edward Miles was a member of B. H. Miller & Company, which in April 1869 bought a seven-and-a-half-acre parcel on the north side of the railroad tracks.[22] The land likely adjoined Miles's large new distillery, and the purchase likely allowed him to expand his warehouses, livestock feeding sheds, and other support facilities. In 1870 Miles was one of eight commissioners who formed the New Hope and Rolling Fork Turnpike Road Company, which built a five-mile-long turnpike that connected New Hope to the Bardstown-Greensburg Road at the Marion-Nelson County line.

In the late 1860s and 1870s Miles, in partnership with whiskey producer and wholesaler Thomas H. Sherley of Louisville, built a new distillery beside the railroad tracks just west of the existing works. It operated as the New Hope Distillery and had a mashing capacity of 200 bushels per day.[23] On Saturday, May 19, 1883, a fire destroyed both the Miles and the New Hope Distilleries. The conflagration also consumed two granaries and nine cattle pens. Two warehouses containing whiskey worth more than $500,000 caught fire,

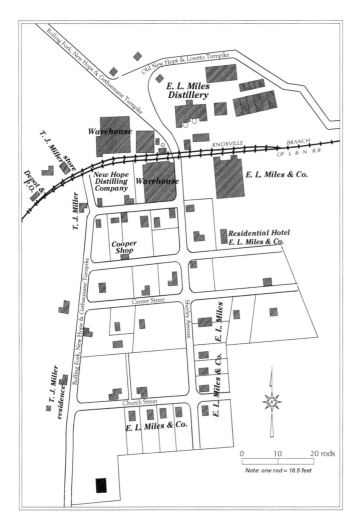

E. L. Miles and New Hope Distilleries, Nelson County. (From D. J. Lake, *An Atlas of Nelson and Spencer Counties, Kentucky* [Philadelphia, 1882]; US Geological Survey Topographic Quadrangle, New Haven, KY, 1953)

but they were saved. Though insured for $30,000, the loss was valued at $40,000.[24] Miles and his business partners rebuilt their distilleries in tandem, standing side by side on the east side of the Rolling Fork, New Hope, and Gethsemane Turnpike and north of the railroad tracks.[25]

New Hope's distilleries embraced the railroad. A 6,000-bushel grain storage elevator stood on the north side of a dedicated siding, and warehouses stood on both sides of the tracks. Elevated whiskey pipes carried spirits from the distilleries north of the tracks to warehouses and barreling and bottling facilities on the south side. The railroad depot attracted service businesses related to moving freight and telegraph operations, as well as a large lumber company. The distilleries offered seasonal employment, and their size was sufficient to attract permanent residents, among them merchants and grocers who operated three stores, a cooper, a blacksmith and wagon maker, a schoolteacher, and a physician.[26] By the 1880s, New Hope resembled a small town sited at the junction of three turnpikes and the railroad tracks. The E. L. Miles Company owned a residential hotel and houses on nine lots, including Miles's residence. Sherley Avenue became the town's primary north-south street.[27]

Marion County

Upon crossing into Marion County, the Lebanon branch connected the small settlements of Chicago, Loretto, and St. Mary with Lebanon and eventually extended southeast to Crab Orchard and Knoxville, Tennessee. Marion County residents subscribed $200,000 for the Lebanon branch construction.[28] The first L & N train reached Lebanon in 1858, and regularly scheduled trains served the line soon thereafter.[29] J. W. Dant built a distillery on his farm west of Loretto on Pottinger Creek in 1836. The L & N surveyors routed the tracks through the distillery site and provided a dedicated siding for the aging warehouses. The railroad established Dant Station across the tracks from the distillery.[30]

The L & N eventually extended the branch rail line from Bardstown east to Springfield in Washington County. The national financial panic of 1873 and the subsequent depression halted most railroad construction. By the late 1870s, a business recovery was under way, and railroad construction resumed. The extension to Springfield was not completed until 1888, twenty-eight years after the tracks reached Early Times Station. This last track section may have arrived too late to attract distillers. Though nearly a dozen distilleries operated at roadside or creek-side sites in Washington County by the mid-nineteenth century, nearly all had closed by the early 1880s.

Until the L & N Railroad arrived, country roads and turnpikes served the hamlet of Loretto, some fourteen miles southeast of Bardstown; trains did not stop there until the railroad built a depot sometime before 1866. Today, the railroad tracks and depot are gone, and the town is served by KY 52, the primary east-west highway, and KY 49, the north-south road that connects the county seats of Bardstown, in Nelson County, to Lebanon, in Marion County. A Belgian priest, Father Charles Nerinckx, founded a teaching order, the Sisters of Loretto, in 1812 at St. Charles in western Kentucky; the group moved to the motherhouse at Nerinx, two miles north of Loretto, in 1824. Today, the site is home to 100 sisters and includes a working farm, a retreat center, and a long-term-care facility.[31]

Notably, Loretto is also the gateway to Burks Spring Distillery, known today as Maker's Mark, some two miles east. The hamlet is also the site of a large cluster of Maker's Mark bourbon aging warehouses. A number of older buildings on the south side of KY 52, just west of Loretto's St. Francis High School, have been refurbished and supplemented with new structures—a total of eighteen barrel aging warehouses can now be accessed by gravel roads. Since 2014, Buzick Construction of Bardstown has erected five large warehouses across the highway. Specializing in distillery-related construction since the early 1940s, Buzick has built warehouses and other structures for central Kentucky distillers such as Barton Brands, Buffalo Trace, Four Roses, Heaven Hill, Jim Beam, and Wild Turkey. All the Loretto warehouses are now painted in the distinctive dark brown color used by Maker's Mark.

East of Loretto, one can reach Maker's Mark by way of KY 52. Follow Happy Hollow Road to Don Ryan Road. The first distillery-associated building is the two-story Victorian tollhouse. From the 1830s to the 1890s—Kentucky's toll road or turnpike era—people who wished to travel on reliable stone-surfaced thoroughfares had to build the roads themselves. The state legislature authorized private construction of more than 1,400 turnpikes during this period. Investors received a state charter permitting them to form a road-building company and sell stock to finance construction. Once a road was completed, the company built tollhouses to collect fees to support road maintenance. According to state law, tollhouses had to be spaced at least five miles apart. A gate or pike at each tollhouse controlled access to the road. Once travelers paid the toll, the tollhouse keeper turned the pike, allowing them to proceed. This practice led to use of the term "turnpike" to describe a toll road. The Maker's Mark tollhouse is one of the few remaining in the state.

The tollhouse marks the entrance to the valley of Hardins Creek, which flows north from this point about six and a half miles to Beech Creek. The creek meanders back and forth across a flat, fertile floodplain that is up to 1,000 feet wide in some places and some 120 feet below the surrounding upland—an advantageous place for field agriculture, milling, and distilling. A dam on Hardins Creek provided water power for a gristmill constructed there in 1805 by Charles Burks; he also built a small distillery soon after the mill began operation. By the 1830s, the distillery was fully equipped and operated until about 1889, when George Burks built a new works on the site. The present five-story still house was completed in 1935–1936, after the repeal of Prohibition, and maintains an extraordinary link to the past: the building stands on the original mill's 1805 limestone foundation and contains internal framing made of hand-hewn ten- by ten-inch timbers. The two lower floors house a grain mill; mash tubs; low wine tank; fermenting room; various storage tanks, pumps, filters, and tail boxes; and the five-story copper stills. The upper floors house a yeast room, laboratory, scales, grain handling equipment, and water storage tanks. Auxiliary buildings include a 1935 cistern room and two barrel aging warehouses, one dating from the 1880s and the other completed after 1900. A quart house, dating from 1905, stands on a hillside above the main group of distillery buildings. Passersby could purchase whiskey there in less-than-barrel amounts at retail prices. Such sales were common practice at several nineteenth- and early-twentieth-century distilleries, but this may be the only quart house remaining in Kentucky. In 1902 Burks built a two-and-a-half-story Victorian house on the hill overlooking the mill and distillery. The traditional design features steeply pitched roof gables and a wrap-around porch. The works operated until 1919, the eve of Prohibition. New owners resumed production in 1937, and Taylor William "Bill" Samuels purchased the property in 1953 for $50,000 and began renovations. The following year the distillery was back in production.[32]

Samuels, a sixth-generation descendant of Scots-Irish whiskey makers, bought the distillery with the intention of producing a new type of bourbon. Seeking a smoother, fuller-flavored whiskey than other distillers were producing, Samuels abandoned the family whiskey recipe that called for rye as the secondary or "flavor" grain and substituted soft winter wheat. He retained the traditional methods of grain milling and the small-batch distilling process. Workers rotated barrels in the aging warehouses to equalize the long-term effects of interior top-to-bottom temperature differentials. The whiskey's production, branding, and promotion were a family undertaking. Mrs. Samuels suggested the product name, Maker's Mark, and the bottle and label design. She also suggested dipping the bottle neck in hot red wax, a common practice among the makers of fine distilled cognacs. Although Mr. Samuels was reluctant to engage a professional advertising firm to promote Maker's Mark Whisky (note that the brand name omits the *e* in "whiskey"), word-of-mouth endorsements, positive reviews by trade magazines, and tasting competition awards brought widespread recognition and healthy sales. Bill Samuels Jr. joined the business and, despite a quiescent American whiskey market in the 1980s and 1990s, increased sales with a clever homespun advertising campaign. The Maker's Mark ads that ran in print media and on billboards in the 1980s and 1990s are often credited with creating a national awareness of and demand for premium bourbon whiskeys, and Bill Jr. came to be regarded by many in the business as an inspired promoter.[33] In the process, Maker's Mark became one of the industry's iconic brands.[34]

Historic properties deemed to have exceptional value as illustrations of America's heritage may be designated National Historic Landmarks by the US secretary of the interior. Nationally, only 2,500 properties have achieved this designation.[35] To qualify as a landmark, a structure or property must represent nationally important historic events, places, or persons in American history. Such a place may illustrate the achievements of a significant individual, or it may be an exceptional representation of a particular building or engineering method.[36] Kentucky has thirty National Historic Landmark sites, three of which are distilleries: Burks Spring Distillery (Maker's Mark), George T. Stagg (Buffalo Trace), and Labrot & Graham (Woodford Reserve). The Maker's Mark Distillery was listed on the National Register of Historic Places in December 1974 and was designated a National Historic Landmark in December 1980. Maker's Mark was the first distillery in America where the landmark buildings were in active use for distilling when it was so recognized.

Larue County

John McDougall Atherton built and operated his first distillery on Knob Creek in northeastern Larue County in 1867. The works stood beside the Bardstown and Green River Turnpike in open farm country. New Haven was the nearest town. Athertonville, the village that eventually grew up beside the distillery, did not exist at the time. Knob Creek is one of dozens of small streams that slice into the western face of the Muldraugh Hill escarpment, the limestone bluff that marks the divide between the Outer Bluegrass to the east and the Pennyroyal upland to the west. Fronting the escarpment, a narrow belt of conical hills, Pennyroyal remnants, forms a topographically distinct area called the Knobs. Neither Bluegrass nor Pennyroyal, the steep-sided Knobs region stands apart, separated by alluvial floodplains created by the region's rivers. From its head atop the escarpment, the aptly named Knob Creek flows north, dropping some 450 feet over five miles and passing Thomas Lincoln's family farm on the way to its junction with Rolling Fork, the regional trunk stream.[37] Another tributary, the westward-flowing Pottinger Creek, joins Rolling Fork slightly more than a mile above Knob Creek. Each stream has created its own broad, nearly level floodplain; at their junction, south of New Haven, their composite floodplain is more than 7,000 feet wide. Though forested when Anglo pioneers arrived in the 1780s and 1790s, the bottomland was fertile and productive when cleared of trees. By the mid-nineteenth century, the Rolling Fork–Pottinger Creek–Knob Creek lowland was producing grain surpluses that supported the development of Atherton's distillery.

Peter Lee Atherton of Fauquier County, Virginia, obtained a land grant on the Knob Creek drainage and moved to the area in about 1791. The fertile lands produced grains and corn that Atherton processed in a small farm distillery that he operated on the west bank of Knob Creek from 1800 to 1830. Peter's son, John M. Atherton, was born there in 1841 and later owned much of the land in his father's original grant. One mile south of its junction with Rolling Fork, near the foot of the Muldraugh escarpment, the Knob Creek floodplain is about 1,000 feet wide, with an elevated alluvial terrace on the west side above the creek. The Bardstown and Green River Turnpike followed the terrace.

John Atherton attended St. Joseph College in nearby Bardstown and Georgetown College in Scott County. In August 1867 he formed a partnership with Miles Hagan of Nelson County and Marshall Key of Larue County to build a distillery. Atherton donated firewood for the distillery, designating that it be cut from the 180 acres of land he owned along Knob Creek. The works stood on the terrace beside the turnpike and began making sweet-mash whiskey, processing about 100 bushels of grain a day, which yielded about seven barrels of spirits. Over the next twenty years, Atherton acquired land near his Knob Creek distillery in large and small parcels. Some tracts he likely subdivided into small residential lots; others he may have used to expand distillery operations. In September 1868 business partner Miles Hagan sold his share of the distillery and part interest in a storage warehouse to Atherton.[38]

In 1879 Atherton built a new brick distillery with brick warehouses across the turnpike from his 1867 works. Alexander Mayfield, a relative of Mr. Atherton, operated that distillery under his own name. In June 1879, to facilitate access to the expanding distillery complex, Atherton's company leased for ninety-nine years a strip of land two miles long and forty feet wide as a right-of-way for a spur rail line connecting the distillery to the

L & N Railroad's Knoxville branch line in New Haven. Between 1880 and 1882 Atherton added two additional brick distilleries, named Clifton and Winsor, to his distilling complex. Steam powered the distilleries and heated the warehouses in the winter. Automatic sprinklers provided fire suppression, and a gravity-flow pipe delivered water from a hillside reservoir.[39]

Considering its agrarian surroundings, the distillery complex assembled by Atherton and his business partners must have seemed an industrial marvel. Masons built the entire works, except for the cattle sheds, with 11 million bricks. The distilling machinery was the newest available. Two batteries of boilers fed 60,000 feet of steam pipes installed in the aging warehouses. Atherton believed that maintaining a constant interior warehouse temperature year-round accelerated aging and resulted in a uniform, high-quality product.[40] For some fifteen years, from 1879 to 1895, Atherton's four distilleries operated five to seven months a year, drawing water from wells and Knob Creek.[41] Collectively, the distilleries processed roughly 2,200 bushels of grain per day; the aging warehouses stored more than 150,000 barrels.[42] Assuming that wagoners delivered grain to the Atherton distilleries in large farm wagons with a forty-bushel capacity, each day's operation would have required fifty-five wagonloads. Wagons drawn by mule or horse teams were awkward to maneuver, and traffic of this magnitude would have congested the distillery grounds. The amount of grain required to sustain such high-capacity distilling would have quickly consumed locally produced grains, obligating the distillers to deal with grain brokers at some distance from the works. A railroad connection would alleviate many of these concerns, and once it was completed, Atherton's two-mile rail spur was active. Regular train shipments delivered grain, coal, and other supplies and carried away barreled whiskey.

During the distilling season, the Atherton works produced slop in large quantities. An elaborate system of tubs and delivery pipes carried the liquid slop some 900 feet to three large feeding sheds built near Knob Creek, north of and downstream from the distillery buildings. As whiskey production increased during the 1880s and 1890s, Kentucky's distillers expanded their livestock feeding operations, which focused on fattening feeder cattle. During the 1890s, area distilleries fed slop to about 6,000 cattle a year.[43]

As John Atherton's industrial distillery complex increased in size and number of employees, the village of Athertonville grew up at the site. Though situated in a rural area, the distilleries were a hub of business activity that required appropriate infrastructure to function: residential housing, educational facilities, retail stores, blacksmiths, carpenters, and transport. Housing workers at rural industrial sites was a common problem for nineteenth- and early-twentieth-century mining and manufacturing companies. Industrial firms often addressed the issue by building residential factory towns that were referred to generically as "company towns." Nineteenth-century textile mills in New England and the Carolina Piedmont were tethered to streamside water power sites that were often remote from established urban centers and ports and roadways. To provide housing for their workers, these companies often built mills, housing, service buildings, and streets and roads as centrally planned and company-managed projects.[44]

John Atherton's distillery works operated on family farmland located ten miles from Hodgenville, the county seat, and two miles from New Haven and the L & N Railroad depot. The village of Athertonville developed to serve the distilleries. In 1880 Athertonville's 118 residents included two engineers and a baker, bookkeeper, brick mason, fireman, foreman, merchant, and miller. Initially, a stave maker and nine coopers made barrels; by the mid-1880s, the works employed more than twenty coopers and consumed some 600,000 staves annually.[45] Some laborers lived in Athertonville; others lived on neighboring farms and may have worked both on the farms and at the distilleries during the appropriate seasons. Several households had two or more distillery employees. Taylor Whitehead, Atherton's distiller, and his wife Alice boarded twelve men in their home, including six coopers, a stave maker, a steam engine fireman, and a government warehouseman and storekeeper. Brick mason J. W. Eblin operated a brick kiln in Athertonville, and his household included nine African American borders who worked as brick molders, setters, and laborers.[46]

By 1890, Athertonville was said to be the largest employment center in Larue County. It had a three-story, five-bay clapboard hotel (later called a boardinghouse), a schoolhouse, a general store, and a railroad depot. Although John Atherton, through his company partnerships, owned the distilleries and the other buildings, he did not own the entire town. The distilleries employed 150 to 200 people during the fall-to-spring distilling season.[47] Laborers employed only during the distilling season may have lived on nearby farms and walked or rode horses to work. But other employees in skilled positions may have worked at the distilleries year-round, making it more convenient to live nearby. For example, federal revenue agents monitored the bonded warehouses, recorded tax payments, and approved the withdrawal of whiskey from bond for shipment to customers.[48] Engineers and mechanics repaired and updated equipment. Bookkeepers (primarily men) and stenographers (primarily women) handled record keeping and correspondence.[49] The town's residents, about evenly divided between Catholic and Protestant, established Catholic and Methodist Episcopal churches. John Atherton built the public school and contributed funds for its operation. The school was said to be the largest in the county—larger than the one in Hodgenville, the county seat.[50] At the turn of the century, Athertonville businesses included a hotel, general store, blacksmith shops, saloon, livery stable, and post office. Counted among the residents were John Lougherty, the thirty-year-old distillery superintendent, and twenty-one distillery laborers, as well as a dressmaker, shoemaker, harness maker, millwright, teacher, slop feeder, and seven railroad employees.[51]

The J. M. Atherton & Company distilling business continued in Athertonville until 1899, when the Kentucky Distillers and Warehouse Company bought the works and operated the distillery until Prohibition.[52] After repeal in 1933, the distillery was rebuilt and resumed production. After several ownership changes, Seagram purchased the works in

1946. Production stopped in 1987, and the remaining buildings are presently used by ZAK Cooperage. Athertonville retains a few of its original houses and a one-story church, while accruing new houses and trailer homes. The rail spur tracks have been removed, but the raised track bed is visible west of US 31E south of New Haven.

Bullitt County

The countryside between Nelson County and Louisville is a theater of contrasting landscapes. A railroad transect from Bardstown in Nelson County northwest to Shepherdsville, the Bullitt County seat, is a transition in geologic time that is announced by dramatic changes in surface topography. From Bardstown, tracks for the Springfield branch of the L & N Railroad run northwest across the rolling Ordovician limestones of the Outer Bluegrass. Rocks just below the surface date to roughly 440 million years ago. At Deatsville, site of the 1933 T. W. Samuels Distillery, the topography abruptly breaks into wooded hills. There, the railroad surveyors threaded their track through a 300-foot-deep crease between the hills. Crossing into Bullitt County, the rail bed segues into Silurian and Devonian limestones and shales, 395 million to 435 million years old. About twelve miles farther west, a steep escarpment, Muldraugh Hill, marks the western edge of the hills and the eastern edge of the Pennyroyal region, which is composed largely of Mississippian-age limestones and sandstones that are 310 million to 345 million years old. Erosional remnants of the Pennyroyal stand in front of the escarpment, forming clusters of conical hills that are collectively known as the Knobs. Mississippian limestones cap the knobby hills, which stand on bases of blackish gold Devonian shales. Springs emerge on hillsides at the limestone-shale junction, and two distilleries near Clermont—Chapeze and Jim Beam—have historically used water from these springs.

Adam and Ben Chapeze built a distillery between Long Lick Creek and the L & N track in 1867. The track and distillery site stand on stout Silurian limestones; the creek flows across a nearly level floodplain comprising relatively recent deposits of alluvial sand and gravel that, just downstream to the west, transition into much older glacial lake deposits dating from the Pleistocene period. The lake deposits are largely limestone gravel and cobbles and may reach sixty feet deep before contacting bedrock. All this is disguised by a very gently rolling surface, where farms are being replaced by subdivisions and shopping centers that serve Shepherdsville and Louisville's distant suburbs. A short distance to the east, another distillery started by the Murphy Barber Company began operations in 1880; that works eventually became the contemporary Jim Beam Distillery.

The Chapezes' still house stood beside a dedicated railroad siding, and in 1894 it mashed about ninety-two bushels of grain per day; the primary brand was Old Charter. The grounds initially included a cooper's shop, a corncrib, and two large sheds where cattle were fed on distillery slop. A single 4,400-barrel storage warehouse was supplemented with a second and later a third. The striking office was built at a later date in Craftsman style, with half-timbered exterior walls and large gable-roofed dormers supported by ex-tended brackets. Distillery remnants onsite can be accessed by way of KY 245 and Chapeze Road. The remaining structures include the still house, warehouses, a water tower, and the office building. Production stopped in 1951. The property is currently owned by the nearby Jim Beam Distillery, which uses some of the warehouses for barrel storage.[53]

Less than a mile to the east, Clermont (also known as Limestone Springs) was a stop on the L & N Railroad. Squire Murphy, A. M. Barber, and Calvin Brown built the 1880s Murphy Barber Distillery just above the springs; like the Chapezes, they placed their works beside the railroad tracks and Long Lick Creek. Cane Spring was their primary bourbon brand. The works operated on a twenty-horsepower wood-fired steam engine. In the 1890s the column still was mashing about 150 bushels of grain per day during the six- to eight-month distilling season. A large pump inside the still building drew water from a deep well. Three warehouses had a total storage capacity of 10,000 barrels. A dedi-cated cooperage shop operated adjacent to the railroad tracks and the loading platform. By 1910, ownership had changed, but the works continued to operate as the Murphy Barber Company. The railroad loading platform was moved to the opposite side of tracks, and a dedicated railroad siding now made grain and coal deliveries directly to the still house. A new, larger steam engine provided power, and new storage was built for grain and barrels. The works had grown to four warehouses with a storage capacity of 45,000 barrels; one of the warehouses accommodated a new bottling house. The old cooper shop was vacant, replaced by a much larger structure with a dedicated branding furnace. Murphy Barber operated the works until 1917. Jim Beam and Son purchased the property during Prohibi-tion and razed most of the buildings. The new owners rebuilt the property after the repeal of Prohibition in 1933 and began mashing in 1934, producing the venerable Old Tub and Jim Beam brands.[54]

The present-day Clermont distillery has the capacity to mash more than 8,000 bush-els of grain per day and some twenty warehouses with a storage capacity of 400,000 bar-rels. The property has been configured to accommodate visitors. A walking tour features a display of a small nineteenth-century farm distillery, with mashing barrels and a stone fire box topped by a copper pot still. The grounds contain two structures of special inter-est: the T. Jeremiah Beam house and the American Stillhouse Visitors' Center. The Beam house stands on the crest of a low hill, overlooking the Long Lick Creek valley and the modern and expansive Jim Beam Distillery. Built in 1911 as a boardinghouse for coopers, gaugers, and visiting salespeople, the building became a farmhouse and Jeremiah Beam's residence when the Murphy Barber operation closed in 1917. The two-story frame house is sheathed in clapboard. The primary south-facing façade has three windows on the ground floor and two on the second. An unadorned front door opens into the structure's right-side wall—an unusual placement, but practical, given the building's original purpose. A two-story cross-gable section is attached to the rear. A large wrap-around porch extends across the front of the house and along each side.[55] The Beam house is an ordinary frame structure, similar to those found on farms and in small towns throughout the region, and it serves as a reminder that distillers lived in ordinary dwellings as well as outsized mansions. The new American Stillhouse Visitors' Center building is a replica of the old post-Prohibition still house. Inside, a protective glass case holds an exquisite copper miniature of a nineteenth-century still, with three pot stills sitting atop three stone fire boxes and all the mashing tubs, fermenting vats, flake stands, and other equipment required to produce bourbon whiskey—a work of industrial art!

The expansive woodland across KY 245 in front of the Jim Beam works is the renowned Bernheim Arboretum and Forest Research Center. In 1928 Isaac Bernheim, Kentucky bourbon distiller and founder of the I. W. Harper brand, bought more than 15,000 acres of land that had been timbered and mined. Bernheim's purpose was to restore the forest and create a nature preserve. He hired the Frederick Law Olmsted landscape-architecture firm to develop a site plan in 1931. Less than twenty years later, after extensive replanting and construction work, the arboretum was opened to the public.

The Outer Bluegrass counties of Bullitt, Marion, Nelson, and Washington were intensively developed by nineteenth-century distillers. When cleared of woodland, farms produced surplus grains. The oldest distilleries were often sited at springs or along creeks, but when railroads extended through the countryside, those distillers who wished to increase their production and industrialize their works relocated trackside. Moving large quantities of grain, staves, coal, and other materials required reliable and comparatively low-cost transportation. Large distilleries operating in the rural countryside also required a larger labor force than was available on neighboring farms, and small villages grew up at some sites, the remnants of which still stand.

8

Distilling in the Ohio River Valley

The navigational potential of two substantial rivers—the Ohio and its northwest-flowing tributary the Kentucky—offered supporting infrastructure for the initial transformation of nineteenth-century whiskey production from small-scale farmer-distillers to industrial works capable of sustained high-volume output.

During the nineteenth century, five of Kentucky's largest cities became industrial distilling centers, and three of them were Ohio River towns: Covington, Louisville, and Owensboro. Frankfort's Kentucky River waterfront also accommodated several distilleries. Building and operating a large, successful distillery were less dependent on city size than on direct river access. By the 1880s, three medium-capacity distilleries, processing 200 to 600 bushels of grain per day, operated in Maysville, one of Kentucky's early Ohio River ports, sixty-two miles upstream from Cincinnati. One of the state's largest pre–Civil War distilleries operated at Petersburg, a small Ohio River village some twenty-four miles downstream from Cincinnati. Water transport was comparatively cheap and provided ready access to supplies of grains, oak barrel staves, and bituminous coal for distillers with riverside works. Large-capacity cargo boats, whether flatboats or steam-powered packets, required streams with a substantial volume of water and minimal seasonal variation in water level—neither hazardous high water nor levels too low to permit safe passage. After

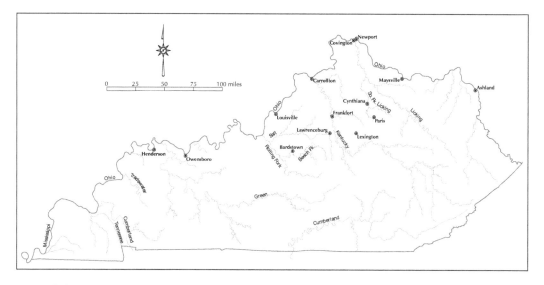

Kentucky's major rivers.

the Civil War, railroads began to link riverside settlements such as Covington, Louisville, Frankfort, and Owensboro to interior hinterlands, permitting distilleries to go much farther afield to obtain grain and cooperage lumber and to extend their whiskey sales to markets across the nation.

Reaching Riverine Markets

Moving Kentucky farm products to market in the late eighteenth and early nineteenth centuries—whether grain, tobacco, livestock, salted meat, or whiskey—was difficult and expensive in terms of time, labor, and tractive power. Commodity transport was seasonal, in part because farmwork and commodity shipments were seasonal, and in part because water levels in Kentucky's navigable creeks and rivers were reliably high enough only in late winter and early spring to accommodate cargo boats. Everyone engaged in waterborne commodity shipment was subject to the vagaries of weather. The annual river navigation cycle in the Ohio River Valley included three primary high-water shipping periods: a short season in November, followed by another short season in February. High water during the late spring in May and June usually sustained shipping for several weeks. An extended low-water period could be expected during the summer and early fall, as well as a shorter low-water winter season.[1] Given the size of the Ohio River watershed (nearly 190,000 square miles) and the valley's whimsical weather, no one could reliably predict when the high-water season would begin nor divine its duration. Only experienced crews piloting the shallow-draft vessels known as low-water packets could chance navigating rivers in summer, given the hazards of exposed rocks and sunken snags. In midwinter streams and rivers would often freeze over, halting riverboat traffic until the icy waterways began to clear. But even then, open water often harbored large ice floes moving downstream with the current, their mass and movement sufficient to crush and sink boats and barges tied up at the river's edge and shear wharf boats from their moorings.

Kentucky lay near the headwaters of the Mississippi–Ohio River system and therefore had access to several downriver markets, among them Memphis, Natchez, and New Orleans. Farmers could build or buy flatboats, keelboats, or barges and float their cargo downstream with the current. Boatbuilders frequented the Ohio River's banks from Pittsburgh to Paducah. A major boatbuilding center developed at Brownsville, Pennsylvania, on the Monongahela River south of Pittsburgh. In the middle Ohio Valley, Cincinnati, Ohio; Newport, Louisville, and Portland, Kentucky; and New Albany and Jeffersonville, Indiana, all became large boatbuilding centers.[2] Smaller boat construction operations were commonplace. Thomas Hart, a Lexington boatbuilder and sales agent, conducted business at the mouth of Tates Creek on the Kentucky River. He sold flatboats on short-term credit. Buyers loaded their newly purchased boats with goods and set off downriver to the lower Mississippi ports; there, they sold their cargo and their boats and paid one of Hart's business representatives. This generous financial arrangement implies a recognition that local shippers had insufficient operating capital to purchase a boat outright, whether with personal funds or through an obliging banker. It also suggests that, despite the elementary state of communications at the time, Hart understood the rather sophisticated business practices on the lower Mississippi, even though that market lay more than 1,400 river miles from his Kentucky River boat works. Even more incredible is that Hart instituted this credit policy knowing that unless the boats he sold survived the trip's navigational hazards with their cargo intact, payment would likely not be forthcoming.

Riverine Distilleries

Maysville

Limestone Landing, as Maysville was known in the late eighteenth century, was an early Ohio River shipping point for whiskey distilled in northeastern Kentucky's Mason and Bourbon Counties. Five hundred feet above the river, the Outer Bluegrass limestones terminate at a steep bluff. At the base of the bluff, a narrow alluvial terrace extends to the river's edge. The town developed on the terrace, crowding against the bluff's base and leaving little level land on which to establish large-scale industrial works. After the Civil War, three distillers found sufficient space to establish operations. In 1869 O. H. P. Thomas's distillery operated on Maysville's west side. Henry Pogue bought the Thomas works in 1876, moved it to the river's edge, and renamed it the Old Pogue Distillery. Pogue produced several different branded whiskeys, including Sour Mash Copper Whisky and Fire Copper Whisky. The site included four large aging and shipping warehouses. Production ended, except for a small amount of medicinal whiskey, with the enforcement of Prohibition in 1920. Although production resumed after 1933, the distillery and warehouses were torn down sometime thereafter. The Pogue family home remained, however—a bluff-side Greek Revival brick house built in 1845 for hemp merchant Michael Ryan. The three-story house with a central-hall plan featured a distinctive stepped-gable roof and, at 4,800 square feet, was among Maysville's largest and finest homes. The Pogue family sold the property in 1955, and subsequent owners allowed the house and grounds to deteriorate. Henry Pogue's descendants repurchased the house and surrounding property and began renovations in 2005. The house is now listed on the National Register of Historic Places. A new double garage–size building houses the Old Pogue Distillery, a revival craft operation that began producing a bourbon and two rye malt whiskeys in 2012.[3]

Covington, Newport, and Surrounds

Covington's site was surveyed and platted in 1815 on an expansive alluvial basin inside the right angle formed by the confluence of the Licking and Ohio Rivers. The Licking's narrow watershed extends from the Ohio's south bank 300 miles southeast to its headwaters in eastern Kentucky's Appalachian Plateau. The Covington basin, directly across the

Ohio River from Cincinnati, was the terminus for early buffalo trails and roads, including the Covington-Lexington Turnpike, incorporated in 1834, and the Covington & Lexington Railroad, which was completed south to Paris with connections to Lexington in 1854.

Industrial distilling and manufacturing in northern Kentucky were abetted by the opportune coincidence of navigable rivers, broad, flat floodplains, and highly productive agricultural hinterlands—not by abundant calcium-rich limestone spring water. The Ohio River represents a seam between two different but complementary regions: Kentucky's Bluegrass region to the south, and Ohio's Miami Valley to the north. Though physically and culturally distinct, both regions were important frontier farming areas, and by the 1830s, they served as incubators for the development of specialized corn and livestock agriculture, which spread across the Middle West and came to characterize the Corn Belt.[4] Nineteenth-century farmers in southwestern Ohio and the Kentucky Bluegrass country produced large surpluses of hogs, cattle, and grain, especially corn. Drovers directed livestock herds to Covington and Cincinnati slaughterhouses, and corn moved by wagon and railcar to Covington distilleries.

Four tributaries form a confluence with the Ohio River at or near Covington and Cincinnati. The Great and Little Miami Rivers, the Licking River, and a smaller stream, Mill Creek, flow into the Ohio just east of the great meander curve where the trunk stream's valley changes course. The Ohio's general direction of flow pivots ninety degrees from northwest to southwest at a point marked by an Ohio town appropriately named North Bend. Mill Creek and the Great and Little Miami Rivers flow out of southwestern Ohio to enter the Ohio River immediately up- and downstream from Cincinnati. The Licking River flows into the Ohio opposite present-day Cincinnati's business district. In cross-section width, each tributary stream valley differs dramatically from the Ohio Valley.[5] Just downstream from Cincinnati, the Ohio Valley is about 4,500 feet wide. The valley of the Great Miami west of Cincinnati is about 5,000 feet wide near its confluence with the Ohio. Upstream from Cincinnati, the Little Miami valley is 8,500 feet wide near the Ohio. Mill Creek is presently a small stream running in a concrete conduit for much of its lower reach before trickling into the Ohio. Its valley, however, is about two miles wide. For the last mile or more above the confluence with the Ohio, the Licking valley is 9,000 feet wide—and much wider than that near the river, where the bluffs recede to accommodate the riverside towns of Covington, Newport, Bellevue, and Dayton. Six miles upstream at DeCoursey, the Licking valley is still 4,500 feet wide, the same width as the Ohio River Valley.

The unusual stream configuration at Covington was brought about by Pleistocene glaciation. The northward flow of the Old Licking and Old Kentucky Rivers was blocked during the Illinoian glacial advance about 300,000 years ago, and the Ohio drainage was reconfigured during the Wisconsin glacial epoch, circa 15,000 years ago.[6] Vast quantities of glacial meltwater runoff widened old river channels and deposited significant volumes of alluvial silt, sand, and gravel in their beds. At Covington, the depth of alluvial deposits reaches 150 feet. The present-day Licking and Ohio River channels occupy only a small part of the old alluvial surface at Covington, allowing expansive urban development across the valley floor.[7]

The rivers' expansive floodplains offered square miles of nearly level land, and the river nexus was a popular place for urban and industrial development. Steel mills, stockyards, slaughterhouses, packing plants, tanneries, flour mills, lumber and coal yards, and industrial distilleries were avid consumers of the Ohio and Licking River floodplain flats, a rare resource in the otherwise deeply stream-dissected country near the Ohio River. These industries also required access to Ohio and Licking River shipping.[8] Nineteen distilleries operated in the Covington area during the nineteenth century; all but two were established after the Civil War and operated as high-volume, industrial-scale works with links to valley railroad lines and riverfront landings and wharf boats.[9]

While transport access and level land were the primary attractions for distillery development at the confluence of the Licking and Ohio Rivers, access to fresh water was another plus. Water could be obtained in quantity from both surface and ground sources, although nineteenth-century water quality was problematic at best. Water for industrial and residential use could be drawn from different sources at Covington: from the Licking and Ohio Rivers, from the deep alluvial sands and gravels of the river flats, and from deep bedrock. During the second half of the nineteenth century, when distilling flourished in this area, river water contained silt and a heavy pollution load, and it had to be treated before use. The Pleistocene alluvial material was a valuable aquifer, with moderate to large amounts of fair- to excellent-quality water. Water pumped from wells drilled into the Ordovician limestone and shale bedrock below the city was meager in quantity and generally too salty and sulfurous for use. The water obtained from several area wells had an iron content too high for use in beverage manufacturing or food processing.[10]

The Cincinnati firm Walsh, Brooks & Kellogg operated a rectifying distillery and built a second rectifying-redistilling operation beside the Roebling Bridge on the Ohio River in Covington in about 1859. Irish immigrant James Walsh and other business partners reorganized the company and renamed it the James Walsh Company. The Covington distillery drew water from six bored wells and processed it at a private waterworks.[11] The New England Distillery Company operated another small works in the crowded industrial area near the Covington railroad station and the Kentucky Central Railroad freight warehouse. A lumberyard, livery stables, and carriage factory operated nearby. The New England Distillery used water from two wells for cooling and condensing.[12] The Old '76 Distillery on the Licking River south of the Ohio River drilled a 1,200-foot well to the St. Peter sandstone formation, which was characterized as salty and sulfurous; this variation on "Blue Lick" water was used for cooling, but it was so corrosive to pipes that the well was abandoned.[13] "Blue Lick" is the term applied to the sulfurous brine that occurred in northern Kentucky, implying that it resembled the water found at Lower Blue Licks on the central Licking River west of Flemingsburg; the "blue" mineral water, thought to have medicinal qualities, was the main attraction at the nineteenth-century resort that grew up at that site.

In the 1880s at least three distilleries operated along the Licking River as part of an intensive rail and river industrial development that extended south of Covington for more than three miles.[14] Northernmost in this alignment was the Dorsel & Wulftange works, which produced bourbon and rye whiskey at Rickey Street, in the shadow of a large steel rolling mill. The distillery used city water and received whole-ear corn that was stored in a crib and shelled onsite. Dorsel & Wulftange did not operate a livestock feeding lot; it stored its slop in a large tub that stood beside the street, suggesting that the by-product was sold, given away, or hauled to the Licking River and dumped.

The B. K. Reynolds or Kenton County Distillery operated beside the Licking River about one and a half miles south of the courthouse. A high-production plant, the distillery mashed 800 bushels per day; the works included a corncrib and sheller but had no direct railroad connections. Cattle and pigs were fed on slop piped to large pens beside the Licking River—effectively livestock latrines—with the feedlot runoff likely flowing directly downslope into the river. The Willow Run or Milldale Distillery operated about three miles south of the Covington courthouse. A coal-fired steam plant powered the works, which mashed about 400 bushels of grain per day. Willow Run had access to railroad tracks and stored grain shipments in an onsite elevator. Seven small warehouses stored the barreled whiskey. The Willow Run works used well water in its operation. Given the heavy pollution load carried by the Licking and Ohio Rivers from industrial and residential contamination, it is likely that distilleries were reluctant to sully their product with river water.[15]

Petersburg

William and John Snyder moved from Albemarle County, on Virginia's Piedmont, to Petersburg, Kentucky, on the Ohio River in Boone County, in 1833. The brothers bought a riverside steam-powered gristmill and later added a distillery. Capitalizing on ready access to steamboat shipping, William Snyder steadily expanded the milling-distilling operation, drawing water from the Ohio River and a deep well. By 1850, the works employed sixteen hands who produced 7,000 barrels of flour and 164,000 gallons of whiskey. John Snyder's son David worked as a distiller; son James was a cooper. Snyder employed two millers, one from Germany and the other from Pennsylvania. The distillery dispatched whiskey to river markets, especially Cincinnati. Corn shipped from St. Louis arrived at the Petersburg wharf by steamboat barge, upward of 2,000 sacks in each delivery.[16] Cincinnati coal merchants delivered coal to the distillery by river barge several times a year. Given the distillery's demand for white oak barrels, it is likely that river shipments included large numbers of barrel staves. The works likely employed part-time laborers to load and unload cargo.[17]

By 1860, William Snyder's mill had 80,000 bushels of wheat and 300,000 bushels of corn stored in bins and cribs. He employed sixteen coopers and thirty distillery hands and day laborers to produce 1.125 million gallons that year.[18] The production of spirits in that quantity suggests that he had fitted the Petersburg Distillery with high-volume column stills.[19] Snyder lost the distillery to creditors in 1861, but the new owners continued production. In the 1880s the distillery works contained more than twenty-five buildings. Three structures remain, including the superintendent's house.[20]

Shipping grains, fuel, and whisky in volume by water was inexpensive, safe, and reliable, but it was dependent on benign river conditions. Petersburg was not served by a railroad, although a track ran along the north side of the river through Lawrenceburg, Indiana. Operators of the Petersburg Distillery made frequent river crossings to deliver whiskey to the Lawrenceburg depot for transshipment to regional customers. They shipped goods by boat when the river was open and by sled when the river was ice covered. Ice gorges sometimes blocked the Ohio River; for instance, in the winter of 1877, "the Ice was from Shore to Shore & over 100 barges past down in the Ice Some 8 or 10 of them loaded some Barges with the end Stoved in Some with their sides mashed in &c." The floating ice hazard was especially pronounced that winter, causing "the Greatest Destruction of Boats by the ice from Pittsburg to Louisville that ever has been Known by the Oldest River Men."[21] Barges bearing barreled whiskey often lost part or all of their cargoes when they were smashed by floating ice, and errant barrels were sometimes seen floating with the current.[22] To avoid such difficulties, distillers often held their whiskey in riverside warehouses or on open docks, awaiting favorable conditions for low-risk navigation.

Louisville

Basic whiskey production requirements for urban and rural distilleries were similar—access to a fresh water source and grain. For that reason, country distillers initially sited their works near springs or creeks. But for city distilleries, the primary locational criterion was access to a railroad or a river port. City distillers were therefore obliged to drill wells or draw water from the Ohio or Kentucky River—hardly an endorsement of the time-worn "pure limestone water" narrative. Both rural and urban distillers fed their spent grain by-product to livestock. But operating cattle and hog pens in or near a city was much different from feeding livestock in the country, where odors were carried away on the breeze and manure disposal was a straightforward matter of fertilizing adjacent farm fields.

The Ohio River's 981-mile course from its head at Pittsburgh to its confluence with the Mississippi at Cairo, Illinois, follows a deeply incised valley through the western uplands of the Allegheny Plateau past Cincinnati and Louisville to Tell City, Indiana. There, the river emerges from its picturesque vale to flow in great looping meanders across a broad alluvial plain on its way southwest to the Mississippi. The river's natural channel includes shoals, near-shore islands, and deep channel sections, but the most dramatic feature, and its only geological obstruction, is the Falls of the Ohio. About 606 miles below Pittsburgh, the Ohio cascades across the exceptionally competent Jeffersonville limestone—coral rich and, at 390 million years old, Devonian in age—dropping twenty-six feet over a distance of two miles. The rapids are especially vigorous in low water, which, given the Ohio Valley's precipitation pattern, could persist for nine months out of the year. Nineteenth-century boat captains moving downstream might attempt to run the rapids by one of three chutes. Those with better judgment landed above the falls and off-loaded cargo and passengers for portage to another landing below the obstruction. Overland trails, including the western branch of the Wilderness Road, coalesced at the falls. Given the imperative of riverine and overland travel, frontier settlements developed at this geographic nexus.[23]

The two-mile rapids became less of a focal point than the corridor along the falls' south and north banks, which invited development. From the first years of European settlement in the Ohio Valley, not one village but five developed near the falls. Pioneers founded Louisville at a site above the falls in 1779; Clarksville materialized on the north bank and below the falls four years later. These were followed by Jeffersonville above the falls and across the river from Louisville in 1802; Shippingport below the falls and west of Louisville in 1806; and Portland, also below the falls, in 1814. Commercial flatboats carrying Ohio Valley goods to New Orleans were active from the first years of settlement, prompting the US Congress to declare Louisville a port of entry in 1789.[24] By 1800, Louisville had 359 inhabitants. The first steam-powered boat arrived at Louisville in 1814; by 1819, nearly seventy steamboats operated on the Ohio River. As railroads developed in the mid-nineteenth century, they focused on established river landings near the falls, initially making water-to-interior links with inland towns. By 1882, more than 5,000 miles of railroad track linked the falls corridor to the national rail network.[25] Engineers and laborers completed the two-mile-long Louisville and Portland Canal, bypassing the falls, in 1830.[26] The following year, 406 steamboats passed through the canal. In 1837 more than 1,500 boats negotiated the lock, or a fourfold increase in six years. That count did not include the boats that landed above and below the falls without passing through the canal.[27]

Ohio Valley industrialization was abetted, in part, by the availability of coal to fire steam engines. Beginning in 1814 and for some eight decades thereafter, coal mined in southwestern Pennsylvania fueled Louisville's industrial development. The first coal barges from the Monongahela Valley arrived in 1814. In the mid-1850s steamboat-powered tows delivered coal, supplemented in the 1870s by the railroads.[28] By the mid-nineteenth century, manufacturing and related commercial businesses clustered in the five settlements near the falls, especially at Louisville. Factories processed farm products and prepared them for shipment, including salted beef and pork, smoked bacon, lard, flour, tobacco, and hemp rope and bags. Maltsters produced malted barley and rye for Kentucky distillers and brewers.[29] Wholesalers' warehouses stored and routed produce and products for shipment via river or rail. By the 1880s, Louisville's manufactured and processed goods

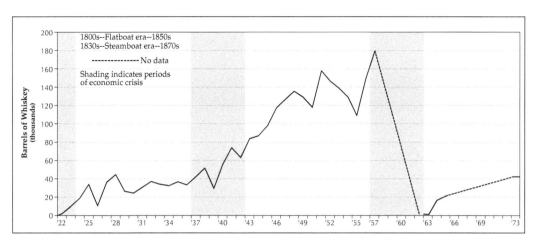

Whiskey imported into New Orleans via the Mississippi River, 1822–1873. (From US Treasury Department, Bureau of Statistics, *Report on the Internal Commerce of the United States* [Washington, DC, 1888])

were available throughout the South and Middle West, with deliveries extending as far as the new railroad towns on the Great Plains. Kentucky whiskey, whether measured in volume or value, was a major export.

City Distilling

Paradoxically, before the 1860s, little of the whiskey shipped through Louisville's river port was distilled in the city at the falls. A few pioneer distillers such as Evan Williams operated works in Louisville and Jefferson County in the late eighteenth century, but their production was small and intermittent. New England investors led by Rhode Island resident James D'Wolf Jr. built the large Hope Distillery near the Ohio River in Portland in 1816. The steam-powered works produced 1,200 gallons of whiskey per day but closed in 1820.[30]

Two firms, Schrodt & Laval Company and N. D. Smith & Company, built distilleries in Louisville in 1857. The Smith Distillery burned in 1858 and was not rebuilt. The Schrodt & Laval Distillery operated near the Ohio River on Second Street, between Washington and Water Streets, approximately where the KFC Yum Center currently stands. The distillery had an operating capacity of sixty barrels per day, or 12,000 barrels during a 200-day operating season, but the steam-powered works made industrial alcohol for lamp fuel and chemical manufacturing, not whiskey.[31]

By the eve of the Civil War, only one small distillery operated in Louisville. After the war, urban industrial distilling expanded rapidly in new large-scale plants at sites with railroad connections; direct river access had become a secondary consideration. While early distillers had oriented their works toward riverside settlements, the new postwar industrial distilleries appeared on the central city's periphery, at level sites that fronted creeks or had access to water through deep drilled wells. As the city industrialized, it also suburban-

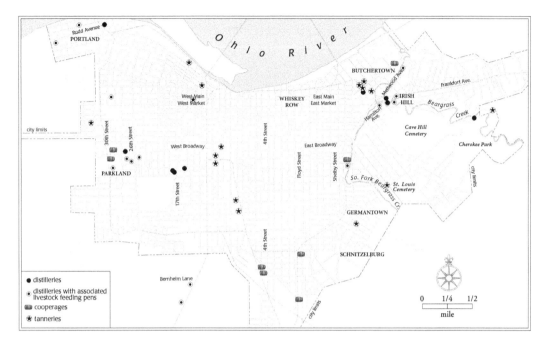

Distilleries, cooperages, and tanneries, Louisville, 1892–1905. (Compiled from *Insurance Maps of Louisville, Kentucky,* vols. 1–3 [New York: Sanborn-Perris Map Company, 1892]; *Insurance Maps of Louisville, Kentucky,* vol. 4 (New York: Sanborn Map Company, 1905]; *Caron's City Directory of the City of Louisville,* vol. 2 [Louisville: Bradley & Gilbert, 1895])

ized as factories and residential neighborhoods expanded into the surrounding farmland. From Louisville's original site on the south bank of the Ohio, urban expansion prior to 1865 extended up- and downriver and south across the near-level glacial outwash plain. Property subdivision was laissez-faire and driven primarily by landowners and speculators, although lot sales were often tepid and desultory. The city started operating a horse-drawn trolley car system in 1865, and by 1889, the network was electrified. Speculators platted small-lot subdivisions along trolley lines to attract working-class residents, many of them Irish and German immigrants, seeking to become home owners.[32] During this same postwar period, railroad companies extended tracks south from the river, creating rail corridors attached to a circumferential belt line. High-density industrial development took place in the city's old riverfront section, as well as along the new railroad corridors.[33]

Louisville's 620 manufacturing establishments in 1860 had nearly doubled to 1,191 by 1880. Factories turned out durable and nondurable goods: tobacco products; wooden furniture; farm machinery, especially steel plows; iron pipes, boilers, and stoves; cotton and woolen goods; glass, brick, and tile products; and, on the banks of the Ohio, steamboats.[34] Pork packing was Louisville's largest industry as measured by monetary value of operations and products; whiskey distilling ranked second. The city's one distillery in 1860 grew to six in 1870 (as Louisville's population reached 100,000); by 1880, thirty-six

Elk Creek Distillery No. 368, Jefferson County, ca. 1910. (Photo from Oscar Getz Museum, Bardstown, KY; map from Kentucky Digital Libraries)

large-capacity distilleries operated across the city. One works covered twenty-five acres and produced some 8 million gallons of fine whiskey annually.[35] At least five Kentucky distillers sold their works and relocated to Louisville: John G. Mattingly and George W. Beall moved from Marion County in 1878, Isaac and Bernard Bernheim moved from Mc-

Cracken County in about 1888, and John G. Roach moved to Louisville from Green County in 1893 to build a new distillery.[36] Adding thirty large distilleries in ten years to Louisville's industrial base would have been an admirable achievement if only local and state capital had been available, but capital markets were national or even international by that time. Distillers had access to funds provided by investors in eastern cities and in Europe, and they expanded their operations at an astonishing rate.

The new high-capacity industrial distilleries bore limited resemblance to long-established farm and mill distilleries. Louisville's postbellum distilleries were housed in multistory brick buildings and warehouses with dedicated rail sidings. During the 1880s and 1890s, the city's collective daily grain mashing capacity was roughly 35,500 bushels, or more than 100 railroad boxcars of grain. A few distilleries had mashing capacities of less than 400 bushels per day; eleven mashed more than 1,000 bushels per day.[37]

Complementary Businesses

Distilling requires certain complementary industries that function as input suppliers or output consumers and are often linked together in a chain of supply and consumption businesses.[38] Farmers supplied corn and rye, and coopers furnished oak barrels. In 1870 fifteen Louisville cooperages employed 129 coopers.[39] Coopers obtained staves from Kentucky and Indiana lumberyards and shipped their barrels to both local and more distant distilleries; therefore, most coopers positioned their shops in rail corridors.

Distillers fed their spent grains to livestock. James D'Wolf's distillery at Portland fed slop to cattle in 1816. In the 1880s and 1890s fourteen Louisville distilleries operated cattle feedlots, and others sold or gave slop to area farmers. Meat processors and distillery feedlots were also complementary businesses. Butchertown, an east Louisville neighborhood near Beargrass Creek, was a small nineteenth-century slaughterhouse and processing center at the terminus of the Frankfort and Lexington Turnpike. Prior to the development of a regional railroad network, farmers drove livestock overland to Butchertown for slaughter and processing. The Bourbon Stockyards started there in 1836 as a place to consolidate livestock for feeding and watering prior to sale and slaughter. Fresh meat was perishable and had to be sold promptly at local urban markets or salted or smoked and packed in barrels for storage or shipment to markets elsewhere. Operators usually sited stockyards, slaughterhouses, and packing plants in close proximity. Many of Butchertown's shops were small family-operated businesses that could process a limited volume of livestock, but these operations began to fade during the 1880s and 1890s. Commercial meatpackers built several large processing plants in Louisville, motivated in part by the ease of livestock shipment by rail, the availability of refrigerated railcars to haul processed carcasses, and increased livestock feeding at the city's distilleries.[40]

In turn, tanneries were reliant on slaughterhouses and butcher shops to supply hides. Awkward overland transport motivated tanners to locate on good roads, near hide suppliers, and close to a ready market for tanned hides.[41] Six small tanneries operated in Louisville in 1860, and eleven in 1870; by 1880, seventeen large industrial tanneries operated in the city.[42] Enabled by steam-powered mechanization, railroad transport, and increased livestock production, the tanning industry flourished, and Louisville became a major leather manufacturing center. Tanneries supported boot and shoe, belt, and harness manufacturers. By the 1880s, as the national rail net matured, established Louisville tanneries processed more than 150,000 hides annually, many of them shipped in from as far away as Texas and Colorado.[43]

Nineteenth-century Kentucky tanners followed traditional Old World practices, which required only two raw materials to process animal hides: lime and tannic acid.[44] When burned in kilns at high temperatures, crushed limestone yields calcium oxide; when hydrated, it produces caustic lime water that can be used to remove hair from animal hides. Tanners extracted tannic acid from hemlock and oak bark. After receiving bark shipments by wagon or rail, tanners stored the bark in covered sheds to dry it thoroughly before pulverizing it in a bark mill. The bark powder was then soaked in warm water to extract tannic acid. The traditional tannery was a simple operation: an open tan yard, a rude cluster of wooden tanning vats sunk into the ground, a small mill with bark-grinding stones turned by water power or a draft animal, and an open shed or beam house for working hides.[45] Nineteenth-century tanneries were noisome places, but they were often surrounded by working-class residential neighborhoods.

By the late 1860s, Louisville's tanning industry was industrialized. The tanneries proper were arranged in clusters of large four-story, factory-type brick buildings with vat rooms, curry and finish rooms, bark mill, beam house, hide house, and engine room. Wooden frame buildings contained bark storage and leeching rooms. The industrial tannery closely resembled a brick whiskey aging warehouse, although tanneries were outfitted with more windows for interior illumination. The Conrad, Ohio Falls, Phoenix, and Shuff tanneries were all located between Eleventh and Twelfth Streets, adjacent to the L & N Railroad shops, and together occupied one and a half city blocks.[46]

Factory clustering reduced procurement, processing, and distribution costs and made attractive destinations for railroad sidings. But clustering also increased the risk of catastrophic fire. In August 1890 fire destroyed a Kentucky Distilling Company warehouse containing 25,000 barrels of whiskey, the distillery itself, and cattle sheds, at an estimated loss of $800,000. The adjoining Conrad Seller slaughterhouse and pork packing plant was also destroyed, at a loss of about $50,000.[47]

Whiskey Row

Louisville's Ohio River wharf attracted a broad range of commercial and industrial businesses that built structures adjacent to the riverfront. The river also attracted railroad development, and the combined water and land transportation nexus drew commercial businesses like a magnet. Many of Louisville's industrial distilleries and associated businesses, such as whiskey wholesaling and storage, bought lots fronting Main Street, a few hundred feet and upslope from the river, where they established works and warehouses in the 1870s. Large firms, including W. H. Thomas & Son, J. T. S. Brown & Sons, and George P. Weller, participated in Main Street development, and the cluster soon became known as Whiskey Row.[48] Some rural distillers operating elsewhere in the state opened offices on East or West Main Street or on adjacent streets. Several buildings in this district, including structures with grand Romanesque Revival, Beaux Arts, and Chicago-style façades made of stone, brick, terra-cotta, and cast iron, remain intact. East and West Main Street represents a heritage location for bourbon history and lore and is undergoing redevelopment by whiskey-related businesses. Angel's Envy Bourbon, Old Forester Distillery, Evan Williams Bourbon Experience, and Michter's Distillery all operate visitors' centers and distilling works. On the east, this venerable corridor now extends to include the renowned Vendome Copper and Brass works at 729 Franklin Street and the Copper & Kings American Brandy Company at 1121 East Washington Street.

Footloose Distilling in Louisville

Louisville's rapid growth during the nineteenth century was spurred by several intertwined influences: rapid farm and forestry development in the hinterland, the application of new transport technologies both inside and outside the city, multifaceted industrial expansion, the growth of banking and financial institutions, and rapid population growth due to immigration from Europe and from elsewhere in the state and region. Industrial, commercial, and residential transformations prompted changes in land use. Industry venues were in a state of continuous flux and geographically footloose; few locations retained the same owners and occupants for more than a decade. The high-density industrial, business, and residential activity along the Ohio River waterfront during the first third of the nineteenth century gave way to dispersal inland along railroad and trolley car tracks.

Distillers and their complementary industries and businesses participated in this transitional process. Some distillers reorganized or sold their business, and subsequent owners moved the works to new locations. Others retired, and their children or business partners assumed control of operations, perhaps combining them with other works in which they had a financial and management interest. Fires destroyed some distilleries, prompting the owners to either rebuild on the same site or move to a new location with better access to transport or other advantages. Finally, Prohibition terminated most distilling; works closed, and many sites never reestablished operations after repeal in 1933.

The evolution of the distilling works operated by members of the Stitzel and Weller families illustrates the complexity of multigenerational urban-industrial distilling. German-born brothers Frederick and Philip Stitzel built a distillery at Twenty-Sixth Street and Broadway in a developing industrial district on Louisville's west side in 1872. Frederick

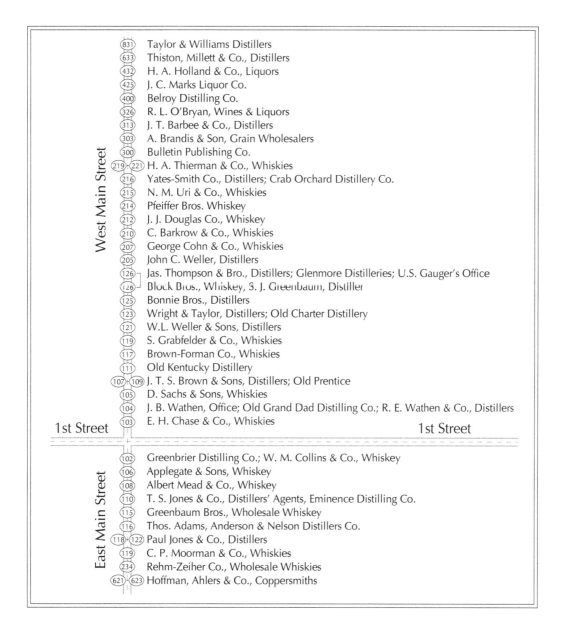

Louisville's Whiskey Row, 1909. Actual distances between addresses are not accurately depicted. (Compiled from *Caron's Annual Directory of the City of Louisville,* vol. 39 [Louisville: Bradley & Gilbert, 1909], 2046–54)

was a gifted "mechanic," in the idiom of the day. As noted in chapter 4, he invented a new type of multilevel rack system for storing whiskey barrels, which he patented in 1879. The distilling complex burned in 1883, and the Stitzels rebuilt it on the same site. By the 1890s, the distillery was mashing 350 bushels of grain per day and storing whiskey in three onsite warehouses. Cattle, housed in large sheds, consumed the slop produced. J. B. Wathen &

Brother Company operated a six-warehouse distillery across Twenty-Sixth Street to the west. And at Twenty-Eighth Street and Broadway, Old Times Distillery and Kentucky Comfort Distillery operated side by side, sharing warehouses and cattle sheds. The nearest railroad line ran north-south along Thirtieth Street, so each distillery in this group obtained its grains and fuel and shipped its barreled whiskey by wagon. In 1902 Frederick and Philip selected a site some three miles to the east near Beargrass Creek, the Bourbon Stockyards, and Butchertown, where they built Stitzel Brothers Registered Distillery No. 17. Although the new works was modestly sized, mashing 200 bushels of grain per day and having only one small storage warehouse, its location at Story Avenue and Johnson Street placed it within a cluster of rail-oriented, large-capacity works, including the Allen Bradley, Elk Run, Anderson, Nelson, Mellwood, and Crystal Spring distilleries.

Philip Stitzel bought his brother's share of the company, and the works was subsequently managed by Philip's son Arthur, who was also a partner in a whiskey distribution business with Hilmar Ehrmann. In addition, Arthur managed business operations at the Stitzel Brothers works at Twenty-Sixth Street and Broadway in west Louisville and oversaw the first stages of the family company's merger with W. L. Weller & Sons. Arthur Stitzel and his wife lived in Clifton, near Stitzel Brothers Registered Distillery No. 17, but in 1922 they built a Georgian Revival home in the country east of Louisville at 9707 Shelbyville Road. The house was designed by Alfred and Oscar Joseph, of the well-regarded Louisville architecture firm Joseph and Joseph. The house is one of several distilling-related Kentucky structures listed on the National Register of Historic Places.

In 1903 the west-side distillery was sold to W. L. Weller & Sons and business partner Philip Hollenback, who operated the works as the Glencoe Distilling Company. The east-side distillery (No. 17) operated as the Stitzel Brothers Distillery, where Julian Van Winkle and Alexander Farnsley directed business activities. During Prohibition, the distillery operated as a warehouse facility and bottling works for medicinal whiskeys. When Prohibition was repealed in 1933, the distillery resumed operations as Stitzel-Weller for a short time, while construction of a new distillery was completed. The new works, designed by architects Joseph and Joseph and located southwest of Louisville in the suburb of Shively, was finished in 1935, whereupon all production was transferred there. The Shively distillery had direct railroad access, as well as a lower tax rate than that exacted by the city of Louisville. These advantages attracted seven other distilleries to the area, including Brown-Forman, Frankfort, National, Schenley, Seagram, and Yellowstone. Eventually, the No. 17 works was largely demolished. Only a two-story brick building remains at 1033 Story Avenue; the site is now utilized by trucking businesses and scrap metal processors.[49]

During Prohibition, W. L. Weller acquired the brand name Old Fitzgerald from a distiller in Frankfort. This became the company's leading brand at the new Shively distillery on Fitzgerald Road. Norton-Simon Inc., a subsidiary of Somerset Importers Ltd., bought the family-owned Stitzel-Weller Distillery in 1972 and changed the name to Old

Fitzgerald Distillery. The works was resold several times thereafter. It was eventually acquired by beverage conglomerate Diageo, but distilling operations ended in 1992. Diageo continues to use the warehouses for whiskey storage, and it has turned the Stitzel-Weller office building into a venue for the exhibition of company history.

Tom Bulleit, great-great-grandson of distiller Augustus Bulleit, began distilling a high-rye-content "revival" bourbon in 1987. Seagram bought the brand a decade later and distilled the whiskey at the Four Roses Distillery in Lawrenceburg. Diageo then bought the brand, and in 2017 it built the new Bulleit Distillery east of Shelbyville in rural Shelby County. The distillery is on the Kentucky Bourbon Trail and offers a site tour that is packaged as the "Bulleit Bourbon Experience." Diageo's new Shelby County distillery is a technological showplace that employs numerous innovations but also deliberately retains a degree of design heritage. Each single-story aging warehouse has a capacity that exceeds 55,000 barrels. Workers stack the barrels on pallets vertically on end, rather than laying them horizontally on multilevel wooden racks. The warehouse exterior walls are set atop four- to five-foot poured concrete "dike" walls that form a fully enclosed perimeter around the building base. In the event of a fire and the collapse of barrel stacks, the walls and concrete floors will contain the burning whiskey within the building's base, preventing it from flowing downslope and endangering other structures. The fire-suppression system includes twin diesel engines running high-pressure pumps that draw water from a 200,000-gallon pond and a nearby reservoir. A pressurized sprinkler system protects the building interiors, and exterior fire hydrants connect to large hydrant-mounted nozzles that can direct the spray onto building and grain storage tank exteriors.[50]

Remnants and Rejuvenation

The Stitzel-Weller–Old Fitzgerald works in Shively is a rare example of a largely intact historical industrial distillery. Most such sites were razed and cleared for other uses; where scattered buildings remain, they may be vacant or converted to other uses. A cluster of four whiskey aging warehouses still stands near the original Stitzel Brothers distillery at the corner of Payne Street and Lexington Road in the industrial triangle between east Louisville's Butchertown, Clifton, and Irish Hill neighborhoods. The floodplain site, inside a tight meander in the Middle Fork of Beargrass Creek, was likely first developed in the early 1860s by John G. Mattingly & Brother. By 1885, the Anderson Distillery and the Nelson Distillery operated side by side, and their warehouses, cooperage shops, grain storage bins, bottling plants, and associated buildings occupied most of the available land. Anderson produced sour-mash bourbon and rye whiskeys, processing some 450 bushels of grain each day; Nelson made sweet-mash bourbon and rye, mashing 800 bushels a day. Immediately across Beargrass Creek to the west, adjacent to a large Louisville & Nashville Railroad yard and roundhouse, the outsized Allen Bradley–Elk Run Distillery complex produced both sweet- and sour-mash whiskeys. This site was accessible to the Anderson and Nelson Distilleries by a footbridge. At present, three large, five-story apartment buildings stand on the footprint of the old Anderson-Nelson complex. The Allen Bradley–Elk Run site is vacant, the only remnants being some asphalt access roads and the concrete floors of several distillery buildings.

The four remaining aging warehouses stand across Lexington Road (formerly Hamilton Avenue) from the Anderson-Nelson site. The easternmost warehouse in the group, the Nelson Distilling Company Warehouse, stands in the angle between Payne Street and Lexington Road. The solid brick exterior side walls are 240 feet long and are reinforced by twenty-four nearly full-height pilasters. The 100-foot-long end walls are similarly supported. The internal space was filled with barrel racks eighteen tiers high, giving the structure a capacity of 30,000 barrels. An elevator on the west end lifted barrels to the various levels, and the roof was capped by a small shed-like monitor roof that admitted light and provided ventilation.

Immediately to the west, the Williams Bonded Warehouse and the Central Bonded Warehouse stand side by side. Part of the Slocum Bonded Warehouse, which adjoined this group in 1905, has been torn down; the space is now a parking lot. The three-story brick Williams building is 132 feet wide and 350 feet long and held more than 65,000 barrels. The pilaster-reinforced side walls support a low-angle roof. West of the Williams building, the Central Bonded Warehouse had an internal capacity of 23,000 barrels, and the full Slocum structure held more than 52,000 barrels. A special "whiskey sewer" ran below Lexington Road in front of the Williams, Central, and Slocum warehouses. In the event of a catastrophic fire, as barrels fell from the collapsing racks and smashed, the burning whiskey would pour from the building and drain into twenty-six roadside catch basins, which would direct the liquid into the whiskey sewer. The flaming liquid would then surge down the gradient into Beargrass Creek, a few hundred feet to the west. The sewer's draining capacity was 66,000 barrels per hour. The catch basins are no longer functional, but their location may be represented by tree boxes set into the sidewalk in front of the warehouses at about the same intervals as the original catch basins.

Although the Nelson warehouse stands empty and is in need of a new roof, the structure is on the National Register of Historic Places. The Williams and Central warehouses have been rejuvenated as Distillery Commons, which offers office space for rent. Across the parking lot to the west stands a small brick building that may have once functioned as a bottling plant; it now serves as a community theater.[51]

Owensboro

West of Louisville, distilling was a minor antebellum activity practiced by a small number of farmer-distillers in environmental circumstances that were profoundly different from those in central Kentucky's Bluegrass region. Only five distilleries in Owensboro and Daviess County predated the Civil War. The presence of distilling there was based not on the availability of pure limestone spring water but on the experience of a few early settlers whose families came from Maryland and Pennsylvania. After a generation in Washington, Marion, and Nelson Counties in the Outer Bluegrass, they moved to western Kentucky.[52] The Ohio River or shallow wells provided water for distilling. Land near the Ohio River above Owensboro was lightly settled by 1810, but the low-lying swamplands to the south and west were slow to develop; by 1850, those lands were still undeveloped or occupied by squatters.[53]

The rationale for lagging farm and industrial development was straightforward. On the eve of Daviess County's great post–Civil War distillery boom, the county's farmland inventory included 115,000 acres of improved land and 107,226 acres of woodland.[54] The southern third of Daviess County, the area south of Panther Creek, was largely forested uplands. Extensive alluvial plains extended from the creek north to the Ohio River. Some sections near the Ohio River drained well, but the rest was nearly level and largely covered by old-growth swamp forest.[55] Creating agricultural land that would support an extensive distilling industry out of waterlogged swamp required cutting the timber and organizing extensive drainage projects.[56] An 1888 US Treasury report summarized the industry's grain supply: a "large amount of corn received from the adjacent country loaded on flat-boats and barges and towed in for consumption by the eight distilleries here."[57]

Although accurate tabulation is difficult, more than thirty distilleries operated in Daviess County as small farm and industrial works between 1810 and 1900. Fourteen distilleries were in operation in 1899, ten of which were large industrial works.[58] During the nineteenth century, some distilleries were shut down and abandoned; others burned. In some cases, new distilleries were rebuilt on the sites of previous works. Distillers built at least two distilleries near the Green River in the southwestern part of the county, and more than twenty distilleries operated on the Ohio River's south bank, several on adjoining riverfront property. Only five distilleries operated in Owensboro itself or within walking distance of the city's residential areas.[59] Most distilleries in and near Owensboro were built between 1869 and 1895 as industrial works financed by local distillers and businesspeople; by distillers from Nelson, Marion, and Washington Counties; and by investors from Louisville and New York.[60]

The Owensboro and Daviess County economies were closely tied to river transport, and most postbellum distilleries fronted the Ohio at river landings. Owensboro was dependent on road and riverboat transport until 1884, when the north-south Owensboro & Russellville rail line connected Owensboro to Central City and Russellville. The Louisville, St. Louis & Texas Railroad completed an east-west track from Louisville to Owensboro, paralleling the Ohio River, in 1888. The following year, it completed a line west from Owensboro to the Green River, Henderson, and Evansville, Indiana.[61] Most riverfront distilleries were already in operation in 1889; by the 1890s, they could have obtained dedicated rail spurs, but several continued to operate as river distilleries.

The Owensboro riverfront distilleries were configured differently from the rural Bluegrass distilleries or the large industrial distilleries in Louisville and Jefferson County, where farmers' wagons or railcars could be depended on to deliver grain or coal on a regular schedule—daily, if needed. Barges served the riverfront distilleries and moved at the whim of river conditions. Low water, floods, and winter ice impeded deliveries.[62] At each distillery river landing, grains and coal arrived on barges; the cargo had to be off-loaded and elevated by steam-powered conveyors or trams to the distillery's large corncrib, granary, or coal storage building. Filled whiskey barrels were carried via the same trams to riverboats for shipment to market. Outsized storage buildings allowed the riverfront distilleries to accommodate irregular delivery schedules, and tramways reduced the awkwardness of moving raw materials and finished products up and down the steep riverbank.[63] Shippers delivered corn "on the ear," and distillers shelled and milled the corn into mashing meal. Corncobs supplemented coal as a fuel source. Coal could have been obtained from several sources, including a local commercial mine that opened in 1905. Most Daviess County distilleries maintained feeding yards, where they fed slop to hogs or cattle. A complementary livestock butchering and meatpacking industry did not develop until the 1890s, when four slaughterhouses were established on a small creek adjacent to the Daviess County Distillery northwest of Owensboro.

At least three Kentucky towns—Lawrenceburg, Bardstown, and Owensboro—had residential streets where clusters of distillers built large houses. Distilling in Owensboro and Daviess County began in the early 1800s. The Monarch family moved from Maryland to Owensboro in the 1830s and became prominent among Daviess County distillers. Thomas J. Monarch Sr. was born in Owensboro in about 1836. He and his wife Eliza Jane had a daughter, Miranda, and sons William, Daniel, Henry, Thomas, Richard, Martin, and Sylvester. Several Monarch sons became distillers. Peter E. Payne, a family member by marriage, was a distilling company partner. Payne and Monarch brothers Richard, Martin, and Sylvester built large Queen Anne–style mansions on Highland Avenue in the 1880s and 1890s. Richard's and Martin's houses were razed, but Sylvester's red brick home (known now as the Le Vega Clements house) and Payne's house (the Monarch-Payne house) remain.[64] Sylvester Monarch's house overlooks the present-day Glenmore Distillery site, and Payne's house stands a short distance to the west. Architects designed each Owensboro "Distillery Row" house according to period style and used exotic building materials not obtainable locally. Artisanal carpenters and other tradespeople provided the skills required; the distilling business provided the financial wherewithal.

While farm-related craft distilling could be accomplished in semi-isolation, industrial distilling required support from related and complementary industries such as machine shops, coppersmiths, coopers, lumberyards, stockyards, and slaughterhouses. Large industrial works required multiple suppliers, including farmers and specialized businesses dealing in grains and coal. City distilleries were hives of seasonal activity. Access streets were frequently filled with wagons making deliveries and hauling away spent grains. Auxiliary structures included grain bins, corncribs, and livestock feeding sheds. Railroad tracks and sidings harbored boxcars loaded with grains or staves for delivery or full whiskey barrels awaiting shipment to wholesalers. Residential neighborhoods near distillery clusters were often occupied by distillery employees or those who worked in nearby complementary industries. In river cities, wholesalers constructed warehouses near the riverfront to facilitate whiskey shipments, and distillers and related businesses opened offices in the area to take advantage of the business synergy created by propinquity. Successful distillery owners might build large private homes in high-amenity neighborhoods, often on the hills near the river or the bluffs fringing the low-lying alluvial floodplain. All this constituted a distinctive landscape unlike that of other industries operating in the same places and at the same time. Today, remnants of this landscape are rare, but those that remain are now part of the distilling industry's tactile heritage. Researchers actively study these structures and archive them on the National Register of Historic Places and in biographies of distillers. Contemporary distillers promote their heritage and attract tourists with innovations such as the Bourbon Trail. The remnants of nineteenth- and early-twentieth-century distilleries that remain bear the cachet of authenticity and represent places associated with memorable, and sometimes profitable, achievements. These places reside along the backroads, in the sense that their geographic placement is "off the main track," and in the sense that, historically, they demarcate a "landscape of yesteryear."

Epilogue

Backroads and the Reservoir of Tradition

Kentucky's whiskey distilling ancestry and legacy descend from eighteenth-century Europe, especially Celtic Eire, Ulster Ireland, and Scotland, and from colonial settlements in Virginia, Maryland, and Pennsylvania. Distilling's traditions and present-day operations are widely recorded in scholarly and popular literature and media, but they are also present in "hard copy" on the contemporary landscape, often on backroads and in out-of-the-way places not frequented by visitors. Landscapes are heritage reservoirs filled with historic and contemporary structures such as distillery works. But they also harbor infrastructure that enabled a distilling industry to thrive, such as hard-surface turnpikes, river ports, and railroads. Rural distillers, their families, and their labor forces lived onsite, on neighboring farms, or in rail-side villages. Urban distillery laborers often lived in nearby working-class neighborhoods, while the owner may have resided in an upscale neighborhood elsewhere.

Distilleries do not stand alone; they operate in concert with complementary industries. During the nineteenth century's first three decades, Kentucky's farm and mill distilleries were codependent on agriculture for both grain supplies and livestock; they needed draft animals to move wagons, and those that maintained their own feedlots needed cattle and hogs. Some distillers remained small-scale craft producers, while others bought steam engines and adopted other enabling technology. Whiskey production increasingly focused on the most accessible sections of the Greater Bluegrass, especially the Inner and Outer Bluegrass subregions. These areas enjoyed the mutual advantages of fertile soils and productive farms, a near ubiquitous distribution of cool-water springs and perennial streams, and hard-surface turnpikes. By the 1820s and 1830s, distillers increasingly adopted products produced by complementary industries, which were also changing. Steamboat builders superseded flatboat carpenters; coopers increased their use of barrel stave stock and were supported by an expanding lumber industry; coppersmiths obtained their materials from East Coast rolling mills or ship salvage yards. Railroads laid ballast beds and iron rails from river ports into the countryside. Rural distillers recognized the advantage of trackside access and often moved to a depot or arranged for the construction of dedicated sidings. Riverfront settlements large and small underwrote the development of the state's largest distilleries before the Civil War. River ports often became railroad hubs; these attracted distillers, who built new works along railroad beltways. Inventions and innovations enhanced distillery mechanization, especially during the second half of the nineteenth century, furthering the drive toward industrial-scale production. The gradual mechanization of complementary enterprises such as power generation, agriculture, lumber processing, mining, and glassmaking also enhanced whiskey production.

As distilling became more transport and urban oriented after the Civil War, city distillers enjoyed the advantage of direct access to wholesalers, banks, and insurers. Early commercial distilleries were often family ventures that were either self-financed or funded from local or regional sources. By the 1880s, companies with access to national and international financial markets owned many of Kentucky's large industrial distilleries. When considered in the aggregate, commercial distilling created an industrial landscape comprising the distillery and its associated works, sawmills, coopers' shops, lumberyards, grain fields, corncribs, livestock barns and feedlots, iron foundries, and machinery manufacturers.

Appreciation of Kentucky's bourbon distilling traditions can be enhanced by closely examining distilleries and their associated landscapes. Tradition is also sustained in narratives or stories that distillers and others construct to explain what they have created.[1] Stories record those places and events that people deem important and that contribute to their identity, whatever their relationship to the industry. Because these narratives are selectively constructed, they often retain and embellish some aspects of the past while allowing others to slip into obscurity. And importantly, although these narratives originate within the industry, they are often adopted by the public.

Kentucky's distilling industry is notable for the way it engages its past—retaining old structures, mash bill and yeast recipes, still house methods, and brand names—while also embracing experimentation and modern business practices. Distillers recognize landscapes as containing sites of origin—places where their heritage and traditions reside. Distillers' narratives have bonded with those of associated trades: coopers, coppersmiths, grain farmers, bankers, and a large cadre of other related businesses. While appreciative of their traditions, contemporary distillers do not live *in* the past but *with* the past. They also recognize that, if tutored, the consuming public will come to appreciate these qualities and will associate product with place and tradition in a gainful manner.

Acknowledgments

Books and essays are, for me, not solely the product of my own devices but a summation of what my mentors and colleagues have taught me through their own ruminations, written and verbal. My interest in observing and interpreting our world, both the visible and the concealed, was fostered and guided by my teachers and advisers: Eugene C. Mather, John Fraser Hart, Fred Luckermann, John Borchert, Robert Kiste, Philip Porter, Dwight Brown, John A. Wolter, Russell Adams, Ward Barrett, John Webb, Leslie Hewes, and J. B. Jackson.

Many generous colleagues provided guidance, ideas, and insights: Ron Abler, John Adams, Charles Aiken, Arne Alenan, Daniel Arreola, Tom Bell, Stephen Birdsall, Stanley Brunn, Geoffrey Buckley, Harry Caudill, Grady Clay, Craig Colton, Michael Conzen, Ronald Eller, Nikky Finney, Philip Gersmehl, Glenn Harper, George Herring, Warren Hofstra, John Hudson, John Jakle, John Paul Jones III, Penny Kaiserlian, Kathi Kern, James Klotter, Karen Koegler, Charles Kovacik, Thomas Leinbach, Pierce Lewis, Kent Mathewson, Thomas McIlwraith, Donald Meinig, Tyrel Moore, Keith Mountain, Edward K. Muller, Wolfgang Natter, Gary O'Dell, Robert Ostergren, Risa Palm, Kevin Patrick, Ken Pavelchak, Chip Peterson, Jonathan Phillips, John Pickles, Richard Pillsbury, Susan Roberts, Robert Sack, Ted Schatzki, Thomas Schlereth, Keith Sculle, James Shortridge, Gerald L. Smith, Jonathan M. Smith, Paul Starrs, John Stephenson, George F. Thompson, Stanley Trimble, Monica Udvardy, Richard Ulack, Dell Upton, Richard Walker, Jon L. Walstrom, Charles Walters, Joseph Wood, Nan Woodruff, William Wyckoff, Don Yaeger, Wilbur Zelinsky, and Chester Zoeller.

I am indebted to library staff colleagues for their generous and insightful assistance: William Marshall, Sarah Dorpinghaus, Matt Harris, Gordon Hogg, Terry Kopana, James Birchfield, Tina Brooks, and Kate Black at the University of Kentucky Library and Library Special Collections, Lexington; Gwen Curtis and Sarah Watson, Science and Engineering Library, University of Kentucky; Faith Harders and Lalana Powell, Hunter M. Adams College of Design Library, University of Kentucky; B. J. Gooch, Transylvania University Library Special Collections, Lexington; Amy Hanaford Purcell, University of Louisville Library Special Collections; Johna L. Ebling and Aaron Rosenblum, Filson Historical Society, Louisville; Nancy Richey, Western Kentucky University Library Special Collections, Bowling Green; Erin Campbell and Devhra Bennett Jones, Lloyd Library and Museum, Cincinnati, OH; Francis Alba, Center for Research Libraries, Chicago; and Kenneth Butcher, National Institute of Standards and Technology, Washington, DC.

Colleagues Nancy O'Malley, former assistant director of the William S. Webb Museum of Anthropology, University of Kentucky, and Professor Richard Schein, Department of Geography and Arts & Sciences, University of Kentucky, contributed enlightenment and enriching critique over the years. Master cartographer Richard Gilbreath, director of the Gyula Pauer Center for Cartography and GIS, University of Kentucky, crafted the maps, graphs, and tables, and Jeffrey E. Levy, Geographic Information Systems Program coordinator, Department of Geography, University of Kentucky, assisted with the line drawings and photographic work.

I also wish to extend my deep appreciation to friends and colleagues for their assistance and wise counsel: Professor David Hamilton, Department of History, University of Kentucky; Professor Mary Gilmartin, Department of Geography, National University of Ireland, Maynooth; Emeritus Professor William Nolan, Department of Geography, University College, Dublin, Ireland; Hal Craven, Skerries, Ireland; Seamus Daugherty, Draperstown, Northern Ireland; Mark Brown and Meredith Moody, Buffalo Trace Distillery, Frankfort, KY; Bill Samuels Jr., Maker's Mark Distillery, Loretto, KY; Drew Kulsveen, Willett Distillery, Bardstown, KY; Kevin Didio, Bulleit Frontier Whiskey Experience, Bulleit Distillery, Shelbyville, KY; Dwayne Kozlowski, Bulleit Distillery, Shelbyville, KY; John Pogue, Old Pogue Distillery, Maysville, KY; Amanda Craft, Phillip Miles, and Samuel Hamilton, Barton Distillery, Bardstown, KY; Kentucky Cooperage, Independent Stave Company, Lebanon, KY; Vendome Copper & Brass Works, Louisville, KY; Oscar Getz Museum of Whiskey History, Bardstown, KY; Mackenzie Morris, Saffell House, Lawrenceburg, KY; Adam Johnson, Kentucky Distiller's Association, Frankfort; Samantha Davis and Tim Tharpe, Kentucky Transportation Cabinet, Frankfort; Nicholas Laracuente, archaeologist, Kentucky Heritage Council, Frankfort; Marty Perry, Kelli Carmean, Margaret Rogers, Kim McBride, James Montgomery, Julie Riesenweber, and Natalie Wilkerson of the Kentucky Heritage Council's Kentucky Historic Preservation Review Board, Frankfort.

And I wish to express my deep gratitude to Leila Salisbury, director of the University Press of Kentucky; Anne Dean Dotson, senior acquisitions editor; and Natalie O'Neal, acquisitions assistant, for their encouragement and guidance in seeing this project and its companion volume, *Making Bourbon: A Geographical History of Distilling in Nineteenth-Century Kentucky,* through to completion.

Appendix

Weights and Measures Circa 1882

The following weights constitute a bushel:

Barley, 47 pounds
Malted barley, 34 pounds
Bluegrass seed, 14 pounds
Bran, 20 pounds
Corn—on the cob, 70 pounds
Corn—shelled, 56 pounds
Cornmeal, 50 pounds
Clover seed, 60 pounds
Rye, 56 pounds
Salt, 50 pounds
Fine salt, 55 pounds
Timothy seed, 45 pounds
Wheat, 60 pounds
Distiller's Bushel, always 56 pounds regardless of the type of grain.
Stone coal, 76 pounds (stone coal includes all mined coals).
Liquids, 42 gallons per barrel (or 160 liters, historic), 53 gallons (or 200 liters, contemporary measure)

Weights

Water, 8.34 pounds per gallon
Ethyl alcohol, 6.79 pounds per gallon at 190 proof and 60° F
Empty white oak whiskey barrel, by the contemporary American Standard Barrel (ASB) measure of 53 US gallons volume, about 110 pounds; full barrel about 520 pounds.
Barreled whiskey may evaporate through the wood at a rate of roughly 2 percent per year subject to warehouse temperature and humidity, stave wood moisture content, proof, and other factors

Source: C. E. **Bowman**, *Annual Report of the Kentucky Bureau of Agriculture, Horticulture, and Statistics* (Frankfort, KY: S. I. M. Major, Printer, 1882), 290–91, and Herman F. Willkie and Joseph A. Prochaska, *Fundamentals of Distillery Practice* (Louisville, KY: Joseph E. Seagram & Sons, 1943), 180.

Further Reading

Concepts

Balee, William, ed. *Advances in Historical Ecology.* New York: Columbia University Press, 1998.

Brown, Ralph H. *Historical Geography of the United States.* New York: Harcourt, Brace & World, 1948.

Cronon, William. *Nature's Metropolis: Chicago and the Great West.* New York: W. W. Norton, 1991.

Crumley, Carole L., ed. *Historical Ecology: Cultural Knowledge and Changing Landscapes.* Santa Fe, NM: School of American Research Press, 1994.

Earle, Carville. *Geographical Inquiry and American Historical Problems.* Stanford, CA: Stanford University Press, 1992.

Glassie, Henry. *Pattern in the Material Folk Culture of the Eastern United States.* Philadelphia: University of Pennsylvania Press, 1968.

Gomez, Basil, and John Paul Jones III, eds. *Research Methods in Geography.* West Sussex, UK: Wiley-Blackwell, 2010.

Ingold, Tim. *Making: Anthropology, Archaeology, Art and Architecture.* London: Routledge, 2013.

———. *The Perception of the Environment: Essays on Livelihood, Dwelling, and Skill.* London: Routledge, 2000.

Kragh, Helge. *An Introduction to the Historiography of Science.* Cambridge: Cambridge University Press, 1987.

Le Goff, Jacques. *History and Memory.* New York: Columbia University Press, 1992.

Lowenthal, David. *The Heritage Crusade and the Spoils of History.* Cambridge: Cambridge University Press, 1998.

———. *The Past Is a Foreign Country.* Cambridge: Cambridge University Press, 1985.

———. *The Past Is a Foreign Country Revisited.* Cambridge: Cambridge University Press, 2015.

———. *Possessed by the Past: The Heritage Crusade and the Spoils of History.* New York: Free Press, 1996.

Lynes, Russell. *The Taste-Makers.* New York: Harper & Brothers, 1955.

Meinig, D. W. *The Shaping of America: A Geographical Perspective on 500 Years of History.* Vol. 2, *Continental America 1800–1867.* New Haven, CT: Yale University Press, 1993.

Miller, Daniel, ed. *The Power of Making.* London: V & A Publishing, 2011.

Munslow, Alun. *Narrative and History.* New York: Palgrave Macmillan, 2007.

Rickman, H. P., ed. *Pattern & Meaning in History: Wilhelm Dilthey, Thoughts on History & Society.* New York: Harper & Row, 1961.

Schatzki, Theodore R. *The Site of the Social: A Philosophical Account of the Constitution of Social Life and Change.* University Park: Pennsylvania State University Press, 2002.

Schein, Richard H. "A Conceptual Framework for Interpreting an American Scene." *Annals of the Association of American Geographers* 87, no. 4 (1997): 660–80.

Landscape

Hart, John Fraser. *The Rural Landscape.* Baltimore: Johns Hopkins University Press, 1998.

Hoskins, W. G. *The Making of the English Landscape.* London: Hodder & Stoughton, 1955.

Ingold, Tim. "The Temporality of the Landscape." *World Archaeology* 25, no. 2 (1993): 152–74.

Jackson, John Brinckerhoff. *Discovering the Vernacular Landscape.* New Haven, CT: Yale University Press, 1984.

———. *Landscape in Sight: Looking for America.* Edited by Helen Lefkowitz Horowitz. New Haven, CT: Yale University Press, 1997.

———. *A Sense of Place, a Sense of Time.* New Haven, CT: Yale University Press, 1994.

Lewis, Peirce. "The Future of the Past: Our Clouded Vision of Historic Preservation." *Pioneer America* 7, no. 2 (1975): 1–20.

Meinig, D. W., ed. *The Interpretation of Ordinary Landscapes: Geographical Essays.* New York: Oxford University Press, 1979.

Stilgoe, John R. *Landscape and Images.* Charlottesville: University of Virginia Press, 2005.

Upton, Dell. *Another City: Urban Life and Urban Spaces in the New American Republic.* New Haven, CT: Yale University Press, 2008.

Wilson, Chris, and Paul Groth, eds. *Everyday America: Cultural Landscape Studies after J. B. Jackson.* Berkeley: University of California Press, 2003.

Zube, Ervin H., ed. *Landscapes: Selected Writings of J. B. Jackson.* Amherst: University of Massachusetts Press, 1970.

Environment

Anderson, Roger C., James S. Fralish, and Jerry M. Baskin. *Savannas, Barrens, and Rock Outcrop Plant Communities of North America.* New York: Cambridge University Press, 1999.

Bailey, Robert G. *Ecosystem Geography: From Ecoregions to Sites.* 2d ed. New York: Springer Science, 2009.

Bell, Edwin A., Robert W. Kellogg, and Willis K. Kulp. *Progress Report on the Ground-Water Resources of the Louisville Area Kentucky, 1949–55.* US Geological Survey Water Supply Paper 1579. Washington, DC: GPO, 1963.

Black, Douglas F. B., Earle R. Cressman, and William C. MacQuown Jr. *The Lexington Limestone (Middle Ordovician) of Central Kentucky.* US Geological Survey Bulletin 1224-C. Washington, DC: GPO, 1965.

Matson, George C. *Water Resources of the Blue Grass Region of Kentucky.* US Geological Survey Water Supply Paper 233. Washington, DC: GPO, 1909.

Mugerauer, Robert. *Interpreting Environments: Tradition, Deconstruction, Hermeneutics.* Austin: University of Texas Press, 1995.

O'Dell, Gary. "Water Supply and the Early Development of Lexington, Kentucky." *Filson Club History Quarterly* 67, no. 4 (1993): 431–61.

Palmquist, W. N., and F. R. Hall. *Public and Industrial Water Supplies of the Blue Grass Region Kentucky.* US Geological Survey Circular 299. Washington, DC: GPO, 1953.

Scanlon, B. R. "Physical Controls on Hydrochemical Variability in the Inner Bluegrass Karst Region of Central Kentucky." *Ground Water* 27, no. 5 (1989): 639–46.

Scanlon, B. R., and J. Thrailkill. "Chemical Similarities among Physically Distinct Spring Types in a Karst Terrain." *Journal of Hydrology* 89 (1987): 259–79.

Stabler, Herman. *Prevention of Stream Pollution by Distillery Refuse.* US Geological Survey Water Supply and Irrigation Paper 179. Washington, DC: GPO, 1906.

Walker, Eugene H. *The Deep Channel and Alluvial Deposits of the Ohio Valley in Kentucky.* US Geological Survey Water Supply Paper 1411. Washington, DC: GPO, 1957.

Agriculture

Ardrey, P. L. *American Agricultural Implements.* Chicago: P. L. Ardrey, 1894.

Beatty, Adam. *Southern Agriculture.* New York: C. M. Saxon, 1843.

Brooks, Eugene C. *The Story of Corn and the Westward Migration.* New York: Rand McNally, 1916.

Danhof, Clarence H. *Change in Agriculture: The Northern United States, 1820–1870.* Cambridge, MA: Harvard University Press, 1969.

Henlein, Paul C. *Cattle Kingdom in the Ohio Valley, 1783–1860.* Lexington: University of Kentucky Press, 1959.

Hudson, John C. *Making the Corn Belt: A Geographical History of Middle-Western Agriculture.* Bloomington: Indiana University Press, 1994.

Hutchinson, William T. *Cyrus Hall McCormick: Seed-Time, 1809–1856.* New York: Century, 1930.

———. *Cyrus Hall McCormick: Harvest, 1856–1884.* New York: D. Appleton-Century, 1935.

Mangelsdorf, Paul C. *Corn: Its Origin, Evolution and Improvement.* Cambridge, MA: Belknap Press, 1974.

Olmstead, Alan L., and Paul W. Rhode. *Arresting Contagion: Science, Policy, and Conflicts over Animal Disease Control.* Cambridge, MA: Harvard University Press, 2015.

Wallace, Henry A., and William L. Brown. *Corn and Its Early Fathers.* East Lansing: Michigan State University Press, 1956.

Weaver, John C. "United States Malting Barley Production." *Annals of the Association of American Geographers* 34, no. 2 (1944): 97–131.

Culture and Economy

Bernstein, Peter L. *Against the Gods: The Remarkable Story of Risk.* New York: John Wiley, 1996.

Cromley, Elizabeth C., and Carter L. Hudgins, eds. *Gender, Class, and Shelter: Perspectives in Vernacular Architecture V.* Knoxville: University of Tennessee Press, 1995.

Hindle, Brooke, ed. *Material Culture of the Wooden Age.* Tarrytown, NY: Sleepy Hollow Press, 1981.

Hoover, Edgar M. *The Location of Economic Activity.* New York: McGraw Hill, 1948.

Hunter, Louis C. *Studies in the Economic History of the Ohio Valley.* New York: DaCapo Press, 1973.

Jones, Geoffrey, and Nicholas J. Morgan, eds. *Adding Value: Brands and Marketing in Food and Drink.* New York: Routledge, 1994.

Knight, Frank H. *Risk, Uncertainty and Profit.* Boston: Houghton Mifflin, 1921. Reprint, Mansfield Centre, CT: Martino Publishing, 2014.

Lucas, Marion B. *A History of Blacks in Kentucky: From Slavery to Segregation, 1760–1891.* 2d ed. Frankfort: Kentucky Historical Society, 2003.

Martin, Jonathan D. *Divided Mastery: Slave Hiring in the American South.* Cambridge, MA: Harvard University Press, 2004.

McCracken, Grant. *Culture & Consumption: New Approaches to the Symbolic Character of Consumer Goods and Activities.* Bloomington: Indiana University Press, 1988.

McGovern, Charles F. *Sold American: Consumption and Citizenship, 1890–1945.* Chapel Hill: University of North Carolina Press, 2006.

Schein, Richard H. "Cultural Landscapes." In *Research Methods in Geography,* ed. Basil Gomez and John Paul Jones III, 222–39. West Sussex, UK: Wiley-Blackwell, 2010.

Schlereth, Thomas J. *Cultural History and Material Culture: Everyday Life, Landscapes, Museums.* Charlottesville: University Press of Virginia, 1990.

———. *Victorian America: Transformations in Everyday Life, 1876–1915.* New York: HarperCollins, 1991.

Smith, John D., and Thomas H. Appleton Jr., eds. *A Mythic Land Apart: Reassessing Southerners and Their History.* Westport, CT: Greenwood Press, 1997.

Spooner, Walter W., ed. *The Political Prohibitionist for 1888: A Handbook for the Aggressive Temperance People of the United States.* New York: Funk & Wagnalls, 1888.

Starobin, Robert S. *Industrial Slavery in the Old South.* New York: Oxford University Press, 1970.

Tallant, Harold D. *Evil Necessity: Slavery and Political Culture in Antebellum Kentucky.* Lexington: University Press of Kentucky, 2003.

Zaborney, John J. *Slaves for Hire: Renting Enslaved Laborers in Antebellum Virginia.* Baton Rouge: Louisiana State University Press, 2012.

Distilling

Ambrose, William M. *Bottled in Bond under U.S. Government Supervision.* Lexington, KY: William M. Ambrose, 2007.

Barnard, Alfred. *The Whiskey Distilleries of the United Kingdom.* 1887. Reprint, Edinburgh: Birlinn, 2008.

Boucherie, Anthony. *The Art of Making Whiskey.* Lexington, KY: Worsley & Smith, 1819.

Buxton, Ian, and Paul S. Hughes. *The Science and Commerce of Whiskey.* Cambridge: Royal Society of Chemistry, 2014.

Campbell, Sally Van Winkle. *But Always Fine Bourbon.* Frankfort, KY: Old Rip Van Winkle Distillery, 1999.

Carlton, Carla Harris. *Barrel Strength Bourbon: The Explosive Growth of America's Whiskey.* Birmingham, AL: Clerisy Press, 2017.

Carson, Gerald. *The Social History of Bourbon.* Lexington: University Press of Kentucky, 1963.

Cecil, Sam K. *Bourbon: The Evolution of Kentucky Whiskey.* New York: Turner Publishing, 2010.

Clay, Karen, and Werner Troesken. "Strategic Behavior in Whiskey Distilling, 1887–1895." *Journal of Economic History* 62, no. 1 (2002): 999–1023.

Cowdery, Charles K. *Bourbon Straight: The Uncut and Unfiltered Story of American Whiskey.* Chicago: Made and Bottled in Kentucky, 2004.

Crowgey, Henry G. *Kentucky Bourbon: The Early Years of Whiskeymaking.* Lexington: University Press of Kentucky, 1971.

Fleischman, Joseph. *The Art of Blending and Compounding Liquors and Wines.* New York: Dick & Fitzgerald, 1885.

Fosdick, Raymond B., and Albert L. Scott. *Toward Liquor Control.* New York: Harper & Brothers, 1933.

Getz, Oscar. *Whiskey: An American Pictorial History.* New York: David McKay, 1978.

Hall, Harrison. *The Distiller.* Philadelphia: J. Bioren, 1818. 2d rev. ed., Hayward, CA: White Mule Press, 2015.

Harrison, Barry, Olivier Fagnen, Frances Jack, and James Brosnan. "The Impact of Copper in Different Parts of Malt Whisky Pot Stills on New Make Spirit Composition and Aroma." *Journal of the Institute of Brewing* 117, no. 1 (2011): 106–12.

Hibbs, Dixie. *Before Prohibition: Distilleries in Nelson County, Kentucky, 1880–1920.* New Hope, KY: St. Martin de Porres Print Shop, 2012.

Krafft, Michael. *The American Distiller or, the Theory and Practice of Distilling.* Philadelphia: Archibald Bariram, 1804. Reprint, Gale, Sabin Americana Print Editions, n.d.

Minnick, Fred. *Bourbon: The Rise, Fall, and Rebirth of an American Whiskey.* Minneapolis, MN: Voyageur Press, 2016.

Pacult, F. Paul. *American Still Life: The Jim Beam Story and the Making of the World's #1 Bourbon.* Hoboken, NJ: John Wiley & Sons, 2003.

Pearce, John Ed. *Nothing Better in the Market.* Louisville, KY: Brown-Forman Distillers, 1970.

Purcell, Aaron D. "Bourbon to Bullets: Louisville's Distilling Industry during World War II." *Register of the Kentucky Historical Society* 96, no. 2 (1998): 61–87.

Reaich, Donna. "The Influence of Copper on Malt Whisky Character." In *Proceedings of the Fifth Aviemore Conference on Malting, Brewing and Distilling,* Aviemore, Inverness-Shire, Scotland, May 25–28, 1998, 141–52.

Regan, Gary, and Mardee Haidin Regan. *The Book of Bourbon and Other Fine American Whiskeys.* Shelburne, VT: Chapters Publishing, 1995.

Russell, Inge, and Graham Stewart. *Whiskey: Technology, Production and Marketing.* 2d ed. Oxford: Academic Press, 2014.

Samuels, Bill, Jr. *My Autobiography.* Louisville, KY: Saber Publishing–Butler Books, 2009.

Taylor, F. Sherwood. "The Evolution of the Still." *Annals of Science* 5, no. 3 (1945): 185–202.

Taylor, Richard. *The Great Crossing: A Historic Journey to Buffalo Trace Distillery.* Frankfort, KY: Buffalo Trace Distillery, 2002.

Veach, Michael R. *Kentucky Bourbon Whiskey: An American Heritage.* Lexington: University Press of Kentucky, 2013.

Willkie, Herman F., and Joseph A. Prochaska. *Fundamentals of Distillery Practice.* Louisville, KY: Joseph E. Seagram & Sons, 1943.

Work, Henry H. *Wood, Whiskey, and Wine: A History of Barrels.* London: Reaktion Books, 2014.

Young, Al. *Four Roses: The Return of a Whiskey Legend.* Louisville, KY: Butler Books, 2010.

Zoeller, Chester. *Bourbon in Kentucky: A History of Distilleries in Kentucky.* 2d ed. Louisville, KY: Butler Books, 2010.

———. *Kentucky Bourbon Barons: Legendary Distillers from the Golden Age of Whiskey Making.* Louisville, KY: Butler Books, 2014.

Industry and Engineering

Alderman, Neil. "Industrial Innovation Diffusion: The Extent of Use and Disuse of Process Technologies in Engineering." *Area* 30, no. 2 (1998): 107–16.

Bain, Joe S. *Industrial Organization.* New York: John Wiley & Sons, 1959.

Barnett, George E. *Chapters on Machinery and Labor.* Cambridge, MA: Harvard University Press, 1926.

Bathe, Greville, and Dorothy Bathe. *Oliver Evans: A Chronicle of Early American Engineering.* Philadelphia: Historical Society of Pennsylvania, 1935.

Biggs, Lindy. *The Rational Factory: Architecture, Technology, and Work in America's Age of Mass Production.* Baltimore: Johns Hopkins University Press, 1996.

Bishop, J. Leander. *A History of American Manufactures from 1608 to 1860.* Vol. 1. London: Edward Young, 1866.

Bradley, Betsy Hunter. *The Works: The Industrial Architecture of the United States.* New York: Oxford University Press, 1999.

Clark, Victor S. *History of Manufactures in the United States 1607–1860.* Washington, DC: Carnegie Institution, 1916.

Cope, Kenneth L. *American Cooperage Machinery and Tools.* Mendham, NJ: Astragal Press, 2003.

Cowan, Ruth Schwartz. *A Social History of American Technology.* New York: Oxford University Press, 1997.

Fuller, John. *Art of Coppersmithing: A Practical Treatise on Working Sheet Copper into All Forms.* New York: David Williams, 1894. Reprint, Mendham, NJ: Astragal Press, 1993.

George, Peter. *The Emergence of Industrial America: Strategic Factors in American Economic Growth since 1870.* Albany: State University of New York Press, 1882.

Hindle, Brooke, and Steven Lubar. *Engines of Change: The American Industrial Revolution, 1790–1860.* Washington, DC: Smithsonian Institution Press, 1986.

Hunter, Louis C. *A History of Industrial Power in the United States, 1780–1930.* Vol. 1, *Waterpower in the Century of the Steam Engine.* Charlottesville: University Press of Virginia, 1979.

———. *A History of Industrial Power in America, 1780–1930.* Vol. 2, *Steam Power.* Charlottesville: University Press of Virginia, 1985.

Kauffman, Henry J. *American Copper & Brass.* Camden, NJ: Thomas Nelson & Sons, 1968.

Kilby, Kenneth. *The Cooper and His Trade.* Fresno, CA: Linden Publishing, 1971.

———. *Coopers and Coopering.* Princes Risborough, UK: Shire Publications, 2004.

Meigh, Edward. *The Story of the Glass Bottle.* Stoke-on-Trent, UK: C. E. Ramsden, 1972.

Melosi, Martin. *The Sanitary City: Urban Infrastructure in America from Colonial Times to the Present.* Baltimore: Johns Hopkins University Press, 2000.

Novak, William J. *The People's Welfare: Law & Regulation in Nineteenth-Century America.* Chapel Hill: University of North Carolina Press, 1996.

Nye, David E. *American Technological Sublime.* Cambridge, MA: MIT Press, 1996.

———. *Narratives and Spaces: Technology and the Construction of American Culture.* New York: Columbia University Press, 1997.

Pursell, Carroll W., Jr. *Early Stationary Steam Engines in America: A Study in the Migration of a Technology.* Washington, DC: Smithsonian Institution Press, 1969.

Reynolds, Terry S. *Stronger than a Hundred Men: A History of the Vertical Water Wheel.* Baltimore: Johns Hopkins University Press, 1983.

Richards, James M. *The Functional Tradition in Early Industrial Buildings.* London: Architectural Press, 1958.

Rogers, Everett M. *Diffusion of Innovations.* 5th ed. New York: Free Press, 2003.

Rogers, Everett M., and F. Floyd Shoemaker. *Communication of Innovations.* 2d ed. New York: Free Press, 1971.

Rogin, Leo. *The Introduction of Farm Machinery in Its Relation to the Productivity of Labor in the Agriculture of the United States during the Nineteenth Century.* Berkeley: University of California Press, 1931.

Rosenberg, Nathan. *Exploring the Black Box: Technology, Economics, and History.* Cambridge: Cambridge University Press, 1994.

Scoville, Warren C. *Revolution in Glassmaking: Entrepreneurship and Technological Change in the American Industry, 1880–1920.* Cambridge, MA: Harvard University Press, 1948.

Skrabec, Quentin R. *Michael Owens and the Glass Industry.* Gretna, LA: Pelican Publishing, 2007.

Strassman, W. Paul. *Risk and Technological Innovation: American Manufacturing Methods in the Nineteenth Century.* Ithaca, NY: Cornell University Press, 1959.

Wagner, Joseph B. *Cooperage: A Treatise on Modern Shop Practice and Methods, from the Tree to the Finished Article.* Yonkers, NY: J. B. Wagner, 1910.

Wermiel, Sara E. *The Fireproof Building: Technology and Public Safety in the Nineteenth-Century American City.* Baltimore: Johns Hopkins University Press, 2000.

Transportation

Borchert, John R. "American Metropolitan Evolution." *Geographical Review* 57, no. 3 (1967): 301–32.

Hunter, Louis C. *Steamboats on the Western Rivers: An Economic and Technological History.* New York: Dover Publications, 1949.

Klein, Maury. *History of the Louisville & Nashville Railroad.* New York: Macmillan, 1972. Reprint, Lexington: University Press of Kentucky, 2003.

MacGill, Caroline E. *History of Transportation in the United States before 1860.* Washington, DC: Carnegie Institution, 1917.

Raitz, Karl, and Nancy O'Malley. *Kentucky's Frontier Highway: Historical Landscapes along the Maysville Road.* Lexington: University Press of Kentucky, 2012.

———. "Local-Scale Turnpike Roads in Nineteenth-Century Kentucky." *Journal of Historical Geography* 33, no. 1 (2007): 1–23.

———. "The Nineteenth-Century Evolution of Local-Scale Roads in Kentucky's Bluegrass." *Geographical Review* 94, no. 4 (2004): 415–39.

Taylor, George Rogers. *The Transportation Revolution, 1815–1860.* New York: Harper & Row, 1951.

Verhoeff, Mary. *The Kentucky River Navigation.* Filson Club Publication 28. Louisville, KY: John P. Morton, 1917.

White, John H., Jr. *The American Railroad Freight Car: From the Wood-Car Era to the Coming of Steel.* Baltimore: Johns Hopkins University Press, 1993.

Heritage, Marketing, and Tourism

Laird, Pamela W. *Advertising Progress: American Business and the Rise of Consumer Marketing.* Baltimore: Johns Hopkins University Press, 1998.

Levy, Sidney J. *The Theory of the Brand.* Wilmette, IL: DecaBooks, 2016.

MacCannell, Dean. *Empty Meeting Grounds: The Tourist Papers.* London: Routledge, 1992.

———. *The Tourist: A New Theory of the Leisure Class.* Berkeley: University of California Press, 2013.

Pike, Andy. "Geographies of Brands and Branding." *Progress in Human Geography* 33, no. 5 (2009): 619–45.

Urry, John, and Jonas Larsen. *The Tourist Gaze 3.0.* Los Angeles: Sage, 2011.

Yale, Pat. *From Tourist Attractions to Heritage Tourism.* 3d ed. Huntingdon, UK: ELM Publications, 2004.

Manuscript Collections

Cleaveland, Emma Jane, Journal, 1820–1932. Lyne-Smith Family Papers (Woodford County, KY). 1997 MS387. Special Collections, University of Kentucky.

Coyte, H. W. "History of Kentucky Distilleries," 1940–1987. Manuscript. University Archives and Records Center, University of Louisville. KDL-help@KDL.KYVL.org.

Daviess County Distilling Company Records, 1850–1940. Medley, Meschendorf, Owensboro. Microfilm, 1F67M-621. Special Collections, University of Kentucky.

Elkhorn Distillery Records (Scott County, KY), 1868–1872. 1997 MS419. Special Collections, University of Kentucky.

Jones, John W., Papers (Bourbon County, KY), 1857–1896, 1857–1889 (bulk dates). 75M26. Special Collections, University of Kentucky.

Loder, Lewis. *The Loder Diary, 1857–1903.* Transcribed by William Conrad. Florence, KY: Boone County Schools, 1985–1988. Microfilm and http://bcpl.org/cbc/doku.php/lewis_loder.

McKenna, Marcella, Distillery Collection (Nelson County, KY), 1824–1945, 1858–1942 (bulk dates). 1 F65M-593. Special Collections, University of Kentucky.

McKenna, Marcella, Distillery Papers. Oscar Getz Bourbon Museum, Bardstown, KY.

Moylan, John. Ledger A, Lexington (Fayette County, KY), 1792. MS042. Special Collections, University of Kentucky.

Oots, Andrew J. Cooper Shop Records (Fayette County, KY), 1880–1926, 1880–1910 (bulk dates). 1 FM-49. Special Collections, University of Kentucky.

Ripy Family Papers (Anderson County, KY), 1888–1963 (bulk dates). 1 F66M-725. Special Collections, University of Kentucky.

Taylor-Hay Family Papers (Franklin County, KY), 1783–1991. MssAT238d. Filson Historical Society, Louisville, KY.

Notes

Introduction

1. US Department of the Treasury, Alcohol and Tobacco Tax and Trade Bureau Regulations, Title 27, Alcohol, Tobacco Products and Firearms; Part 5, Labeling and Advertising of Distilled Spirits; Subpart C, Standards of Identity; Section 5.22, Standards of Identity for Distilled Spirits, pp. 48–52, https://www.gpo.gov/fdsys/pkg/CFR-2011-title27-vol1/pdf/CFR-2011-title27-vol1-chapI.pdf.

1. Kentucky's Distilling Heritage

1. Esther Kellner, *Moonshine: Its History and Folklore* (New York: Weathervane Books, 1971), 15–17.

2. Malachy Magee, *1000 Years of Irish Whiskey* (Dublin, Ireland: O'Brien Press, 1980), 7; Alfred Barnard, *The Whiskey Distilleries of the United Kingdom* (Edinburgh: Harper's Weekly Gazette, 1887), 3.

3. Thomas P. Slaughter, *The Whiskey Rebellion: Frontier Epilogue to the American Revolution* (New York: Oxford University Press, 1986), 223–24.

4. Henry G. Crowgey, *Kentucky Bourbon: The Early Years of Whiskey Making* (Lexington: University Press of Kentucky, 2008), 28–29.

5. "James Crow, Whiskey Maker," *Sun* 65, no. 5 (1897): 5.

6. Gerald Carson, *The Social History of Bourbon* (Lexington: University of Kentucky Press, 1963), 47.

7. Howard T. Walden, *Native Inheritance: The Story of Corn in America* (New York: Harper & Row, 1966), 135.

8. US Congress, House, *The Reports of Committees: H.R. 4165,* 50th Cong., 2d sess., 1888–1889, 12.

9. The American alcohol scale ranges from 0 to 200. A spirit containing 50 percent alcohol is 100 proof.

10. The popular explanation for the change in barrel size is that the 53-gallon barrel maximized the use of available space in warehouse storage racks; it was the maximum size that would fit in the commonly used Stitzel-style rack system. But it is probably not a coincidence that 53 gallons equals 200 liters, the standard barrel size used extensively by European distillers and wine makers.

11. US Department of the Treasury, Alcohol and Tobacco Tax and Trade Bureau Regulations, Title 27, Alcohol, Tobacco Products and Firearms; Part 5—Labeling and Advertising of Distilled Spirits; Subpart C—Standards of Identity; Section 5.22, Standards of Identity for Distilled Spirits, pp. 48–52, https://www.gpo.gov/fdsys/pkg/CFR-2011-title27-vol1/pdf/CFR-2011-title27-vol1-chapI.pdf.

12. Nineteenth-century Kentucky distillers also made whiskeys with rye, wheat, barley, and malting barley as the primary grain. These whiskeys were not bourbons but had distinctive tastes and aromas that some consumers preferred.

13. Barry Kornstein and Jay Luckett, "The Economic and Fiscal Impacts of the Distilling Industry in Kentucky" (Urban Studies Institute, University of Louisville, 2014), 34.

14. John W. Alexander, *Economic Geography* (Englewood Cliffs, NJ: Prentice Hall, 1963), 309–10.

15. US Congress, *Reports of Committees*, 55.

16. Thomas H. Appleton Jr., "'Moral Suasion Has Had Its Day': From Temperance to Prohibition in Antebellum Kentucky," in *A Mythic Land Apart: Reassessing Southerners and Their History*, ed. John D. Smith and Thomas H. Appleton Jr. (Westport, CT: Greenwood Press, 1997), 19–42.

17. Lewis Loder, *The Loder Diary, 1857–1903*, transcribed by William Conrad (Florence, KY: Boone County Schools, 1985–1988), 82.

18. Alexander, *Economic Geography*, 309–10; Harrison Hall, *The Distiller*, 2d rev. ed. (1818; reprint, Hayward, CA: White Mule Press, 2015), 35.

19. Gerald Carson, *The Social History of Bourbon* (Lexington: University of Kentucky Press, 1963), 24–28.

20. Victor S. Clark, *History of Manufactures in the United States, 1607–1860* (Washington, DC: Carnegie Institution, 1916), 480.

21. John Moylan, Ledger A, Lexington, 1792, 2011MS042, Special Collections, University of Kentucky Library, Lexington, 12, 23, 47, 49, 116, 124, 135, 216.

22. Warren R. Hofstra, *The Planting of New Virginia: Settlement and Landscape in the Shenandoah Valley* (Baltimore: Johns Hopkins University Press, 2004), 224; Priscilla Ann Evans, "Merchant Gristmills and Communities, 1820–1880: An Economic Relationship," *Missouri Historical Review* 68, no. 3 (1974): 317–26.

23. Hofstra, *Planting of New Virginia*, 156.

24. Clark, *History of Manufactures*, 480. Kentucky's population in 1810 was 406,571, or 203 people per distillery. Distilleries produced 2,220,773 gallons of whiskey in 1810, or 5.4 gallons per capita. By 1840, the population had increased to 779,828, but the number of distilleries had declined to yield a ratio of 877 people per distillery.

25. Brian Page and Richard Walker, "From Settlement to Fordism: The Agro-Industrial Revolution in the American Midwest," *Economic Geography* 67, no. 4 (1991): 291.

26. Clarence H. Danhof, "Agriculture," in *The Growth of the American Economy*, ed. Harold F. Williamson (New York: Prentice-Hall, 1951), 182.

27. Ibid., 133–53.

28. Ibid., 151.

29. Page and Walker, "From Settlement to Fordism," 293.

30. Arthur G. Peterson, "Flour and Grist Milling in Virginia: A Brief History," *Virginia Magazine of History and Biography* 43, no. 2 (1935): 103.

31. The county boundaries depicted in the maps for 1810 changed as the legislature created additional counties in subsequent decades. Although census marshals tabulated distilleries, locational information was scarce.

32. Loder, *Loder Diary*, 82.

33. Hall, *Distiller*, 23.

34. Page and Walker, "From Settlement to Fordism," 294.

35. Ibid., 294–96.

36. Leo Rogin, *The Introduction of Farm Machinery in Its Relation to the Productivity of Labor in the Agriculture of the United States during the Nineteenth Century* (Berkeley: University of California Press, 1931), 83.

37. William T. Hutchinson, *Cyrus Hall McCormick: Seed-Time, 1809–1856* (New York: Century Company, 1930), 351.

38. George H. Cook and John C. Smock, *Report on the Clay Deposits of Woodbridge, South Amboy, and Other Places in New Jersey, Together with Their Uses for Fire Brick, Pottery, etc.* (Trenton: Geological Survey

of New Jersey, 1878); R. E. Lamborn, C. R. Austin, and Downs Schaaf, *Shales and Surface Clays of Ohio,* Bulletin 39 (Columbus: Ohio Geological Survey, 1938).

2. Distilling's Backstory

1. Carville Earle, *Geographical Inquiry and American Historical Problems* (Stanford, CA: Stanford University Press, 1992), 5–7.

2. William Cronon, "A Place for Stories: Nature, History, and Narrative," *Journal of American History* 78, no. 4 (1992): 1349.

3. C. E. Bowman, *Annual Report of the Kentucky Bureau of Agriculture, Horticulture, and Statistics, 1881,* Legislative Document no. 7 (Frankfort, KY: S. I. M. Major, 1881), 14 (emphasis in original).

4. Eugene H. Walker, *The Deep Channel and Alluvial Deposits of the Ohio Valley in Kentucky,* US Geological Survey Water Supply Paper 1411 (Washington, DC: GPO, 1957), 5–14.

5. W. N. Palmquist and F. R. Hall, *Public and Industrial Water Supplies of the Blue Grass Region Kentucky,* US Geological Survey Circular 299 (Washington, DC: US Geological Survey, 1953), 13.

6. "Strike Fine Spring on Elkhorn Creek," *Frankfort Weekly News and Roundabout* 31, no. 43 (1908): 1.

7. John H. Procter, "Map of Kentucky" (Frankfort: Kentucky Geological Survey, 1881).

8. E. H. Taylor Jr., *Description of the O.F.C., Carlisle, and J. S. Taylor Distilleries* (Frankfort, KY: E. H. Taylor Jr., [1886]), 20. See also advertising card, "The Whiskey," Taylor-Hay Family Papers (Franklin County, KY), 1783–1991, folder 73, MssAT238d, Filson Historical Society, Louisville, KY.

9. Taylor, *Description of the O.F.C., Carlisle, and J. S. Taylor Distilleries,* 9. The Procter map labels the Ordovician-age strata as Lower Silurian. The massive and dense Tyrone limestone does indeed outcrop near the bottom of the Kentucky River gorge from Frankfort upstream to southern Fayette County. The Tyrone, also known as Birdseye limestone, is some sixty feet thick, exceedingly dense, and overlain by multiple members of the thin-bedded Lexington limestone formation. Groundwater at Frankfort likely moved through several of these Lexington formations, but percolation through the Tyrone would have been a protracted process. See A. M. Miller, *Geology of Franklin County,* Kentucky Geological Survey Reports, 4th series, vol. 2, pt. 3 (Frankfort: Kentucky Geological Survey, 1914).

10. "Whisky Trade," *Louisville Courier-Journal,* n.s., 38, no. 148 (1868): 1. It is possible that Van Hook meant that he preferred to use high-sulfur water only for cleaning purposes, but that interpretation seems implausible because it implies the availability of "pure" water and sulfur water at the same distilling site.

11. Robert Peter, *Lower Blue Lick Spring: The Quantitative Chemical Analysis of the Water in the Lower Blue Lick Spring, in Nicholas County, Kentucky* (n.p., 1850), 2–3.

12. Walker, *Deep Channel and Alluvial Deposits of the Ohio Valley.*

13. Chester Zoeller, *Bourbon in Kentucky: A History of Distilleries in Kentucky,* 2d ed. (Louisville, KY: Butler Books, 2010), 59–60.

14. Edward Orton, *Report of the Occurrence of Petroleum, Natural Gas and Asphalt Rock in Western Kentucky: Based on Examinations Made in 1888 and 1889,* Kentucky Geological Survey and State Museum report (Frankfort, KY: E. Polk Johnson, 1891), 194.

15. Herman Stabler, *Prevention of Stream Pollution by Distillery Refuse,* US Geological Survey Water Supply and Irrigation Paper 179 (Washington, DC: GPO, 1906), 6.

16. M. I. Rorabaugh, F. F. Schrader, and L. B. Laird, *Water Resources of the Louisville Area, Kentucky and Indiana,* US Geological Survey Circular 276 (Washington, DC: GPO, 1953), 43.

17. US Department of Health, Education, and Welfare, Public Health Service, *Public Health Service Drinking Water Standards,* Publication no. 956 (Washington, DC: GPO, 1962), 42–43.

18. Ralph C. Heath, *Basic Ground-Water Hydrology*, US Geological Survey Water Supply Paper 2220, rev. (Washington, DC: GPO, 2004), 64–67.

19. Palmquist and Hall, *Public and Industrial Water Supplies of the Blue Grass Region;* B. R. Scanlon, and J. Thrailkill, "Chemical Similarities among Physically Distinct Spring Types in a Karst Terrain," *Journal of Hydrology* 89, no. 3–4 (1987): 259–79; Alan E. Fryer, "Springs and the Origin of Bourbon," *Ground Water* 47, no. 4 (2009): 605–10.

20. Palmquist and Hall, *Public and Industrial Water Supplies of the Blue Grass Region,* 41.

21. Ibid., 48.

22. Ibid., 52.

23. Ibid., 74.

24. Edwin A. Bell, Robert W. Kellogg, and Willis K. Kulp, *Progress Report on the Ground-Water Resources of the Louisville Area Kentucky, 1949–55,* US Geological Survey Water Supply Paper 1579 (Washington, DC: GPO, 1963), 45.

25. Ibid., 37–39; cf. Michael R. Veach, *Kentucky Bourbon Whiskey: An American Heritage* (Lexington: University Press of Kentucky, 2013), 19.

26. Martin Mayer, "The Volatile Business," *Esquire* 52, no. 2 (1959): 104.

27. Ibid.

28. Tim Ingold, "Toward an Ecology of Materials," *Annual Review of Anthropology* 41 (2012): 433–35.

29. "The Drought," *Franklin Farmer* 3, no. 3 (1839): 1.

30. Edgar M. Hoover, *The Location of Economic Activity* (New York: McGraw Hill, 1948), 83–84.

31. Carville Earle, "A Staple Interpretation of Slavery and Free Labor," *Geographical Review* 68, no. 1 (1978): 51–65.

32. Carville Earle and Ronald Hoffman, "The Foundation of the Modern Economy: Agriculture and the Costs of Labor in the United States and England, 1800–1860," *American Historical Review* 85, no. 5 (1980): 1056–60.

33. Peter Mathias, "Agriculture and the Brewing and Distilling Industries in the Eighteenth Century," *Economic History Review,* n.s., 5, no. 2 (1952): 249.

34. Harry G. Enoch, *Colonel John Holder, Boonesborough Defender & Kentucky Entrepreneur* (Morley, MO: Acclaim Press, 2009), 189–211.

35. Harry G. Enoch, *Grimes Mill: Kentucky Landmark on Boone Creek, Fayette County* (Bowie, MD: Heritage Books, 2002), 11–14.

36. John R. Robertson, *Petitions of the Early Inhabitants of Kentucky to the General Assembly of Virginia, 1769–1792* (Louisville, KY: John P. Morton, 1914), 144–45 (petition no. 77).

37. Nancy O'Malley, "Ruddle's Mills, Bourbon County, Kentucky: Early Industry in the Kentucky Bluegrass," *Mill Stone* 5, no. 2 (2006): 21–29. The person's name (Ruddell) and the place (Ruddles) are spelled differently.

38. Harry G. Enoch and Nancy O'Malley, "Early Mills of Bourbon County," *Mill Stone* 4, no. 1 (2005): 25–38.

39. *Franklin Farmer* 3, no. 5 (1839): 40.

40. *Franklin Farmer* 2, no. 43 (1839): 343.

41. US Census Bureau, 1850 Census, table IX, 623.

42. Tim Ingold, *The Perception of the Environment: Essays on Livelihood, Dwelling, and Skill* (London: Routledge, 2000), 320.

43. Frank Cox, *Soil Survey of Daviess and Hancock Counties, Kentucky,* USDA Soil Conservation Service and Kentucky Agricultural Experiment Station survey (Washington, DC: GPO, 1974); Steven J. Blan-

ford, Patrick S. Aldridge, and Robert A. Eigel, *Soil Survey of Jefferson County, Kentucky,* USDA Soil Conservation Service and Kentucky Agricultural Experiment Station survey (Washington, DC: GPO, 1991).

44. Karl Raitz and Nancy O'Malley, "An Index of Soil Production Potential as Applied to Historical Agricultural Adaptation: A Kentucky Example," *Historical Methods* 18, no. 5 (1985): 137.

45. Cf. Adam Beatty, *Southern Agriculture* (New York: C. M. Saxon, 1843), 201–40.

46. Alfred J. Richardson, Rudy Forsythe, and Hubert B. Odor, *Soil Survey of Bourbon and Nicholas Counties, Kentucky,* USDA Soil Conservation Service survey (Washington, DC: GPO, 1982).

47. Douglas F. B. Black, Earle R. Cressman, and William C. MacQuown Jr., *The Lexington Limestone (Middle Ordovician) of Central Kentucky,* US Geological Survey Bulletin 1224-C (Washington, DC: GPO, 1965).

48. Herman P. McDonald, David Keltner, Pamela Wood, Bruce A. Waters, and Orville J. Whitaker, *Soil Survey of Anderson and Franklin Counties, Kentucky,* USDA Soil Conservation Service survey (Washington, DC: GPO, 1985); Herman P. McDonald, Raymond P. Sims, and Dan Isgrig, *Soil Survey of Jessamine and Woodford Counties, Kentucky,* USDA Soil Conservation Service and Kentucky Agricultural Experiment Station survey (Washington, DC: GPO, 1983).

49. Fred S. Arms, James P. Fehr, David T. Carroll, Byron L. Wilson, Herman P. McDonald, and James C. Ross, *Soil Survey of Nelson County, Kentucky,* USDA Soil Conservation Service and Kentucky Agricultural Experiment Station survey (Washington, DC: GPO, 1971); John A. Kelley and William H. Craddock, *Soil Survey of Marion County, Kentucky,* USDA Soil Conservation Service and Kentucky Agricultural Experiment Station survey (Washington, DC: GPO, 1991); William H. Craddock, *Soil Survey of Washington County, Kentucky,* USDA Soil Conservation Service and Kentucky Agricultural Experiment Station survey (Washington, DC: GPO, 1986).

50. US Congress, House, *The Reports of Committees: H.R. 4165,* 50th Cong., 2d sess., 1888–1889, 3.

51. *Cynthiana Democrat* 1, no. 25 (1869): 3.

52. J. F. D. Smyth, *A Tour of the United States of America,* vol. 1 (London: G. Robinson, 1784), 298–99. Smyth's calculation was based on the measure of five bushels of corn per barrel. Other volume measures were also used. If Smyth's count was correct, eighteenth-century planting rates were substantially lower than in contemporary corn farming. A twenty-first-century corn farmer likely plants about 30,000 seeds per acre. Seed counts per bushel vary from 65,000 to 100,000, so a bushel of seed plants only two to three acres.

53. George Imlay, *A Topographical Description of the Western Territory of North America,* 2d ed. (London: J. Debrett, 1793), 166–69.

54. C. E. Bowman, *Annual Report of the Kentucky Bureau of Agriculture, Horticulture, and Statistics, 1880* (Frankfort, KY: E. H. Porter, 1880), 51.

55. Neal O. Hammon, "Settlers, Land Jobbers, and Outlyers: A Quantitative Analysis of Land Acquisition on the Kentucky Frontier," *Register of the Kentucky Historical Society* 84, no. 3 (1986): 247–48.

56. Ellen Eslinger, "Farming on the Kentucky Frontier," *Register of the Kentucky Historical Society* 107, no. 1 (2009): 4–5.

57. Ibid., 8.

58. Neal O. Hammon, "Land Acquisition on the Kentucky Frontier," *Register of the Kentucky Historical Society* 78, no. 4 (1980): 297–98.

59. Henry A. Wallace and William L. Brown, *Corn and Its Early Fathers* (East Lansing: Michigan State University Press, 1956), 34–35.

60. US Census Bureau, *Report of the Superintendent of the Census, 1852* (Washington, DC: Robert Armstrong, 1853), 60.

61. Wallace and Brown, *Corn and Its Early Fathers*, 54–63.

62. Arthur M. Schlesinger, "A Dietary Interpretation of American History," *Massachusetts Historical Society Proceedings* 68 (1944–1947): 202.

63. Caroline E. MacGill, *History of Transportation in the United States before 1860* (Washington, DC: Carnegie Institution, 1917), 111.

64. US Census Bureau, *Report of the Productions of Agriculture* (Washington, DC: GPO, 1883), 103.

65. US Census Bureau, *Report of the Superintendent of the Census, 1852*, 88–89, 61.

66. "Corn Wanted," *Lexington Observer and Reporter* 60, no. 16 (1867): 1. Ashland Distillery was later known as the William Tarr & Company Distillery.

67. Compiled from US Census Bureau, *Agriculture, 1880* and *1890*; Bowman, *Annual Report of the Kentucky Bureau of Agriculture, Horticulture, and Statistics, 1881*; William H. Perrin, ed., *History of Bourbon, Scott, Harrison and Nicholas Counties, Kentucky* (Chicago: O. L. Baskin, 1882), 66.

68. US Census Bureau, *Report of the Superintendent of the Census, 1852*, 56.

69. *National Magazine* 2, no. 9 (1846): 801.

70. Clarence Danhof, *Change in Agriculture: The Northern United States, 1820–1870* (Cambridge, MA: Harvard University Press, 1969), 31.

71. Bowman, *Annual Report of the Kentucky Bureau of Agriculture, Horticulture, and Statistics, 1880*, 42–45.

72. Ibid., 46.

73. *National Magazine* 2, no. 11 (1846): 1033–37.

74. William Cronon, *Nature's Metropolis: Chicago and the Great West* (New York: W. W. Norton, 1991), 104–8.

75. US Department of Agriculture, *Yearbook, 1922* (Washington, DC: GPO, 1943), 503.

76. US Census Bureau, *Report of the Productions of Agriculture*, 123.

77. US Census Bureau, *Report of the Superintendent of the Census, 1852*, 58.

78. Ibid., 59.

79. Twentieth-century farmers often used rye as a winter cover and green manure crop, although the production of fine-grade rye declined. In the twenty-first century, distillers import rye from producers on the American Great Plains, Canada, and Scandinavia.

80. US Census Bureau, *Report of the Productions of Agriculture*, 124.

81. "Winter and Spring Pasture," *Franklin Farmer* 3, no. 4 (1839): 30; Bowman, *Annual Report of the Kentucky Bureau of Agriculture, Horticulture, and Statistics, 1881*, 126–27.

82. John C. Weaver, "Barley in the United States: A Historical Sketch," *Geographical Review* 33, no. 1 (1943): 56.

83. Ibid., 58.

84. Warren M. Parsons, *Beer and Brewing in America: An Economic Study* (New York: United Brewers Industrial Foundation, 1941), 5; John C. Weaver, "United States Malting Barley Production," *Annals of the Association of American Geographers* 34, no. 2 (1944): 98.

85. US Census Bureau, *Report of the Superintendent of the Census, 1852*, 71.

86. "Agriculture," *National Magazine* 1, no. 1 (1845): 91.

87. US Census Bureau, *Report of the Productions of Agriculture*, 117.

88. Weaver, "Barley in the United States," 60–65; John C. Weaver, "Climatic Relations of American Barley Production," *Geographical Review* 33, no. 4 (1943): 569–72.

89. H. V. Harlan and G. A. Wiebe, *Growing Barley for Malt and Feed*, USDA Farmers' Bulletin 1732 (Washington, DC: GPO, 1934), 1–7.

90. US Census Bureau, *Report of the Productions of Agriculture*, 121; H. L. Shands and A. D. Dickson,

"Barley: Botany, Production, Harvesting, Processing, Utilization, and Economics," *Economic Botany* 7, no. 1 (1953): 19.

91. Shands and Dickson, "Barley," 21.

92. Weaver, "United States Malting Barley Production," 98.

93. Elkhorn Distillery Records, 1868–1872, book 1, 323, 1997 MS419, Special Collections, University of Kentucky.

94. Joseph Nimmo Jr., *Report on the Internal Commerce of the United States, 1881–1882*, Treasury Department, US Bureau of Statistics, report (Washington, DC: GPO, 1884), 438.

95. R. B. Weir, "Distilling and Agriculture 1870–1939," *Agricultural History Review* 32, no. 1 (1984): 49–62.

96. Bird Smith, "Management and Diseases of Hogs," *Franklin Farmer* 1, no. 46 (1838): 365.

97. "Commissioner's Sale of Distillery Land," *Cynthiana News* 20, no. 22 (1870): 3.

98. Tom Kimmerer, *Venerable Trees: History, Biology, and Conservation in the Bluegrass* (Lexington: University Press of Kentucky, 2015), 15.

99. Lewis Sanders, "On Cattle," *Franklin Farmer* 3, no. 21 (1840): 165–66.

100. Paul C. Henlein, *Cattle Kingdom in the Ohio Valley, 1783–1860* (Lexington: University of Kentucky Press, 1959), 7.

101. Danhof, *Change in Agriculture*, 95.

102. Lewis McKee and Linda K. Bond, *History of Anderson County: 1780–1936* (Frankfort, KY: Roberts Print Company, 1936), 151.

3. Distillery Configurations

1. Otto A. Rothert, *A History of Muhlenberg County, Kentucky* (Louisville, KY: John P. Morton, 1913), 121. See also Edward A. Kendall, *Travels through the Northern Parts of the United States in the Years 1807–1808*, vol. 3 (New York: I. Riley, 1809), 33–34.

2. "To Be Rented on Very Moderate Terms," *Kentucky Gazette* 15, no. 794 (1801): 3.

3. Peter Mathias, "Agriculture and the Brewing and Distilling Industries in the Eighteenth Century," *Economic History Review*, n.s., 5, no. 2 (1952): 249–51, 256.

4. Ibid., 252.

5. Although the chemical action of yeast in the fermentation process was not understood until it was demonstrated by Louis Pasteur in the 1850s, early distillers knew that yeast was necessary for proper fermentation. See Anthony Boucherie, *The Art of Making Whiskey* (Lexington, KY: Worsley & Smith, 1819); Harrison Hall, *The Distiller* (Philadelphia: J. Bioren, 1818), 103.

6. Betsy Hunter Bradley, *The Works: The Industrial Architecture of the United States* (New York: Oxford University Press, 1999), 16; John Stilgoe, *Common Landscape of America, 1580 to 1845* (New Haven, CT: Yale University Press, 1982), 4–5, 300–333.

7. Harry G. Enoch, *Grimes Mill: Kentucky Landmark on Boone Creek, Fayette County* (Bowie, MD: Heritage Books, 2002), 21–48; Kevin Murphy and Stephen C. Gordo, "Guyn's Mill in Woodford County, Kentucky, as Recorded by the Historic American Engineering Record," *Millstone: Journal of the Kentucky Old Mill Association* 12, no. 2 (2013): 33–52.

8. James R. Richards, *The Functional Tradition in Early Industrial Buildings* (London: Architectural Press, 1958), 14–15.

9. Thomas Hubka, "Just Folks Designing: Vernacular Designers and the Generation of Form," *Journal of Architectural Education* 32, no. 3 (1979): 27–29.

10. Terry S. Reynolds, *Stronger than a Hundred Men: A History of the Vertical Waterwheel* (Baltimore: Johns Hopkins University Press, 1983), 170–74.

11. Louis C. Hunter, *A History of Industrial Power in the United States, 1780–1930*, vol. 1, *Waterpower in the Century of the Steam Engine* (Charlottesville: University Press of Virginia, 1979), 104–6.

12. Michael Krafft, *The American Distiller or, the Theory and Practice of Distilling* (Philadelphia: Archibald Bariram, 1804), 56–57.

13. The term "charge" refers to the volume of fermented mash liquid or distillers' beer that is transferred to the still to initiate the distilling process. See William M. Ambrose, *Bottled in Bond under U.S. Government Supervision* (Lexington, KY: William M. Ambrose, 2007), 3.

14. Krafft, *American Distiller,* 8–20; Hall, *Distiller,* 27.

15. John Fuller Sr., *Art of Coppersmithing* (New York: David Williams, 1894), 6–13.

16. Krafft, *American Distiller,* 33–37.

17. J. A. Nettleton, *The Manufacture of Spirit* (London: Marcus Ward, 1893), 19–21, 133–45; cf. Ian Buxton and Paul S. Hughes, *The Science and Commerce of Whiskey* (Cambridge: Royal Society of Chemistry, 2014), 10.

18. Boucherie, *Art of Making Whiskey.*

19. Bradley, *Works,* ix. See Krafft, *American Distiller,* 22, on use of the term "works" to describe the distillery structure and equipment.

20. Krafft, *American Distiller,* 152,157; Hall, *Distiller,* 23.

21. Boucherie, *Art of Making Whiskey;* Hall, *Distiller;* Krafft, *American Distiller.*

22. Nathen Rosenberg, *Exploring the Black Box: Technology, Economics, and History* (Cambridge: Cambridge University Press, 1994), 3–4.

23. Bradley, *Works,* 5–7.

24. *Franklin Farmer* 2, no. 43 (1839): 343.

25. Frederick Overman, *Mechanics for the Millwright, Machinist, Engineer, Civil Engineer, Architect and Student* (Philadelphia: Lippincott, Grambo, 1851), 191–96.

26. Harlan I. Halsey, "The Choice between High-Pressure and Low-Pressure Steam Power in America in the Early Nineteenth Century," *Journal of Economic History* 41, no. 4 (1981): 730–31. Oliver Evans's steam engines were sent primarily to locations accessible by water transport. Four of his engines reached Kentucky by 1811—one in Louisville, one in Frankfort, and two in Lexington. The Lexington engines powered a paper mill and a gristmill. Greville Bathe and Dorothy Bathe, *Oliver Evans: A Chronicle of Early American Engineering* (Philadelphia: Historical Society of Pennsylvania, 1935), 207.

27. Henry M'Murtrie, *Sketches of Louisville* (Louisville, KY: S. Penn, 1819), 55.

28. B. Drake and E. D. Mansfield, *Cincinnati in 1826* (Cincinnati, OH: Morgan, Lodge, & Fisher, 1827), 59.

29. Levi Woodbury, "Steam-Engines: Letter from the Secretary of the Treasury," US Congress, House, 25th Cong., 3d sess., 1838, 325 (doc. no. 21). The treasury secretary's report stated that the national count of stationary steam engines was flawed because states did not report information fully or, as in the case of Kentucky, neglected to file a report. Ibid., 379.

30. Louis C. Hunter, *A History of Industrial Power in the United States, 1780–1930*, vol. 2, *Steam Power* (Charlottesville: University of Virginia Press, 1985), 249.

31. "Jefferson County Kentucky Land for Sale," *Louisville Daily Democrat* 9, no. 44 (1852): 1.

32. "Local Notices," *Louisville Courier-Journal*, n.s., 38, no. 145 (1868): 2.

33. "Paris Machine Shop," *Bourbon News* 2, no. 119 (1883): 4.

34. Charles H. Fitch, *Report on the Manufacture of Engines and Boilers* (Washington, DC: GPO, 1881), 50.

35. David E. Schob, "Woodhawks & Cordwood: Steamboat Fuel on the Ohio and Mississippi Rivers, 1820–1860," *Journal of Forest History* 21, no. 3 (1977): 124–32.

36. US Congress, House, *The Reports of Committees: H.R. 4165*, 50th Cong., 2d sess., 1888–1889, 2.

37. Hunter, *History of Industrial Power*, 2:427; Carroll W. Pursell Jr., *Early Stationary Steam Engines in America: A Study in the Migration of a Technology* (Washington, DC: Smithsonian Institution Press, 1969), 132.

38. Elkhorn Distillery Records, 1868–1872, book 1, February 10, 1869, 1997MS419, Special Collections, University of Kentucky; Don Day, "Corncobs—Burning Them with Coal," *Ag Connection* 12, no. 12 (2006): 1–2.

39. "United States Marshall's Sale," *Cynthiana News* 22, no. 22 (1870): 3.

40. "Commissioner's Sale of Distillery Land," *Cynthiana News* 22, no. 22 (1870): 3.

41. Ed Vasser and Jerry Sudduth, *Frankfort and Cincinnati Railroad: History and Remembrances of the Bourbon Road* (Lexington, KY: CreateSpace.com, 2013), 12–13.

42. See, for example, "No Gates Left," *Paducah Daily Sun* 1, no. 96 (1896): 1.

43. Hunter, *History of Industrial Power*, 2:433.

44. US Congress, *Reports of Committees*, 50.

45. Ibid., 4, 6.

46. Ibid., 50.

47. See, for example, K. Austin Kerr, *Organized for Prohibition: A New History of the Anti-Saloon League* (New Haven, CT: Yale University Press, 1985), 17–18.

48. Charles Cross, *The American Compounder or Cross' Guide for Retail Liquor Dealers* (St. Louis: Charles Cross, 1899), 60, 79.

49. Ibid., 133–34.

50. Ibid., 72–73, 115–16.

51. *Practical Druggist and Pharmaceutical Review of Reviews* 35, no. 11 (1917): 36.

52. US Congress, *Reports of Committees*, 13.

53. Ibid., 3, 12; *Congressional Record*, 46th Cong., 2d sess., vol. 10, pt. 3 (April 28, 1880): 2838.

54. "Big Boost Given the Manufacturers of Straight Whiskies," *Frankfort Weekly News and Roundabout* 31, no. 43, (1908): 1.

55. *Congressional Record*, 2834–45. See also Ambrose, *Bottled in Bond*, 16.

4. Applying Technology

1. Alfred Barnard, introduction to *The Whisky Distilleries of the United Kingdom* (1887; reprint, Edinburgh: Birlinn, 2008).

2. Luke Herbert, *The Engineer's and Mechanic's Encyclopedia*, vol. 1 (London: Thomas Kenny, 1836), 59–62; Charles Tovey, *British & Foreign Spirits* (London: Whittaker, 1864), 15–18.

3. Anthony Perrier, "Sir Anthony Perrier's Improved Apparatus for Distillation," *Register of the Arts and Sciences* 1 (1824): 10–12.

4. "Winter's Patent Distilling Apparatus," *Register of the Arts and Sciences* 11 (1824): 161–64; Herbert, *Engineer's and Mechanic's Encyclopedia*, 62–64.

5. "Patent Granted to Robert Stein," *Repertory of Patent Inventions* 8, no. 51 (1830): 538–40; J. A. Nettleton, *The Manufacture of Spirit* (London: Marcus Ward, 1893), 19; Royal Commission on Whiskey and Other Potable Spirits, *Minutes of Evidence Taken by the Royal Commission on Whiskey and Other Potable Spirits*, vol. 1 (London: Jas. Truscott & Son, 1908), 251–52.

6. "Patent Granted to Aeneas Coffey," *Repertory of Patent Inventions* 11, no. 72 (1831): 190–96; Nettleton, *Manufacture of Spirit,* 133–45; Royal Commission, *Minutes of Evidence,* 252, 382.

7. US Patent Office, "Improvement in Stills," George W. Robson, Cincinnati, OH, and Melvin T. Hughes, Paris, KY, US Patent No. 87,971, March 16, 1869.

8. US Patent Office, "Improvement in Stills for Alcoholic Spirits," William Robson and George W. Robson, Cincinnati, OH, US Patent No. 92,477, July 13, 1869. The patent drawing was a partially sectioned elevation arranged in one plane for illustrative purposes. The various units in the installed apparatus would not have been suspended above the floor.

9. Sam K. Cecil, *Bourbon: The Evolution of Kentucky Whiskey* (New York: Turner, 2010), 158.

10. "A New Distillery," *Cynthiana News* 19, no. 2 (1869): 2.

11. Ibid.

12. Andrew J. Oots Cooper Shop Records, 1880–1926, 1880–1910 (bulk dates), 1 FM-49, Special Collections, University of Kentucky.

13. "Pure Copper Whisky," *Louisville Daily Express* 1, no. 172 (1869): 3.

14. Herman Stabler, *Prevention of Stream Pollution by Distillery Refuse,* US Geological Survey Water Supply and Irrigation Paper 179 (Washington, DC: GPO, 1906), table 11, 26.

15. "Cheap Stock Feed for Sale," *Kentucky Sentinel* 1, no. 19 (1868): 4.

16. "Two Big Concerns," *Bourbon News* 24, no. 104 (1904): 5.

17. "Distillery Slops for Sale," *Daily Evening Bulletin* 6, no. 26 (1886): 2.

18. "Hog Raising Is the Poor Farmer's Fortune and the Rich Farmer's Protection," *Hartford Herald* 42, no. 17 (1916): 7.

19. "Enough to Put the Town 'On the Hog,'" *It* 1, no. 4 (1902): 3.

20. L. F. Allen, "Berkshire Pigs," *American Agriculturalist* 3 (1844): 175.

21. "New York Cattle Market," *Louisville Daily Courier* 28, no. 29 (1859): 4; "New York Cattle Market," *Louisville Daily Courier* 31, no. 212 (1860): 4; "New York Cattle Market," *Louisville Daily Courier* 32, no. 49 (1861): 4.

22. William J. Novak, *The People's Welfare: Law & Regulation in Nineteenth-Century America* (Chapel Hill: University of North Carolina Press, 1996), 227.

23. W. W. Thum, *Supplement to 1909 Kentucky Statutes* (Cincinnati, OH: W. H. Anderson, 1915), 546.

24. Novak, *People's Welfare,* 217–18.

25. "Fine Bourbon County Stock Farm for Sale," *Bourbon News,* August 16, 1904, 8.

26. "Commonwealth v. Kentucky Distilleries & Warehouse Co., et al.," *Southwestern Reporter* 159 (1913): 571.

27. "After Them," *Mt. Sterling Advocate* 11, no. 44 (1901): 2.

28. "Warning," *Mt. Sterling Advocate* 12, no. 41 (1902): 2.

29. Chester Zoeller, *Bourbon in Kentucky: A History of Distilleries in Kentucky,* 2d ed. (Louisville, KY: Butler Books, 2010), 204.

30. "A New Enterprise," *Mt. Sterling Advocate* 13, no. 18 (1902): 3.

31. "A Good Sale," *Mt. Sterling Advocate* 17, no. 2 (1907): 8.

32. "Millville," *Frankfort Roundabout* 22, no. 48 (1899): 6.

33. "Agreement," E. H. Taylor Jr. & Sons Inc. and Simon Weil, September 30, 1906, Taylor-Hay Family Papers (Franklin County, KY), 1783–1991, MssAT238d, Filson Historical Society, Louisville, KY.

34. "Big Warehouses etc.," *Frankfort Roundabout* 29, no. 10 (1906): 5.

35. M. D. Leggett, *Subject-Matter Index of Patents for Inventors Issued by the United States Patent Office, 1790–1873,* vol. 1 (Washington, DC: GPO, 1874), 622–23.

36. The Peter Jepson grain dryer, patented in 1887, was specifically designed to process spent grain.

The design included a vertical cylinder that contained a series of funnel-shaped hoppers and perforated disks mounted on a rotating shaft. Pipes circulated pressurized hot air through the grain; when dried, the grain exited the drying cylinder through a bottom exit chute. See US Patent Office, "Grain-Drying Apparatus," Peter Jepson, Port Chester, NY, US Patent No. 373,140, November 15, 1887.

37. In 1904 a fire in the dryer room at the M. S. Greenbaum Distillery at Midway in Woodford County caused $25,000 to $30,000 in damage.

38. US Patent Office, "Drier," John E. Turney, Louisville, KY, US Patent No. 740,607, October 6, 1903.

39. US Patent Office, "Drier," John E. Turney, Charles E. Geiger, W. K. Koop, and G. W. Fisk, Louisville, KY, US Patent No. 774,859, November 15, 1904.

40. "Business Notes," *Engineering Record* 43, no. 9, (1901): 208; "Business Notes," *Engineering Record* 51, no. 11 (1905): 46; "Turney Drier Company," *Railroad Age* 12 (1905): 394; "Drying Plant," *Wine and Spirit Bulletin* 19, no. 1 (1905): 41.

41. "The Louisville Grains Dryer," *Western Brewer* 30, no. 4 (1906): 192.

42. Michael R. Veach, *Kentucky Bourbon Whiskey* (Lexington: University Press of Kentucky, 2013), 39.

43. See Mike Veach, http://www.bourbonenthusiast.com/forum/viewtopic.php?f=17&t=115.

44. US Patent Office, "Improvement in Racks for Tiering Barrels," Frederick Stitzel, Louisville, KY, US Patent No. 221,945, November 25, 1879, reissued April 27, 1880.

45. Some distillers referred to their aging warehouses as "rick houses." It is possible that, at some point, the term "rack" was transformed into "rick." Alternatively, "rick" refers to a cord of stacked firewood, and distillers may have conflated the terms, given that a rack warehouse under construction has the general appearance of a stack of wood.

46. Betsy Hunter Bradley, *The Works: The Industrial Architecture of the United States* (New York: Oxford University Press, 1999), 184; John R. Stilgoe, *Common Landscape of America, 1580–1845* (New Haven, CT: Yale University Press, 1982), 329; J. M. Richards, *The Functional Tradition in Early Industrial Buildings* (London: Architectural Press, 1958).

47. Bradley, *Works*, 60–65.

48. "Walsh's New Distillery," *Bourbon News* 17, no. 29 (1897): 5.

49. Lewis Loder, *The Loder Diary, 1857–1903*, transcribed by William Conrad (Florence, KY: Boone County Schools, 1985–1988), 82.

50. US Congress, House. *The Reports of Committees: H.R. 4165*. 50th Cong., 2d sess., 1888–1889, 66.

51. Richard Peters, ed., *The Public Statutes at Large of the United States of America from the Organization of the Government in 1789, to March 3, 1845*, vol. 3 (Boston: Charles C. Little & James Brown, 1846), 43.

52. US Congress, *Reports of Committees*, 22.

53. Grant McCracken, *Culture & Consumption: New Approaches to the Symbolic Character of Consumer Goods and Activities* (Bloomington: Indiana University Press, 1988), 106.

5. Complementary Industries

1. J. Leander Bishop, *A History of American Manufactures from 1608 to 1860*, vol. 1 (London: Edward Young, 1866), 492.

2. Henry H. Work, *Wood, Whiskey, and Wine: A History of Barrels* (London: Reaktion Books, 2014), 17.

3. Kenneth Kilby, *The Cooper and His Trade* (Fresno, CA: Linden Publishing, 1971), 65–67.

4. "Wanted Immediately," *Kentucky Gazette Extra*, January 15, 1801, 2.

5. J. B. Wagner, *Cooperage: A Treatise on Modern Shop Practice and Methods; from the Tree to the Finished Article* (Yonkers, NY: J. B. Wagner, 1910), 153–54.

6. Wayne D. Rasmussen, "Wood on the Farm," in *Material Culture of the Wooden Age,* ed. Brooke Hindle (Tarrytown, NY: Sleepy Hollow Press, 1981), 15–34.

7. J. R. Mosedale, "Effects of Oak Wood on the Maturation of Alcoholic Beverages with Particular Reference to Whisky," *Forestry* 68, no. 3 (1998): 211.

8. N. S. Shaler and A. R. Crandall, *Report on the Forests of Greenup, Carter, Boyd & Lawrence Counties,* pt. 1, vol. 1, 2d ser., Geological Survey of Kentucky (Frankfort, KY: Yeoman Press, 1884), 13–14.

9. Henry Hall, *Report on the Ship-Building Industry of the United States* (Washington, DC: Department of the Interior, Census Office, 1884), 191.

10. Simon Difford, "Casks," in *Difford's Guide,* 5, https://www.diffordsguide.com/encyclopedia/481.

11. "How a Barrel Is Made Up," *Paducah Evening Sun* 25, no. 92 (1909): 8.

12. Mary Verhoeff, *The Kentucky River Navigation,* Filson Club Publication no. 28 (Louisville, KY: John P. Morton, 1917), 188–89; Steven A. Schulman, "The Lumber Industry of the Upper Cumberland River Valley," *Tennessee Historical Quarterly* 32, no. 3 (1973): 256; "Correspondence," *Mountain Advocate* 5, no. 8 (1908): 4.

13. Lewis Loder, *The Loder Diary, 1857–1903,* transcribed by William Conrad (Florence, KY: Boone County Schools, 1985–1988), 118.

14. Schulman, "Lumber Industry of Upper Cumberland River Valley," 258.

15. "Along the Cincinnati Southern Railroad," *Farmers' Home Journal* 27, no. 46 (1879): 1.

16. "Good Thing for Patesville," *Breckenridge News* 28, no. 7 (1903): 7.

17. "A Big Business," *Mt. Sterling Advocate* 15, no. 20 (1904): 3.

18. US Congress, House, *The Reports of Committees: H.R. 4165,* 50th Cong., 2d sess., 1888–1889, 2.

19. C. E. Bowman, *Annual Report of the Kentucky Bureau of Agriculture, Horticulture, and Statistics, 1880* (Frankfort, KY: E. H. Porter, 1880), 82. In 1901 the Kern Company of Vienna, Austria, employed 450 men in Magoffin County, Kentucky, where they cut and shipped more than 15 million staves. The stave cutters included 150 men from the county "and 300 . . . Slavonians from Austria." "Facts and Observations," *Mt. Sterling Advocate* 11, no. 30 (1901): 6.

20. Henry Gannett and Jasper E. Whelchel, "Lumber," in US Department of Commerce, *Twelfth Census of the United States,* pt. 3, vol. 9, *Manufacturers* (Washington, DC: GPO, 1900), 853.

21. Verhoeff, *Kentucky River Navigation,* 113.

22. Gannett and Whelchel, "Lumber," 884, 824.

23. Mosedale, "Effects of Oak Wood," 204.

24. Work, *Wood, Whiskey, and Wine,* 126–36.

25. Verhoeff, *Kentucky River Navigation,* 195–96. See also Mosedale, "Effects of Oak Wood," 211.

26. Joseph Fleischman, *The Art of Blending and Compounding Liquors and Wines* (New York: Dick & Fitzgerald, 1885), 10–12.

27. Victor S. Clark, *History of Manufactures in the United States 1607–1860* (Washington, DC: Carnegie Institution, 1916), 472.

28. Kenneth L. Cope, *American Cooperage Machinery and Tools* (Mendham, NJ: Astragal Press, 2003), 6.

29. US Census Bureau, "Table X, Professions, Occupations, and Trades of the Male Population," in *1850 Census* (Washington, DC: Robert Armstrong, 1853), 623.

30. "Our Louisville Letter," *National Coopers Journal* 26, no. 12 (1911): 11.

31. Wagner, *Cooperage,* 193.

32. "Local Matters," *Cynthiana News* 8, no. 44 (1867): 3.

33. "Weekly Roundabout," *Weekly Roundabout* 3, no. 29 (1880): 5.

34. US Congress, *Reports of Committees*, 2.

35. "Queen City Copper Works," *Cynthiana News* 19, no. 44 (1869): 4.

36. William F. Switzler, *Report on the Internal Commerce of the United States* (Washington, DC: GPO, 1888), 437.

37. Louisville Board of Trade, Committee on Industrial and Commercial Improvement, *The City of Louisville and a Glimpse of Kentucky, 1887* (Louisville, KY: Courier-Journal Press, 1887), 17.

38. Switzler, *Report on the Internal Commerce*, 491, 494.

39. "T. B. Ripy and the Anderson County Distilling Company Distilleries," *Anderson News*, Souvenir Supplement, June 1906, 51.

40. "In Neighboring Counties," *Semi-Weekly Interior Journal* 31, no. 9 (1903): 1.

41. Andrew J. Oots Cooper Shop Records, 1880–1926, 1880–1910 (bulk dates), 1 FM-49, Special Collections, University of Kentucky. See also R. L. Polk & Company and A. C. Danser, *Kentucky State Gazetteer and Business Directory, 1881–1882,* vol. 3, pt. 2 (Detroit, MI: R. L. Polk & Company and A. C. Danser, 1882), 629, which lists one cooper in Lexington in 1881–1882 (H. F. Oots); *Prather's Directory of the City of Lexington, Kentucky,* August 1895.

42. Whiskey barrel capacity was changed after World War II from 48 to 53 gallons, or 200 liters, the largest barrel size that would fit in the racks used in most aging warehouses.

43. See *Lexington, Kentucky* (New York: Sanborn-Perris Map Company, 1890), 9.

44. William H. Perrin, *History of Bourbon, Scott, Harrison and Nicholas Counties, Kentucky* (Chicago: O. L. Baskin, 1882), 510.

45. Donna Reaich, "The Influence of Copper on Malt Whisky Character," in *Proceedings of the Fifth Aviemore Conference on Malting, Brewing and Distilling,* Aviemore, Inverness-shire, Scotland, May 25–28, 1998, 141–52; Barry Harrison, Olivier Fagnen, Frances Jack, and James Brosnan, "The Impact of Copper in Different Parts of Malt Whisky Pot Stills on New Make Spirit Composition and Aroma," *Journal of the Institute of Brewing* 117, no. 1 (2011): 106–12; "Copper," *Whisky Science* (blog), http://whiskyscience. blogspot.com/2014/10/copper.html.

46. "Copper Mines and the Copper Trade," *National Magazine* 1, no. 2, (1845): 117–23.

47. James A. Mulholland, *A History of Metals in Colonial America* (University: University of Alabama Press, 1981), 37–43.

48. Bishop, *History of American Manufactures,* 547–48.

49. Otis E. Young, "Origins of the American Copper Industry," *Journal of the Early Republic* 3, no. 2 (1983): 118–25.

50. Ibid., 127, 133. See also Henry J. Kauffman, *American Copper & Brass* (Camden, NJ: Thomas Nelson & Sons, 1968), 21–23.

51. Young, "Origins of the American Copper Industry," 136–37; Clark, *History of Manufactures,* 525; Orris C. Herfindahl, *Copper Costs and Prices: 1870–1957* (Baltimore: Johns Hopkins University Press, 1959), 70–71.

52. M. L. Quinn, "Industry and Environment in the Appalachian Copper Basin, 1890–1930," *Technology and Culture* 34, no. 3 (1993): 575–612.

53. US Census Bureau, *Manufactures 1905,* pt. 4, *Special Reports on Selected Industries* (Washington, DC: GPO, 1908), 162.

54. Thomas J. Schlereth, "The New York Artisan in the Early Republic: A Portrait from Graphic Evidence, 1787–1853," *Landscape, Place, & Material Culture* 20, no. 1 (1988): 3.

55. Shirley Austin referred to this human quality as "the sympathetic touch of the skilled workman." Shirley P. Austin, "Glass," in US Department of Commerce, *Twelfth Census of the United States,* 978.

56. Nicolas R. Laracuente, "Archaeological Investigations of the O.F.C. Building, Buffalo Trace Distillery," (2016), 4, 11, on file at Buffalo Trace Distillery, Frankfort, KY; *Sanborn's Survey of the Whiskey Warehouses of Kentucky and Tennessee* (New York: Sanborn-Perris Map Company, 1894), 52.

57. "Fishel & Gallatine, Copper & Tin Smiths," *Kentucky Gazette* 15, no. 334 (1802): 3.

58. "They Made Moonshine Whisky," *Climax* 10, no. 28 (1896): 4; "Personal," *Climax* 4, no. 38 (1891): 3.

59. The cost of copper sheet or plate was determined by its thickness and weight (ounces per square foot). Twenty-ounce copper weighs twenty ounces per square foot of plate that is about 0.027 inch thick. "Fishel & Gallatine," 3; Kauffman, *American Copper & Brass,* 13.

60. "Stills for Sale," *Kentucky Gazette* 24, no. 1302 (1810): 1 (emphasis in original).

61. Karl Raitz and Nancy O'Malley, *Kentucky's Frontier Highway: Historical Landscapes along the Maysville Road* (Lexington: University Press of Kentucky, 2012), 63.

62. "John Metcalfe & Bro.," *Louisville Daily Courier* 27, no. 155 (1858): 4.

63. "Louisville Manufacturers," *Louisville Daily Courier* 39, no. 46 (1859): 1. See also "Lightburn & Ward," *Louisville Daily Courier* 31, no. 73 (1860): 1.

64. Everett M. Rogers and F. Floyd Shoemaker, *Communication of Innovations: A Cross-Cultural Approach,* 2d ed. (New York: Free Press, 1971), 14–15. See also Everett M. Rogers, *Diffusion of Innovations,* 5th ed. (New York: Free Press, 2003), 305–8; Joe S. Bain, *Industrial Organization* (New York: John Wiley & Sons, 1959), 58–62; Kauffman, *American Copper & Brass,* 107.

65. "Louisville Manufacturers," *Louisville Daily Courier* 39, no. 46 (1859): 1.

66. "Hoffman, Ahlers & Co.," *Kentucky Irish American* 18, no. 12 (1907): 10.

67. The Vendome fabrication business continues in operation at Franklin Street in Louisville, a short distance from the original Main Street location. See http://www.vendomecopper.com.

6. The Inner Bluegrass Region

1. William H. English, *Conquest of the Country Northwest of the River Ohio . . . 1778–1783,* vol. 1 (Indianapolis: n.p., 1896), 83.

2. William H. Perrin, ed., *History of Bourbon, Scott, Harrison and Nicholas Counties, Kentucky* (Chicago: O. L. Baskin, 1882), 59.

3. Industrial slavery in central Kentucky was present in hemp manufacturing and salt boiling. See Robert S. Starobin, *Industrial Slavery in the Old South* (New York: Oxford University Press, 1970), 17–18, 24–25.

4. William H. Perrin, *History of Bourbon, Scott, Harrison and Nicholas Counties,* 66–67.

5. "A New Distillery," *Cynthiana News* 19, no. 2 (1869): 2.

6. Ibid.

7. Andrew J. Oots Cooper Shop Records, 1880–1926, 1880–1910 (bulk dates), 1 FM-49, Special Collections, University of Kentucky; Chester Zoeller, *Bourbon in Kentucky: A History of Distilleries in Kentucky,* 2d ed. (Louisville, KY: Butler Books, 2010), 170–71.

8. See Perrin, *History of Bourbon, Scott, Harrison and Nicholas Counties,* 664.

9. Thelma Taylor, "Monticello," National Register of Historic Places Registration Form, Kentucky Heritage Council, Frankfort, 1974.

10. Nancy O'Malley, "McConnell Springs in Historical Perspective" (University of Kentucky, Department of Anthropology, n.d.), 23.

11. Gary O'Dell, "Water Supply and the Early Development of Lexington, Kentucky," *Filson Club History Quarterly* 67, no. 4 (1993): 443, 447.

12. William H. Perrin, ed., *History of Fayette County, Kentucky* (Chicago: O. L. Baskin, 1882), 35. "Chalybeate" is a substance impregnated with appreciable quantities of salts of iron.

13. George W. Ranck, *History of Lexington, Kentucky* (Cincinnati, OH: Robert Clarke, 1872), 18–19.

14. "Elijah Culpepper," newspaper clipping, January 10, 1894, folder 66, Taylor-Hay Family Papers, Filson Historical Society, Louisville; *Sanborn's Survey of the Whiskey Warehouses of Kentucky and Tennessee* (New York: Sanborn-Perris Map Company, 1894), 61; Zoeller, *Bourbon in Kentucky*, 189.

15. Perrin, *History of Fayette County*, 205.

16. Ibid., 206; *Lexington, Kentucky* (New York: Sanborn Map & Publishing, 1885), 18.

17. Zoeller, *Bourbon in Kentucky*, 191–92.

18. Gary O'Dell, "Hillenmeyer Spring and Boiling Spring (Spring Lake Spring)" (unpublished paper, n.d.).

19. Perrin, *History of Fayette County*, 210; *Lexington, Kentucky* (New York: Sanborn-Perris Map Company, 1891), 22.

20. Julie Riesenweber and Karen Hudson, eds., *Kentucky's Bluegrass Region* (Frankfort: Kentucky Heritage Council, 1990), 86–88.

21. E. A. Hewitt, and G. W. Hewitt, "Topographical Map of the Counties of Bourbon, Fayette, Clark, Jessamine and Woodford, Kentucky" (New York: Smith, Gallup, 1861).

22. "Elijah Culpepper," newspaper clipping, January 10, 1894.

23. "James Crow, Whiskey Maker," *Sun* 65, no. 5 (1897): 5.

24. William Mida, *Mida's Compendium of Information for the Liquor Interests* (Chicago: Criterion Publishing, 1899), 176–78; cf. Zoeller, *Bourbon in Kentucky*, 212.

25. Mida, *Mida's Compendium of Information*, 176–78.

26. Creason quoted in Donovan D. Rypkema, *Historic Preservation and the Economy of the Commonwealth: Kentucky's Past at Work for Kentucky's Future* (Frankfort: Kentucky Heritage Council & Commonwealth Preservation Advocates, 1997). See also Jean K. Wolf, "Labrot & Graham's Old Oscar Pepper Distillery," National Historic Landmark Nomination Form, Kentucky Heritage Council, Frankfort, 1999.

27. Sam K. Cecil, *Bourbon: The Evolution of Kentucky Whiskey* (New York: Turner Publishing, 2010), 285–86; Zoeller, *Bourbon in Kentucky*, 214.

28. "Old Crow Resumes Operations," *Frankfort Roundabout* 31, no. 12 (1907): 7.

29. "To Build Branch Railroad," *Frankfort Roundabout* 30, no. 22 (1907): 7.

30. "Opens Office—Hard at Work," *Frankfort Roundabout* 30, no. 40 (1907): 5.

31. "Kentucky Highland Railroad," *Frankfort Weekly News and Roundabout* 31, no. 33 (1908): 3.

32. Jayne Goddard, Brett Connors, and Amy Crossfield, "Old Taylor Distillery Historic District," National Register of Historic Places Registration Form, Kentucky Heritage Council, Frankfort, 2016, 3–34; Janet Patton, "Former Woodford Distillery to Spring Back to Life," *Lexington Herald-Leader*, July 11, 2016, 1B, 6B.

33. Zoeller, *Bourbon in Kentucky*, 209–10.

34. "All Sorts and Sizes," *Stanford (KY) Semi-Weekly Interior Journal* 16, no. 283 (1887): 4.

35. "Fire Destroys Midway Distillery," *Frankfort Weekly News* 31, no. 48 (1908): 1.

36. "Burned Whisky," *Frankfort Weekly News and Roundabout* 31, no. 49 (1908): 8.

37. "Current Events," *Adair County News* 11, no. 43 (1908): 6.

38. Clerk of Court, Anderson County, *Anderson County Deed Record Book M*, vol. 1, 456.

39. "T. B. Ripy and the Anderson County Distilling Company Distilleries," *Anderson News* (Lawrenceburg, KY), Souvenir Supplement, June 1906, 51.

40. US Census Bureau, 1870 Census, Anderson County.

41. The award is not listed on the official awards list and cannot be confirmed. The exhibition's international jury gave only two awards for whiskey: one to Hannis Distilling of Philadelphia, and the other to Sattler & Company of Baltimore. Both winners were rye whiskies. See US Centennial Commission, *List of Awards, International Exhibition, 1876, at Philadelphia* (Philadelphia: S. T. Souder, 1876), 101.

42. "Cedar Brook," *Anderson News*, Souvenir Supplement, June 1906, 36. See also Cecil, *Bourbon*, 94.

43. As a convenient reference, an acre is 43,560 square feet, or roughly the size of an American football field less one end zone.

44. "Lancaster, Garrard County," *Semi-Weekly Interior Journal* 16, no. 91 (1888): 2; "Farm and Trade Items," *Semi-Weekly Interior Journal* 19, no. 14 (1891): 1; "Farm and Trade Items," *Semi-Weekly Interior Journal* 20, no. 35 (1892), 3.

45. "The Frankfort Roundabout," *Frankfort Roundabout* 9, no. 13 (1885): 1; "Personals," *Frankfort Roundabout* 10, no. 28 (1887): 2.

46. "A New Departure," *Mt. Sterling Advocate* 5, no. 36 (1895): 7; "Local Jottings," *Adair County News* 4, no. 14 (1901): 3.

47. More than thirty resettlement villages for freedmen sprang up in Kentucky's Inner Bluegrass counties in the late 1860s and 1870s, and many others were created in the central and western Pennyroyal. Peter C. Smith and Karl B. Raitz, "Negro Hamlets and Agricultural Estates in Kentucky's Inner Bluegrass," *Geographical Review* 64, no. 2 (1974): 283–404. See also Sallie L. Powell, "African American Hamlets," in *The Kentucky African American Encyclopedia*, ed. Gerald L. Smith, Karen C. McDaniel, and John A. Hardin (Lexington: University Press of Kentucky, 2015), 5.

48. Clerk of Court, Anderson County, *Anderson County Deed Record Book N*, 48, 412; *Book Q*, 156, 356, 423; *Book R*, 433; *Book S*, 197, 215.

49. Ibid., *Book Q*, 156; *Book S*, 217.

50. According to the *Anderson News*, Tyrone was incorporated in 1879, but official incorporation papers filed with the clerk of court were dated December 7, 1881. See ibid., *Book Q*, 469.

51. Ibid.; "Tyrone," *It* 1, no. 15 (1903): 11.

52. Cecil, *Bourbon*, 93.

53. "Tyrone," *Anderson News*, Souvenir Supplement, June 1906, 52.

54. "Tyrone," *It* 1, no. 15 (1903): 11.

55. "Little Jottings by the Way," *Frankfort Roundabout* 29, no. 42 (1906): 1.

56. Zoller, *Bourbon in Kentucky*, 219.

57. "The Commonwealth," *Big Sandy News* 4, no. 45 (1889): 1; "The Great Bridge at Tyrone," *Climax* 3, no. 11 (1889): 3.

58. *Anderson News*, Souvenir Supplement, June 1906, 51; Cecil, *Bourbon*, 93; Zoeller, *Bourbon in Kentucky*, 222.

59. Lewis McKee and Linda K. Bond, *History of Anderson County: 1780–1936* (Frankfort, KY: Roberts Print Company, 1936), 210.

60. Charlotte Schneider, "Dowling House," National Register of Historic Places Registration Form, Kentucky Heritage Council, Frankfort, 1979.

61. Typescript copies of *Anderson News*, June 7, 1888, Ripy Family Papers, 1888–1963, 1F66M-725, Special Collections, University of Kentucky.

62. "T. B. Ripy and the Anderson County Distilling Company Distilleries," *Anderson News*, Souvenir Supplement, June 1906, 51.

63. "T. B. Ripy House," *Anderson News*, November 28, 2012, 8.

64. Cecil, *Bourbon*, 99.

65. *Sanborn's Surveys of the Distilleries and Warehouses of Kentucky and Tennessee* (New York: Sanborn Map Company, 1910), 85.

66. Robert M. Polsgrove, "Old Prentice Distillery (Four Roses Distillery)," National Register of Historic Places Registration Form, Kentucky Heritage Council, Frankfort, 1986.

67. The lineage of the Old Prentice, Old Joe, and Four Roses distilleries is complex and difficult to trace with assurance. See Zoeller, *Bourbon in Kentucky*, 104, 217–18; Al Young, *Four Roses: The Return of a Whiskey Legend* (Louisville, KY: Butler Books, 2010), 26–27.

68. William M. Andrews Jr., "Geological Controls on Plio-Pleistocene Drainage Evolution of the Kentucky River in Central Kentucky" (PhD diss., University of Kentucky, 2004), 77–84.

69. Nicholas Cresswell, *The Journal of Nicholas Cresswell, 1774–1777* (New York: Dial Press, 1924), 77–79.

70. Fortesque Cuming, *Sketches of a Tour to the Western Country, through the States of Ohio and Kentucky* (Pittsburgh, PA: Cramer, Spear & Eichbaum, 1810), 169; B. N. Griffing, *An Atlas of Franklin County, Kentucky* (Philadelphia, PA: D. J. Lake, 1882), 18–19.

71. Cuming, *Sketches of a Tour to the Western Country*, 168.

72. *Frankfort, Kentucky* (New York: Sanborn Map Publishing Company 1886), 10; E. H. Taylor Jr., *Description of the O.F.C., Carlisle, and J. S. Taylor Distilleries* (Frankfort, KY: E. H. Taylor Jr., 1886), 4.

73. John H. Procter, "Map of Kentucky" (Frankfort: Kentucky Geological Survey, 1881). But note that in 1912 geologists characterized the water drawn from the "Birdseye" limestone as "salty." See M. L. Fuller and F. G. Clapp, *The Underground Waters of Southwestern Ohio,* US Geological Survey Water Supply Paper 259 (Washington, DC: GPO, 1912), 23.

74. Taylor, *Description of the O.F.C., Carlisle, and J. S. Taylor Distilleries*, 20. See also advertising card, "The Whiskey," folder 73, Taylor-Hay Family Papers.

75. Taylor, *Description of the O.F.C., Carlisle, and J. S. Taylor Distilleries*, 8.

76. Ibid., 9. The Procter map labels the Ordovician-age strata as Lower Silurian. The massive and dense Tyrone limestone does indeed outcrop near the bottom of the Kentucky River gorge from Frankfort upstream to southern Fayette County. The Tyrone, also known as Birdseye limestone, is some sixty feet thick, exceedingly dense, and overlain by multiple members of the thin-bedded Lexington limestone formation. Groundwater at Frankfort likely moved through several of these Lexington formations, but percolation through the Tyrone would have been a protracted process. See A. M. Miller, *Geology of Franklin County,* Kentucky Geological Survey Reports, 4th ser., vol. 2, pt. 3 (Frankfort: Kentucky Geological Survey, 1914).

77. *Sanborn's Surveys of the Whiskey Warehouses of Kentucky and Tennessee* (New York: Sanborn-Perris Map Company, 1894), 52.

78. Sanborn map, *Frankfort, Kentucky*, 9; Cecil, *Bourbon*, 137–38.

79. Carl E. Kramer, *Capital on the Kentucky* (Frankfort, KY: Historic Frankfort, 1986), 278–81.

80. Zoeller, *Bourbon in Kentucky*, 194–99.

7. The Outer Bluegrass Region

1. Fred S. Arms, James P. Fehr, David T. Carroll, Byron L. Wilson, Herman P. McDonald, and James C. Ross, *Soil Survey of Nelson County, Kentucky,* USDA Soil Conservation Service and Kentucky Agricultural Experiment Station (Washington, DC: GPO, 1971); John A. Kelley and William H. Craddock, *Soil Survey of Marion County, Kentucky,* USDA Soil Conservation Service and Kentucky Agricultural Experiment Station (Washington, DC: GPO, 1991); William H. Craddock, *Soil Survey of Washington County, Kentucky,* USDA Soil Conservation Service and Kentucky Agricultural Experiment Station (Washington, DC: GPO, 1986).

2. Sarah Smith, *Historic Nelson County, Its Towns and People* (Bardstown, KY: GBA/Delmar, 1983), 156.

3. Clerk of Court, Nelson County, Bardstown, Kentucky, *Nelson County Deed Record Book 29,* 100.

4. Information here is based on records in the Marcella McKenna Distillery Collection (Nelson County, KY), 1824–1945, 1858–1942 (bulk dates), 1 F65M-593, Special Collections, University of Kentucky; hereafter cited as McKenna Collection.

5. James S. McKenna, "H. McKenna, Incorporated in Kentucky," Louisville, KY, 1933, reel 2, McKenna Collection. It is difficult to discern who kept the distillery's personal accounts, although there is some consistency in handwriting from the 1850s to the 1870s. Some entries include brief notes relating to Daniel, James, or Stafford McKenna.

6. "H. McKenna Distiller," *Wine and Spirit Bulletin* 18, no. 6 (1904): 41.

7. *Sanborn's Surveys of the Distilleries and Warehouses of Kentucky and Tennessee* (New York: Sanborn Map Company, 1910), 32.

8. John C. Drewry to H. McKenna, October 2, 1903, reel 4, McKenna Collection.

9. Maury Klein, *History of the Louisville & Nashville Railroad* (New York: Macmillan, 1972; reprint, Lexington: University Press of Kentucky, 2003), 6–7.

10. Sam K. Cecil, *Bourbon: The Evolution of Kentucky Whiskey* (New York: Turner Publishing, 2010), 230; Chester Zoeller, *Bourbon in Kentucky: A History of Distilleries in Kentucky,* 2d ed. (Louisville, KY: Butler Books, 2010), 142.

11. Cecil, *Bourbon,* 227; Zoeller, *Bourbon in Kentucky,* 147.

12. Cecil, *Bourbon,* 229; Zoeller, *Bourbon in Kentucky,* 150.

13. *Sanborn's Surveys of the Distilleries and Warehouses of Kentucky and Tennessee,* 45.

14. Cecil, *Bourbon,* 234; Zoeller, *Bourbon in Kentucky,* 153.

15. In 1960 the Kentucky Geological Survey rated the Tom Moore Spring as having a flow rate of about four gallons per minute of hard water, with no objectionable salts or other contaminants and suitable for domestic use. See F. R. Hall and W. N. Palmquist, "Availability of Ground Water in Marion, Nelson, and Washington Counties," Hydrological Investigations Atlas HA-21 (Washington, DC: US Geological Survey and Kentucky Geological Survey, 1960), plate 2.

16. Cecil, *Bourbon,* 266.

17. D. J. Lake, *An Atlas of Nelson and Spencer Counties, Kentucky* (Philadelphia: n.p., 1882), 27.

18. Cecil, *Bourbon,* 230–31.

19. *Nelson County Deed Record Book 26,* 415.

20. *Nelson County Deed Record Book 28,* 366.

21. *Nelson County Deed Record Book 34,* 111.

22. *Nelson County Deed Record Book 35,* 609.

23. Cecil, *Bourbon,* 231.

24. "The Distilleries," *Hartford (KY) Herald* 9, no. 21 (1883), 2; "Notes of Current Events," *Stanford (KY) Semi-Weekly Interior Journal* 10, no. 510 (1883): 2.

25. *Sanborn's Surveys of the Distilleries and Warehouses of Kentucky and Tennessee,* 43.

26. "Equality Echoes," *Hartford (KY) Herald* 9, no. 13 (1883): 3.

27. A street sign spells the name Shirley.

28. Klein, *History of the Louisville & Nashville Railroad,* 9.

29. Cecil, *Bourbon,* 13.

30. *Sanborn's Surveys of the Distilleries and Warehouses of Kentucky and Tennessee,* 45; Zoeller, *Bourbon in Kentucky,* 132.

31. Jennifer Ryall, "Loretto Historic District," National Register of Historic Places Registration Form, Kentucky Heritage Council, Frankfort, 2012.

32. Sam S. Boldrick, "Burk's Distillery or Maker's Mark Distillery," National Register of Historic Places Registration Form, Kentucky Heritage Council, Frankfort, 1974; Cecil, *Bourbon*, 205–9.

33. Bill Samuels Jr., *My Autobiography* (Louisville, KY: Saber Publishing–Butler Books, 2009).

34. Douglas B. Holt, *How Brands Become Icons: The Principles of Cultural Branding* (Boston: Harvard Business School Press, 2004), 3–12.

35. A National Register or National Landmark "property" may be one building or a district with dozens of structures.

36. National Park Service, "National Historic Landmarks Program," 2017, www.nps.gov/nhl.

37. The Thomas Lincoln farm was Abraham Lincoln's birthplace.

38. Clerk of Court, Larue County, *Larue County Deed Record Book 7*, 27–28.

39. *Sanborn's Surveys of the Distilleries and Warehouses of Kentucky and Tennessee*, 41, 42.

40. George C. Buchanan, *Fine Whisky Facts* (Louisville, KY: George Buchanan, 1892), 20.

41. *Sanborn's Survey of the Whiskey Warehouses of Kentucky and Tennessee* (New York: Sanborn-Perris Map Company, 1894), 27.

42. Cecil, *Bourbon*, 188. J. M. Elstner listed the aggregate grain consumption at 1,800 bushels per day in 1886. See J. M. Elstner, *The Industries of Louisville, Kentucky, and New Albany, Indiana* (Louisville, KY: J. M. Elstner, 1886), 93.

43. "A Cattle Shortage," *Maysville (KY) Daily Public Ledger*, February 28, 1898, 4.

44. Leifur Magnusson, *Housing by Employers in the United States*, US Department of Labor, Bureau of Labor Statistics Bulletin 263 (Washington, DC: GPO, 1920), 1–20.

45. Elstner, *Industries of Louisville, Kentucky, and New Albany, Indiana*, 93.

46. US Census Bureau, 1880 Census, Larue County. Census enumerators made their tabulations during the late spring or early summer, after the distilleries had shut down for the season.

47. Elstner, *Industries of Louisville, Kentucky, and New Albany, Indiana*, 93.

48. "Athertonville, KY," *Adair County News* 10, no. 14 (1907): 6.

49. "Athertonville, KY," *Adair County News* 6, no. 18 (1903): 3.

50. "From Larue County," *Adair County News* 11, no. 45 (1908): 5.

51. US Census Bureau, 1900 Census, Larue County.

52. Cecil, *Bourbon*, 188; Zoeller, *Bourbon in Kentucky*, 127.

53. Cecil, *Bourbon*, 107–8; Zoeller, *Bourbon in Kentucky*, 93–94.

54. Cecil, *Bourbon*, 108–10; Zoeller, *Bourbon in Kentucky*, 94; *Sanborn's Survey of the Whiskey Warehouses of Kentucky and Tennessee*, 22; *Sanborn's Surveys of the Distilleries and Warehouses of Kentucky and Tennessee*, 33.

55. Robert M. Polsgrove, "T. Jeremiah Beam House," National Register of Historic Places Registration Form, Kentucky Heritage Council, Frankfort, 1987.

8. Distilling in the Ohio River Valley

1. Henry Hall, *Report on the Ship-Building Industry of the United States*, Department of the Interior, Census Office (Washington, DC: GPO, 1884), 174; Louis C. Hunter, *Studies in the Economic History of the Ohio Valley* (New York: Da Capo Press, 1973), 6–23.

2. Hall, *Report on the Ship-Building Industry*, 177.

3. Chester Zoeller, *Bourbon in Kentucky: A History of Distilleries in Kentucky*, 2d ed. (Louisville, KY: Butler Books, 2010), 202; Phil Breen, "Pogue House," National Register of Historic Places Registration Form, Kentucky Heritage Council, Frankfort, 2005, 1–8.

4. John C. Hudson, *Making the Corn Belt: A Geographical History of Middle-Western Agriculture* (Bloomington: Indiana University Press, 1994), 6–12.

5. J. M. Nickles, "The Geology of Cincinnati," *Journal of the Cincinnati Society of Natural History* 20, no. 2 (1902): 49.

6. Wilton N. Melhorn and John P. Kempton, "The Teays Valley Problem: A Historical Perspective," in *Geology and Hydrology of the Teays-Mahomet Bedrock Valley Systems,* Special Paper 258, ed. Wilton N. Melhorn and John P. Kempton (Boulder, CO: Geological Society of America, 1991), 5. See also Daniel Drake, "Geological Account of the Valley of the Ohio: In a Letter from Daniel Drake, M.D. to Joseph Correa de Serra," *Transactions of the American Philosophical Society* 2, no. 4 (1825): 124–39.

7. Eugene H. Walker, *Geology and Ground-Water Resources of the Covington-Newport Alluvial Area, Kentucky,* US Geological Survey Circular 240 (Washington, DC: GPO, 1953), 7.

8. *Kentucky State Gazetteer and Business Directory, 1881–1882,* vol. 3, pt. 2 (Detroit, MI: R. L. Polk and A. C. Danser, 1882), 634, 821.

9. Zoeller, *Bourbon in Kentucky,* 172–75; Sam K. Cecil, *Bourbon: The Evolution of Kentucky Whiskey* (New York: Turner Publishing, 2010), 111–12, 186–87.

10. W. N. Palmquist and F. R. Hall, *Public and Industrial Water Supplies of the Blue Grass Region Kentucky,* US Geological Survey Circular 299 (Washington, DC: US Geological Survey, 1953).

11. Cf. Paul A. Tenkotte, James C. Claypool, and David E. Schroeder, eds., *Gateway City: Covington, Kentucky, 1815–2015* (Covington, KY: Clerisy Press, 2015), 177.

12. Cf. George C. Matson, *Water Resources of the Blue Grass Region,* Kentucky Water-Supply Paper 233, US Geological Survey (Washington, DC: GPO, 1909), 104–6, 136–38.

13. Walker, *Geology and Ground-Water Resources,* 6, 25.

14. *Covington, Kentucky, 1886* (New York: Sanborn Map and Publishing Company, 1886).

15. From the colonial period to the end of the nineteenth century, Americans fouled their air and water with industrial and household pollutants. Raw sewage poured straight from pipes into streams and rivers, where it mixed with all forms of noxious materials dumped by industries large and small. Waterborne diseases killed thousands each year. In Cincinnati, for example, which drew its water from the Ohio River, typhoid death rates were 70 per 100,000 people in 1880, second only to Pittsburgh's rate of 135 per 100,000. As recently as 1946, the pollution load of untreated sewage and industrial waste dumped into the Ohio River and its tributaries was so heavy that one-fourth of the river's flow during low-water periods was from sewers. Martin Melosi, *The Sanitary City: Urban Infrastructure in America from Colonial Times to the Present* (Baltimore: Johns Hopkins University Press, 2000), 138, 333. See also Chase Palmer, "Quality of the Underground Waters in the Blue Grass Region," in *Water Resources of the Blue Grass Region of Kentucky,* US Geological Survey Water Supply Paper 233, ed. George C. Matson (Washington, DC: GPO, 1909), 82.

16. Lewis Loder, The Loder Diary, 1857–1903, transcribed by William Conrad (Florence, KY: Boone County Schools, 1985–1988), 75; Matthew E. Becher, "The Distillery at Petersburg, Kentucky: Snyder's Old Rye Whiskey," http://bcplfusion.bcpl.org/Repository/Petersburg_Distillery_History_complete.pdf.

17. Loder, *Loder Diary,* 75.

18. Becher, "Distillery at Petersburg, Kentucky: Snyder's Old Rye Whiskey."

19. The Petersburg Distillery was also known as the Boone County Distillery and by some seventy other names. See Zoeller, *Bourbon in Kentucky,* 161.

20. Kenneth T. Gibbs, "Boone County Distillery Superintendent and Guest House," National Register of Historic Places Registration Form, Kentucky Heritage Council, Frankfort, 1986.

21. Loder, *Loder Diary,* 111.

22. Ibid., 123.

23. Zadok Cramer, *The Navigator,* 7th ed. (Pittsburgh, PA: Cramer, Spear & Eichbaum, 1811), 126–27.

24. Mary Verhoeff, *The Kentucky River Navigation,* Filson Club Publication 28 (Louisville, KY: John P. Morton, 1917), 69.

25. C. E. Bowman, *Annual Report of the Kentucky Bureau of Agriculture, Horticulture, and Statistics,* Legislative Document 7 (Frankfort, KY: S. I. M. Major, 1881), 264.

26. Leland R. Johnson and Charles E. Parrish, *Triumph at the Falls: The Louisville and Portland Canal* (Louisville, KY: US Corps of Engineers, 2007), 49–61.

27. Levi Woodbury, "Steam-Engines: Letter from the Secretary of the Treasury," US Congress, House, 25th Cong., 3d sess., doc. no. 21, 1838, 9.

28. Louis C. Hunter, *Steamboats on the Western Rivers: An Economic and Technological History* (New York: Dover Publications, 1949), 569–70.

29. Bowman, *Annual Report of the Kentucky Bureau of Agriculture, Horticulture, and Statistics* (1881), 351–52.

30. Cecil, *Bourbon,* 165; Zoeller, *Bourbon in Kentucky,* 126.

31. "Louisville Manufacture-Alcohol Distillery," *Louisville Daily Courier* 29, no. 12 (1859): 2.

32. Carl E. Kramer, "The Evolution of the Residential Land Subdivision Process in Louisville, 1772–2008," *Register of the Kentucky Historical Society* 107, no. 1 (2009): 38–52.

33. Harland Bartholomew, *Urban Land Uses,* Harvard City Planning Studies, vol. 4 (Cambridge, MA: Harvard University Press, 1932), plate IX (between pp. 100 and 101).

34. C. E. Bowman, *Annual Report of the Kentucky Bureau of Agriculture, Horticulture, and Statistics, 1880* (Frankfort, KY: E. H. Porter, 1880), 264–66.

35. Ibid., 264.

36. Zoeller, *Bourbon in Kentucky,* 104, 105, 117.

37. Tabulated from Zoeller, *Bourbon in Kentucky,* 100–127.

38. Distilling's complementary industries in Louisville in the 1870s and early 1880s included coppersmiths (3), brass and iron foundries (17), steam engine builders (13), maltsters (4), pork and beef packers (13), barrel stave and headings manufacturers (3), and tanners and curriers (17). *Caron's Annual Directory of the City of Louisville,* vol. 1. (Louisville, KY: Bradley & Gilbert, 1871); *Kentucky State Gazetteer & Business Directory 1883–4* (Detroit, MI: R. L. Polk and A. C. Danser, 1884), 749.

39. Francis Walker, "The Statistics of the Wealth and Industry of the United States," US Census, 1870, vol. 3, table XI, Selected Statistics of Manufacturing, the State of Kentucky (Washington, DC: GPO, 1872), 667.

40. George H. Yater, *Two Hundred Years at the Falls of the Ohio: A History of Louisville and Jefferson County* (Louisville, KY: Heritage Corporation, 1979), 106–7.

41. Peter C. Welsh, "A Craft that Resisted Change: American Tanning Practices to 1850," *Technology and Culture* 4, no. 3 (1963): 306.

42. Walker, "Statistics of the Wealth and Industry of the United States," 667.

43. Bowman, *Annual Report of the Kentucky Bureau of Agriculture, Horticulture, and Statistics* (1880), 264–66.

44. Welsh, "Craft that Resisted Change," 317.

45. J. Leander Bishop, *A History of American Manufactures from 1608 to 1860,* vol. 1 (Philadelphia: Edward Young, 1866), 453.

46. *Insurance Maps of Louisville, Kentucky,* vol. 1 (New York: Sanborn-Perris Map Company, 1892), 22, 24.

47. "Fire Wednesday Night," *Frankfort Roundabout* 13, no. 3 (1890): 4.

48. Carl E. Kramer, "J. T. S. Brown & Son's Complex," National Register of Historic Places Registration Form, Kentucky Heritage Council, Frankfort, 1998.

49. Sally Van Winkle Campbell, *But Always Fine Bourbon* (Frankfort, KY: Old Rip Van Winkle Distillery, 1999), 29–53; Cecil, *Bourbon,* 167–72; M. Oppel, T. James, and D. Stern, "Arthur P. Stitzel House," National Register of Historic Places Registration Form, Kentucky Heritage Council, Frankfort, 1988; *Insurance Maps of Louisville,* vol. 1; *Insurance Maps of Louisville, Kentucky,* vol. 4 (New York: Sanborn Map Company, 1905); Michael R. Veach, *Kentucky Bourbon Whiskey: An American Heritage* (Lexington: University Press of Kentucky, 2013), 99–100; Zoeller, *Bourbon in Kentucky,* 106–7.

50. Interview with Dwayne Kozlowski, Bulleit Distillery, Shelbyville, KY, June 7, 2017.

51. *Insurance Maps of Louisville,* 4:424, 425, 426; Zoeller, *Bourbon in Kentucky,* 117–19; Eric Whisman, "Nelson Distillery Warehouse, Anderson-Nelson Distillery," National Register of Historic Places Registration Form, Kentucky Heritage Council, Frankfort, 2014.

52. For example, the Basil Mattingly family lived in Maryland in the 1770s and moved to Washington County, Kentucky, where son George was born in 1802. George married Nancy Johnson of Washington County in 1829, and they moved to thinly settled Daviess County in 1832. The Monarch family moved from Maryland to Washington County in 1801. M. D. Monarch married Susan Davis of Washington County, and in 1834 they moved to Daviess County. Thomas J. Monarch was born in 1836, and in 1885 he married Elisa Mattingly, daughter of George Mattingly. Thomas Monarch built a distillery on the Green River near Birk City in 1859 and later opened another distillery at Grissom's Landing on the Ohio River, ten miles downstream from Owensboro. See Leo McDonough, *An Illustrated Historical Atlas Map of Daviess County, Ky., 1876* (reprint, Evansville, IN: Unigraphic, 1978), 49, 52.

53. Ibid., 21.

54. US Census Bureau, 1870 Agriculture Census. Neighboring Henderson County, also part of the Western Coal Field region, had 101,706 acres of improved farmland and 114,083 acres of woodland, which accounted for about 53 percent of the land in farms in the county.

55. Frank R. Cox, *Soil Survey of Daviess and Hancock Counties, Kentucky,* USDA Soil Conservation Service (Washington, DC: GPO, 1974).

56. Rodger D. Marsden, *Drainage: Kentucky, Statistics for the State and its Counties,* US Census Bulletin (Washington, DC: GPO, 1921), 8–9.

57. William F. Switzler, *Report on the Internal Commerce of the United States* (Washington, DC: GPO, 1888), 491.

58. T. Edgar Harvey, *Commercial History of the State of Kentucky* (Louisville, KY: Courier-Journal Printing, 1899), 180.

59. McDonough, *Illustrated Historical Atlas Map of Daviess County.*

60. Tabulated from Cecil, *Bourbon,* 116–26; Zoeller, *Bourbon in Kentucky,* 58–69; *History of Daviess County, Kentucky* (Chicago: Inter-State Publishing, 1883), 341–45.

61. Lee A. Dew and Aloma W. Dew, *Owensboro: The City on the Yellow Banks* (Owensboro, KY: Rivendell Publications, 1988), 65–79.

62. Loder, *Loder Diary,* 88.

63. See, for example, *Owensboro, Kentucky* (New York: Sanborn Map & Publishing Co., 1885), 8–13.

64. Glenda Thacker, "Le Vega Clements House," National Register of Historic Places Registration Form, Kentucky Heritage Council, Frankfort, 1986.

Epilogue

1. Jorn Rusen, "Historical Narration: Foundation, Types, Reason," *History and Theory* 26, no. 4 (1987): 88.

Index

Page numbers in italics refer to illustrations.

Lightning Source UK Ltd.
Milton Keynes UK
UKHW031248220420
362104UK00007B/428